ALSO BY JOSHUA HAMMER

The Bad-Ass Librarians of Timbuktu: And Their Race to Save the World's Most Precious Manuscripts

Yokohama Burning: The Deadly 1923 Earthquake and Fire That Helped Forge the Path to World War II

A Season in Bethlehem: Unholy War in a Sacred Place

Chosen by God: A Brother's Journey

A TRUE TALE

of

ADVENTURE,

TREACHERY,

and the

HUNT FOR THE

PERFECT BIRD

The
FALCON
THIEF

Joshua Hammer

SIMON & SCHUSTER

NEW YORK   LONDON   TORONTO

SYDNEY   NEW DELHI

Simon & Schuster
1230 Avenue of the Americas
New York, NY 10020

First Simon & Schuster hardcover edition February 2020

SIMON & SCHUSTER and colophon are registered trademarks of Simon & Schuster, Inc.

For information about special discounts for bulk purchases, please contact Simon & Schuster Special Sales at 1-866-506-1949 or business@simonandschuster.com.

The Simon & Schuster Speakers Bureau can bring authors to your live event. For more information or to book an event, contact the Simon & Schuster Speakers Bureau at 1-866-248-3049 or visit our website at www.simonspeakers.com.

Interior design by Carly Loman

Manufactured in the United States of America

10   9   8   7   6   5   4   3   2   1

Library of Congress Cataloging-in-Publication Data

Names: Hammer, Joshua, 1957- author.
Title: The falcon thief : a true tale of adventure, treachery, and the hunt for the perfect bird / Joshua Hammer.
Description: New York : Simon & Schuster, 2020. | Includes bibliographical references and index.
Identifiers: LCCN 2019031607 (print) | LCCN 2019031608 (ebook) | ISBN 9781501191886 (hardcover) | ISBN 9781501191893 (ebook)
Subjects: LCSH: Wildlife crimes. | Falcons—Eggs. | Wild bird trade. | Rare birds.
Classification: LCC HV6410 .H36 2020 (print) | LCC HV6410 (ebook) | DDC 364.16/28598961468092—dc23
LC record available at https://lccn.loc.gov/2019031607
LC ebook record available at https://lccn.loc.gov/2019031608

ISBN 978-1-5011-9188-6
ISBN 978-1-5011-9189-3 (ebook)

CONTENTS

AUTHOR'S NOTE

This book is based on dozens of first-person interviews plus trial transcripts, videotaped interrogations, contemporary media accounts, and secondary source materials. FOIA requests filed with the British government for transcripts of police interviews were not successful, as these transcripts are generally disposed of after five years. In such cases, I reconstructed the exchanges based on extensive interviews with participants. Some other dialogue has also been reconstructed from memory and notes, to the best of my ability.

PROLOGUE

Shortly after New Year's Day in 2017, I was on vacation with my family in England when I happened to pick up a copy of the *Times* of London. A short article buried inside the newspaper caught my eye. "Thief Who Preys on Falcon Eggs Is Back on the Wing," declared the headline. The report by the *Times*'s crime correspondent John Simpson described a notorious wild-bird trafficker who had jumped bail and disappeared in South America:

> He has dangled from helicopters and abseiled down cliffs in search of falcon eggs for wealthy Arab clients . . . Now, the international egg thief is on the wing again after the authorities in Brazil admitted that they had lost him. [Jeffrey] Lendrum, 55, slipped the net after being caught with four albino falcon eggs stolen from Patagonia and jailed for more than four years. He is said to pose a serious threat to falcons in Britain and beyond . . .

The story of the egg thief grabbed my attention. The notion that there was a lucrative black market for wild birds' eggs seemed faintly ridiculous to me, like some wacky quest out of Dr. Seuss's *Scrambled Eggs Super!*, which I'd read aloud many times over the course of a decade to my three boys. I'd never considered that obtaining the world's most valuable eggs would require dangerous, logistically complex missions to the most remote corners of the planet. What kind of character would make a living that way? Was Lendrum one oddball or part of a whole hidden industry? Always a little skeptical of tabloid hype, I also wondered how much of a threat to endangered raptors Lendrum really posed. I tore out the clipping and started making casual inquiries when I got home.

As I found myself falling deeper into the life of Jeffrey Lendrum, discovering his childhood fascination with falcons and his compulsive tree climbing and nest raiding, something not altogether unexpected happened: I began to notice birds. That spring I traveled to southern Wales with two officers from Great Britain's National Wildlife Crime Unit to search for peregrines and their aeries in the cliffs of the Rhondda Valley. Later that summer, on a magazine assignment in the marshes of southern Iraq, I threaded through canals in a motorboat, acutely attuned to the avian life around me. Pied kingfishers, little black-and-white birds with needle-sharp beaks, darted out of the reeds as our craft sped past; a sacred ibis, with enormous black-tipped white wings and a scythe-like black bill, skimmed the surface of the marsh. I reread "My Bird Problem," a 2005 *New Yorker* essay, in which Jonathan Franzen described how his early bird-watching forays had heightened his excitement about venturing into the wild and encountering nature's breathtaking diversity. "A glimpse of dense brush or a rocky shoreline gave me a crush-like feeling, a sense of the world's being full of possibility," he wrote. "There were new birds to look for everywhere."

It wasn't only the rare ones that caught my eye. In April 2018, I returned from one of my last field-research trips about the falcon thief to discover my five-year-old son in a state of high excitement. By a remarkable coincidence, a pair of common pigeons, *Columba livia*, had built a nest on the bathroom window ledge of our third-floor apartment. For a month, as I wrote about the breeding behavior of birds in the wild and excavated the story of Lendrum's transformation from an adolescent nest raider to an international outlaw, I found regular inspiration looking at that ledge, easily visible across the courtyard from our kitchen window. Watching the pigeon incubate her eggs, observing the tiny, down-covered chicks as they huddled beneath their mother and grew in two weeks into awkward fledglings, made Lendrum's crimes more vivid to me—and more outrageous.

The bird-watching urge was proving irresistible. On Martha's Vineyard, in Massachusetts, the next summer I followed by kayak a pair of regal, ruffle-headed ospreys circling high above their man-made nest at the Long Point Wildlife Refuge; lost myself in a canoe for an hour among honking, socializing Canadian geese on Chilmark Pond; admired a red-tailed hawk soaring above the dunes at Great Rock Bight; and called my family outside to watch when an American robin briefly alit in our garden.

And then, as I was writing this book in the fall, came the most serendipitous moment. Early one morning I caught a flash of color just outside my office window in Berlin. A parakeet—an *Australian* parakeet—had landed on the ledge. Its brilliant green body and yellow head, illuminated by the morning sun, matched the changing leaves of the linden tree behind it. The bird must have escaped from somebody's cage and would soon be devoured by the predatory crows that stalk our neighborhood. One year earlier, I would probably have paid no attention to the sight, but now I called my partner excitedly and we watched it together, exhilarated by the bird's vivid presence, aware of its near-certain fate. The parakeet sat on the ledge for a good two minutes. Then it flew off and, pursued by a sparrow, was swallowed up by the leaves of the linden tree.

ONE

THE AIRPORT

The man had been in there far too long, John Struczynski thought. Twenty minutes had elapsed since he had entered the shower facility in the Emirates Lounge for business and first-class passengers at Birmingham International Airport, in the West Midlands region of England, 113 miles north of London. Now Struczynski stood in the corridor outside the shower room, a stack of fresh towels in the cart beside him, a mop, a pail, and a pair of CAUTION WET FLOOR signs at his feet. The janitor was impatient to clean the place.

The man and a female companion had been the first ones that day to enter the lounge, a warmly decorated room with butterscotch armchairs, a powder-blue carpet, dark wood columns, glass coffee tables, and black-shaded Chinese porcelain lamps. It was Monday, May 3, 2010—a bank holiday in the United Kingdom—and the lounge had opened at noon to accommodate passengers booked on the 2:40 p.m. Emirates direct flight to Dubai. The couple had settled into an alcove with a television near the reception desk. Minutes later the man had stood up and headed for the shower, carrying a shoulder bag and two small suitcases. That had struck Struczynski as strange. Who brings all of his luggage into the business-and-first-class shower room? And now he had been in there two or three times longer than any normal passenger.

A tall, lean man in his forties with short-cropped graying hair and a brush mustache, Struczynski had spent a decade monitoring 130 closed-circuit television cameras on the night shift at a Birmingham shopping mall, a job that "gave me a background in watching people," he would later say. That February, after the security firm laid him off, a management company had hired him to clean the Emirates Lounge. The first week he was there, the contractor enrolled him in an on-site training course to identify potential terrorist threats. The course, he would later say, heightened his normal state of suspicion.

As Struczynski puttered around the hallway, the shower room door opened, and the passenger—a balding, slender, middle-aged white man of average height—stepped out. He slipped past Struczynski without looking at him.

The cleaner opened the shower facility door and looked around the room.

My goodness, he thought. *What do we have here?*

The shower floor and glass partition surrounding it were both bone-dry. All the towels remained stacked and neatly folded. The toilet for the disabled hadn't been used. The washbasin didn't have a drop of water in it. Though the man had been inside the room for twenty minutes, he didn't appear to have touched anything.

Struczynski recalled the terrorism workshop that he had taken three months earlier, the exhortations from the instructor to watch out for odd looks and unusual behavior. This passenger was up to something. He knew it. Not sure what he was looking for, he rifled through the towels and facecloths, rummaged beneath the complimentary toothpaste tubes and other toiletries, checked the rubbish bin. He mounted a footstool and dislodged two ceiling tiles, wedging his hand into the hollow space just above them. Nothing.

He shifted his attention to the baby-changing area. In the corner of the alcove stood a plastic waist-high diaper bin with a round flip lid. Struczynski removed the top and looked inside. He noticed something sitting on the bottom: a green cardboard egg carton.

In one of the middle slots sat a single egg, dyed blood-red.

He stared at it, touched it gently. What could it mean?

He recalled the recent arrest at Heathrow Airport outside London of a man trying to smuggle rare Indian box turtles in egg cartons. But that seemed so odd. More likely this passenger was moving narcotics—like the gangsters in Liverpool who wedged packets of heroin and cocaine inside plastic Kinder Egg containers. *That's it*, he thought. *It must have something to do with drugs.*

Struczynski approached the reception area, a few steps from where the man and his traveling companion were sitting, and spoke softly to the two women working at the front desk. We may have a problem, he murmured, describing what he had just observed. He suggested that they call airport security, then returned to the shower and locked the door so that no one could disturb the evidence. Soon two uniformed security men entered the lounge, interviewed Struczynski, and examined the shower. The facility couldn't be seen from the alcove in which the passengers were sitting, and so, absorbed in conversation, the couple failed to notice the sudden activity.

The security guards summoned a pair of airport-based plain-clothes officers from the West Midlands Counter Terrorism Unit. Formed in 2007 in the wake of the London bus-and-underground bombings, the unit had grown from seventy to nearly five hundred officers, and was chiefly concerned with combating Islamist extremism. Counterterrorism forces had recently arrested a gang that had conspired to kidnap and behead a British officer and post the footage online, and had helped foil a plot by a Birmingham-born terrorist to blow up transatlantic airliners using liquid explosives. These men, too, questioned Struczynski, examined the egg box in the diaper bin, and asked the janitor to point out the passenger. They flashed the badges attached to lanyards around their necks, and chatted with him and his companion politely. Struczynski watched discreetly as the pair stood up and, flanked by the police, exited the lounge.

=

As hundreds of people hurried past them to their gates, the Counter Terrorism agents turned the woman over to colleagues and led the man into a small, windowless room near a security checkpoint. Several other officers squeezed into the space. The police asked the passenger to sit down at a table, and informed him that they would be questioning him under schedule seven of the Terrorism Act 2000, which allowed them to detain him for up to twenty-four hours without a lawyer.

"Are you carrying any sharp objects?"

"No," he said, turning his pockets inside out.

"May we see your airline ticket and travel documents?"

The passenger presented an Irish passport identifying him as Jeffrey Paul Lendrum, born in Northern Rhodesia, now Zambia, on October 26, 1961. He was traveling economy gold class in seat 40F on flight EK040 on his Emirates Skywards frequent flyer miles, arriving in Dubai at twelve-fifteen in the morning local time after a nearly seven-hour flight. Then he had a fourteen-hour layover before catching a connecting Royal Emirates flight to Johannesburg at two-thirty in the afternoon. It seemed a roundabout way to travel to South Africa: a journey of more than thirty hours, as opposed to a twelve-hour direct flight from the United Kingdom. Stapled to his boarding pass were baggage-claim stubs for four pieces of luggage, including a mountain bicycle.

A search of his hand luggage turned up an assortment of unusual gear: insulated hot-cold thermal bags, a Leica viewing scope, a thermometer, binoculars, a GPS system, a walkie-talkie, and a golf ball retriever, which used telescopic extensions to stretch up to seventeen feet. Lendrum carried plenty of cash: £5,000, $3,500 in US dollars, and some South African rand. He also had two more egg cartons. The first was empty. The other was filled with ten quail eggs—tiny white orbs with black speckles, about one-quarter the size of a hen's. Lendrum presented a receipt from Waitrose, the British supermarket chain, and explained that he was carrying farm-fresh organic eggs back home, because they were hard to find in Johannesburg.

The police ordered Lendrum to strip to his underwear.

Lendrum unbuttoned his shirt and slipped out of it. He stood there, arms at his sides, a blank expression on his face.

The agents stared.

Ribbons of white surgical tape were wrapped around his abdomen. Tucked snugly beneath the tape were one green, one black, and one blue woolen sock. Plastic zip ties divided each sock into five segments, and inside each segment was an oval-shaped object. The police unwrapped the surgical tape, removed the socks, cut off the ties, and, one by one, extracted the contents. They laid fourteen eggs gently on a table.

They were slightly smaller than ordinary hens' eggs, ranging in hue from marbleized brown to dark red. One was pale, with chocolate speckles; another had a background of caramel, bruised with plum-colored blotches. Yet another, all brown archipelagoes and continental landmasses juxtaposed against bright red lakes, gulfs, and seas, resembled high-resolution telescopic images of the surface of Mars. None of the police had ever seen anything like them.

"What kind of eggs are these?" an officer asked Lendrum.

"They're duck eggs," he replied.

"What were you planning to do with them?"

"Well, actually," he said, "I was taking them down to Zimbabwe, where my father lives." He was going to play a trick on the old man, he explained, hard-boiling every egg but one, and then getting a good laugh when his unsuspecting father cracked them all open.

"Why were you hiding them on your body?"

He was suffering from spinal problems, he explained, and his physiotherapist had recommended that he carry raw eggs strapped to his abdomen. Wearing the fragile objects against his belly would force him to keep his stomach muscles taut, he said, and strengthen his lower back.

The police officers exchanged incredulous looks.

This one, they realized, was entirely out of their league.

TWO

THE INVESTIGATOR

Andy McWilliam was in the rear garden of his home in Liverpool, playing with his two-year-old granddaughter in the late-afternoon sun, and trying to keep the toddler from running through the flower beds, when his cell phone went off in his kitchen. An officer of the Counter Terrorism Unit at Birmingham International Airport was on the line. He apologized for disturbing McWilliam on a bank holiday, but the unit was dealing with an unusual case, and a policewoman from Staffordshire, the neighboring county, had recommended that they contact him for guidance.

McWilliam was a retired policeman who now served as a senior investigative support officer for the National Wildlife Crime Unit (NWCU), a twelve-person team created in 2006 and headquartered in Stirling, outside Edinburgh. The unit employed four former detectives with a comprehensive knowledge of wildlife legislation to travel across Great Britain, helping local police investigate a range of offenses—from the trading of endangered species to animal cruelty. Unlike active-duty policemen, these support officers had no powers of arrest and couldn't obtain search warrants. They were essentially consultants, providing close-at-hand expertise to law enforcement officers who lacked a background in wildlife law.

Before joining the National Wildlife Crime Unit at its 2006 birth, McWilliam had spent thirty years on the police force in Merseyside, the county covering Liverpool and five metropolitan boroughs on both banks of the Mersey Estuary, which flows into the Irish Sea. In his last four years on the Merseyside force, McWilliam had specialized in wildlife crime, pursuing rhino-horn and ivory smugglers, tracking down dodgy taxidermists, and building cases against "badger baiters"—criminals who use dogs fitted with transmitters to corner the short-legged omnivores in their burrows six feet belowground, and then drag them outside to torture and kill them for sport. Now he was doing much the same thing in an advisory capacity, and his beat had expanded to cover half of England. At the moment, the officer was gathering evidence against a trader in endangered-animal skulls, as well as a man who illegally sold protected tortoises over the Internet, and a Chinese-medicine dealer who was clandestinely distributing plasters made from the ground bones of leopards.

McWilliam's particular area of expertise, however, was bird crime. A ferocious rugby player for an amateur police team until his midthirties, he had quit the sport after suffering a series of injuries, and, in an attempt to fill his leisure time, had taken up a pursuit that could not have been a greater departure from the world of blood bins and choke tackles: bird-watching. Since then he had spent many weekends ambling through a wetland reserve north of Liverpool, twelve square miles of marshes and fields that attracted tens of thousands of migrating pink geese, along with snipes, black-tailed godwits, dunlins, lapwings, redshanks, great crested grebes, ospreys, and dozens of other species that rotated in and out throughout the year.

The interest had carried over into his professional life. In the early 2000s, he made a name for himself arresting obsessives who raided eggs from the nests of endangered species, blew out the live embryos, and mounted the hollowed shells in personal collections. He also investigated numerous cases of "bird laundering"—stealing protected birds of prey from the wild and passing them off as the offspring of captive-bred raptors. McWilliam had developed a nearly unmatched expertise in the birds of Great Britain.

McWilliam was a burly man with arched eyebrows, deep-set blue eyes, a broad nose, a square jaw, and a thatch of tousled gray hair that was thinning on top. One unruly strand often dangled down the center of his forehead. His owlish features, accentuated by square-framed spectacles, suggested a keen intelligence and sense of humor, and his powerful physique gave him the appearance of a man not to be trifled with. He had the grace and the quickness of a former athlete, though a modest paunch had crept up on him since the end of his rugby-playing days. He listened intently as the Counter Terrorism officer characterized the case.

"We're not quite sure what we've got here," he said. They had stopped a passenger bound for South Africa with a fourteen-hour layover in Dubai, he explained, and then recounted the body search and discovery of what the passenger had claimed were duck eggs.

"Describe the eggs," McWilliam said.

As his colleague detailed their size, colors, and patterns, McWilliam knew that the passenger had been lying. The eggs, he was all but certain, were those of the peregrine falcon, the fastest animal on the planet, a denizen of all continents except Antarctica. The strong and solitary raptors—with an average wingspan of forty inches, sooty black feathers around the head and neck, blue-gray wings, a black-barred buff-white underside, bright orange-yellow eyes, and a sharply hooked beak—nest in rock quarries and on ledges in the cliffs of England, Wales, and Scotland, and are relatively easy for a backcountry bird-watcher to spot. But the species nearly died out in both Europe and North America during the 1950s and 1960s as their prey—chiefly wood pigeons and pheasants—became riddled with organochloride pesticides, most notably dichlorodiphenyl-trichloroethane, or DDT.

First synthesized by an Austrian chemist in 1874, DDT came into widespread use during World War II as a lice-killer, after the compound was discovered to have pesticidal properties in 1939. Allied doctors successfully dusted thousands of soldiers, refugees, and prisoners with a powdered form of the chemical; none suffered ill effects. Buoyed by the conviction that the compound was harmless, governments and industries began promoting liquid DDT (dissolved in oil) as the perfect way to kill off agricultural pests and yellow-fever-carrying mosquitoes. But when inhaled, ingested, or absorbed by the skin, liquid DDT worked its way to organs that stored fat—such as the liver, testicles, and intestines—and built up with deadly effect. Even a tiny amount, three parts in a million, was capable of disintegrating healthy cells in humans. DDT also passed easily from mother to unborn child, and from species to species.

During surveys in the 1950s, English ornithologist Derek Ratcliffe began to notice dwindling peregrine populations and strange behavior among the remaining birds. Some mothers even seemed to be pecking apart their own eggs. When Ratcliffe, acting on a hunch, later compared newly laid eggs to those in a museum collection gathered before 1946, when DDT was introduced to the United Kingdom, he discovered that the new eggs weighed 19 percent less than the old. The mother peregrines, he realized, hadn't pecked their eggs to pieces. They were feeding on the remains of thin, brittle eggs that had collapsed beneath their weight during incubation.

Laboratory tests at Cornell University would show that DDT increased the size of peregrines' livers, stimulating production of an enzyme that defends the organ against foreign chemicals. This enzyme in turn caused a plunge in female peregrines' production of sex hormones, including estrogen, which regulates the amount of calcium stored in bones. Less calcium in the females' bodies resulted in thinner, more fragile eggs.

The result was, as Ratcliffe wrote in his book *The Peregrine Falcon*, "a spectacular crash of population with a speed and on a scale seldom found in the vertebrate kingdom." By the early 1970s, only 250 breeding pairs of peregrine falcons were left in Great Britain. The losses were even steeper in North America. There, the *New York Times* reported in 1970 that "all peregrine eyries in the East and in the Upper Mississippi Valley, where once the bird flourished, were empty. In the Rocky Mountains and Far West, less than 10 percent of the prepesticide breeding population remains . . . In all the US, excepting Alaska, perhaps a dozen, and certainly no more than two or three dozen, peregrine families mated, laid eggs and hatched and fledged their young this year . . . The birds are gone."

Rachel Carson's seminal 1962 book *Silent Spring* (originally titled *Man Against the Earth*) had already drawn international attention to the link between DDT and the destruction of bird populations across the United States. Calling insecticides "as crude a weapon as the caveman's club," Carson documented how the lethal chemicals worked their way up the food chain. In California, irrigation water laden with pesticides was recycled back into lakes, where it settled in the organs of fish. As herons, pelicans, gulls, and other birds frequented the lakes and ate there, their populations died off. In Wisconsin, the culprit was pesticides sprayed on trees to protect against Dutch elm disease; the pesticides poisoned the earthworms that ate the trees' leaves, which passed the toxins on to robins. American bald eagles vanished across coastal Florida, New Jersey, and Pennsylvania, swan grebes declined in the western states and Canada, and pheasants, ducks, and blackbirds disappeared from the rice-growing regions of California and the South. "This sudden silencing of the song of birds, this obliteration of the colour and beauty and interest they lend to our world," wrote Carson, "have come about swiftly, insidiously, and unnoticed by those whose communities are as yet unaffected." Carson's groundbreaking work, along with research papers by Ratcliffe and other ornithologists on the near-extinction of the peregrine, led to a North American ban on the use of DDT in 1972, and dieldrin, another devastating insecticide, in 1974. The United Kingdom and the rest of Europe followed with legislation a decade later.

Since then, Great Britain's peregrine population had climbed back to fourteen hundred pairs—about five hundred more pairs than there had been in the 1930s, before the DDT disaster struck. In recent years, a few hardy peregrines had also taken up residence in urban areas, including a pair roosting atop the clock tower of City Hall in the Welsh city of Cardiff, and a total of thirty pairs in London. But the birds were still considered at risk. The Convention on International Trade in Endangered Species of Wild Flora and Fauna (CITES), a global wildlife protection agreement signed by 183 countries, had designated the peregrine an Appendix I bird, meaning that it was threatened with extinction and subject to the highest level of commercial restrictions. Following guidelines established by CITES, the British government had enacted the Control of Trade in Endangered Species Enforcement Regulations in 1997, making both the peregrine's removal from the wild and trade in the bird punishable by lengthy prison terms. That legislation was enforced alongside the Customs and Excise Management Act from 1979, which made it a crime to "knowingly and fraudulently evad[e] regulations" on restricted goods, including narcotics, weapons, and protected wildlife.

Still, conservationists were not in complete agreement on the issue: some argued that the number of wild peregrines in the United Kingdom and elsewhere had stabilized, and that the laws should be modified. In 1999 the US government removed peregrines from its endangered species list. At a biannual CITES conference in October 2016, Canada would propose downgrading the peregrine's status from Appendix I to Appendix II, a category for animals considered to be in less immediate danger. But most member countries rejected the proposal, citing "concern over inadequate precautionary measures" to prevent the raptor's disappearance. "As an apex predator [the peregrine falcon] always will have a small population, and be vulnerable to persecution because it sits at the top of the food chain," said Guy Shorrock, the senior investigative officer of the UK's influential Royal Society for the Protection of Birds.

=

Without even seeing the eggs seized at Birmingham Airport, McWilliam had little doubt that they were fertile and close to hatching. Late April to early May was the period in which peregrine chicks would be breaking out of their shells across the northern hemisphere. That the passenger was carrying the eggs strapped to his body suggested he needed to keep them warm until their incubation period was complete.

Plus there was the fact that he was heading for Dubai.

McWilliam's work on bird-related cases with the Merseyside police had introduced him to a thriving international market for birds of prey. This legal trade linked wealthy Arab devotees of the ancient sport of falconry with licensed breeders in the United States, Great Britain, and other countries in Western Europe. The business was tightly regulated, using a system of government-issued metal or plastic rings fitted around the birds' legs and certificates to guarantee that the birds had been born and bred in captivity. No bird of prey could be sold legally in the United Kingdom unless it had an "Article 10"—a document issued by the country's Animal and Plant Health Agency, in accordance with regulations established by the Convention on International Trade in Endangered Species of Wild Flora and Fauna—testifying that it had not been snatched from the wild.

But McWilliam was also aware of a lucrative underground market for falcons. Investigative studies by conservation groups, along with information provided by commercial breeders, had disclosed that the richest Middle Eastern aficionados were spending huge sums, allegedly up to $400,000 for a single bird, to acquire raptors illegally from the wild. Believing that wild birds were faster, stronger, and healthier than those born and raised in captivity, these sheikhs employed "trappers" to snatch young birds from the most remote corners of the globe. The thieves used pigeons and other lures to take fledglings in mid-flight, or, on occasion, scaled cliffs and trees and seized chicks from nests.

Expensive paramilitary-style expeditions to the Kamchatka Peninsula in southeastern Russia, Siberia, Mongolia, the Indian subcontinent, Greenland, and other remote wilderness areas were said to be disturbing the delicate ecological balance of pristine regions by decimating bird populations, threatening the survival of some of the world's most endangered species. In the two decades since the collapse of the Soviet Union, raptor raiders had nearly wiped out saker falcons—a migratory species, larger and slower than the peregrine, that breeds from Central Europe eastward across Asia to Manchuria. It thrives especially in the desert environments of the Altai-Sayan region of Central Asia, a 386,000-square-mile area known for its remarkable biological diversity and home to a variety of threatened species, including the snow leopard and the Lake Baikal seal. The majestic gyrfalcon, the largest and most sought-after falcon of all, was in danger of eradication from huge swaths of the Russian wilderness, including the Chukotka Peninsula near the Bering Strait. Mark Jeter, a former assistant chief of the California Department of Fish and Wildlife, describes the black market trade succinctly: "I always say, if there is a $50,000 bill flying around, someone is going to try to catch it."

The trafficking of live wild falcon eggs was an ingenious variation on this scheme. Back in October 1986, a Welsh falcon breeder named Ceri Griffith had arrived at Manchester Airport, on a flight from Morocco, carrying twenty-seven lanner falcon eggs stitched into secret pockets in his shirt. In a bit of bad timing for Griffith, one egg hatched at the moment that he was passing through customs—and officials, hearing tweeting, ordered him to strip and seized the live contraband. Griffith avoided jail time but paid a £1,350 fine, close to the maximum penalty a wild-bird egg smuggler could receive at that time.

The egg trafficking went in both directions: In April 1990 customs officials at Dover, on the southeast coast of England, pulled over a Mercedes-Benz bound for mainland Europe and, acting on a tip, took the car apart and found a sophisticated incubation system hidden inside the dashboard, heated by the vehicle's engine and filled with a dozen live peregrine falcon eggs taken from cliffs in Wales and Scotland. The two Germans in the vehicle pleaded guilty to smuggling offenses and were sentenced to thirty months in prison.

Since the incident in 1990, however, nobody had been arrested in the United Kingdom for smuggling wild raptor eggs; most law enforcement officials regarded the two busts in Manchester and Dover as isolated incidents. Now the detention of this new suspect at Birmingham Airport en route to Dubai suggested not only that egg trafficking was still a problem, but also that the operation was more ambitious than anybody had believed. Smugglers could be running eggs between Europe and the Arab world in a far-reaching conspiracy to defy international wildlife laws and damage the environment, financed by some of the richest and most powerful men on earth.

It disgusted McWilliam to think about it. Human beings had an obligation, he believed, to protect the environment and to coexist with other species with as little fuss as possible. "All living things were not made for man," the biologist and co-originator of evolutionary theory Alfred Russel Wallace had written in 1869, expressing a philosophy that McWilliam embraced. "Their happiness and enjoyments, their loves and hates, their struggles for existence, their vigorous life and early death, would seem to be immediately related to their own well-being and perpetuation alone." What better reminder that humans were not the sole proprietors of the planet than the birds in your backyard? And as Rachel Carson pointed out in *Silent Spring*, it served man's interests to avoid rupturing the bonds between species—after all, the beauty, variety, and vitality of the planet depended on it. "To the bird watcher, the suburbanite who derives joy from birds in his garden, the hunter, the fisherman or the explorer of wild regions, anything that destroys the wildlife of an area . . . has deprived him of pleasure to which he has a legitimate right," she wrote. Lendrum's crime was a rebuke to the laws that Great Britain had carefully put into place over the decades to safeguard the future. Robbing nests for sport, or for greed, struck McWilliam as an egregious violation of the fragile, symbiotic relationship beween man and the wild.

"Don't let the man go," McWilliam told the officer. He suggested that the Counter Terrorism Unit arrest the suspect on a preliminary charge of possessing endangered species, which constituted a violation of the Wildlife and Countryside Act, a 1981 law passed by Parliament that expanded the protections afforded wild birds and animals and increased penalties for those who harmed them.

"I'm dropping everything and coming down to meet you," McWilliam said, adding, "Whatever you do, keep the eggs warm."

Five minutes later, McWilliam grabbed a toothbrush and a knapsack full of notebooks, said goodbye to his wife, son, daughter-in-law, and granddaughter, and climbed into his leased Peugeot hatchback for the one-hundred-mile trip to Birmingham.

=

As McWilliam drove south from Liverpool on the M6 with the late-afternoon sunlight streaming through the passenger window, he felt a rising sense of anticipation. Since the Welsh lanner-egg smuggler Griffith had walked free after paying a modest fine in 1986, Great Britain's courts had hardened their attitudes toward wildlife crime. Environmental damage and profit motive had become key considerations in determining sentencing: a professional criminal making off with protected species to supply an underground market was a far bigger threat, law enforcement officials believed, than someone stealing birds for a small personal collection. If the eggs were indeed what McWilliam presumed they were, this offense would constitute one of the most serious crimes ever investigated by the National Wildlife Crime Unit in its four years of existence. Until now, McWilliam's cases mostly involved cruelty to animals or the illegal sale by taxidermists of the preserved parts of protected species—crimes considered the equivalent of misdemeanors and usually punishable by a fine. Live falcon smuggling carried a maximum punishment of seven years in prison.

McWilliam had reason to think that the case might be a game-changer. McWilliam had been aware of the role allegedly played by Middle Eastern royal families in the illicit trade of wild raptors, but had never come across hard evidence. Maybe the suspect could lead him to some sheikhs. The oddity of the crime was also likely to attract the interest of the media, giving the National Wildlife Crime Unit, a bare-bones outfit engaged in a permanent struggle with politicians and the police force to obtain enough funding to operate, a chance to prove that its money was being well spent. A headline-making conviction of a notorious wildlife criminal could protect the unit from closure—or even, if McWilliam was very, very lucky, get his budget significantly raised for the next year.

He called the unit's intelligence chief, a Scottish former drug investigator named Colin Pirie, to alert him to the arrest and to request that he begin digging into the suspect's background. Then he reached out to Lee Featherstone, a local raptor expert and a breeder of goshawks—large, red-eyed, white-browed raptors that frequent the forests of Europe and North America. Featherstone and McWilliam had crossed paths during a wild-bird laundering investigation the previous year. McWilliam asked Featherstone, who was on the way home from a birds-of-prey fair in the Midlands, to join him at the airport to verify what species the eggs belonged to, and whether they were viable.

Ninety minutes later, McWilliam parked his car at Birmingham International Airport and made his way to an operational office belonging to the Counter Terrorism Unit. Two of the arresting officers briefed him on Lendrum's detention, and then escorted him down a bland hallway to a cramped room used by the United Kingdom Border Agency, with three desks and an array of 1990s-era computers. The officers showed him the fourteen eggs that now rested, wrapped in their woolen socks, atop a computer monitor. Fluorescent lights and heated air blowing through the bulky machine's fan vents were keeping them warm. Beside them on the officers' desk lay the mysterious egg carton retrieved from the diaper bin inside the Emirates Lounge shower facility. The red-dyed egg that had piqued the janitor's interest—as it turned out, an ordinary chicken egg—was still sitting inside the carton. Next to the carton was the box full of tiny, black-speckled quail eggs that the police had found in Lendrum's luggage.

When Lee Featherstone arrived ten minutes later, he extracted from his backpack a blue digital monitor called an Egg Buddy, a device about the size of a butter tray used by breeders to detect the heartbeat of a chick inside its shell. The breeder untied the socks and carefully removed the eggs. Featherstone noted the size, marbling, and presence of protoporphyrin, a brownish red pigment found in the shells of many raptor eggs. The color could be useful, evolutionary scientists theorize, to protect against solar radiation and for camouflage on rock ledges.

Without a doubt, Featherstone said, these were the eggs of peregrine falcons.

Featherstone gently placed one egg inside the Egg Buddy and closed the lid. On the green rectangular LED screen he and McWilliam watched a black line rise and fall rapidly and rhythmically, registering six hundred beats per minute, the normal heart rate for a peregrine chick. "That's alive," Featherstone said. He placed another egg in the tray. "That's alive." Huddled inside its shell, a tiny creature was preparing to punch with its beak through the internal membrane that protected its body, take its first breaths from an air pocket that lay just beyond, and then peck its way through the shell and into the world. One after another, the eggs registered strong heartbeats. Only one of the fourteen showed a flat line.

To Featherstone, the fact that Lendrum had absconded with fourteen eggs, and that thirteen were still alive, proved that the thief was a professional. Even just locating so many peregrine eggs in the wilderness—at four eggs to a clutch, a minimum of four aeries—must have required patience, acute powers of observation, physical courage, and athletic skill. It took more expertise to ensure that the fragile creatures survived being ripped out of their nests, bounced around in a car for hours, and then strapped to a human body for a four-thousand-mile journey to the Middle East. If the thief snatched the eggs too early—within the first three weeks of the peregrine's thirty-four-day incubation period, when the ambient temperature must remain between 99.1 and 99.5 degrees Fahrenheit at all times—they would die. If he snatched them too late, he risked having them hatch in his pocket or his backpack while he was going through customs or waiting in the airport security line. The falcon thief's calculations had to be perfect.

The decoy quail eggs and the painted hen's egg were further signs of the criminal's attention to detail. It was a clever tactic, probably meant to persuade a customs agent that he was carrying ordinary farm eggs home to eat.

"He knew what he was doing," Featherstone told McWilliam. "You have to wonder how many times he's gotten away with it."

Featherstone placed the eggs back in the socks, secured them with the plastic ties, took off his woolen sweater, and carefully wrapped the socks up inside it. Then he tied the sweater and the socks around his chest, so that the eggs would absorb his body warmth. "They're fertile, they're alive, but they're getting chilled," Featherstone told the police. The raptor breeder drove to his home ten minutes from the airport, where he kept the eggs warm, manually rotating them every hour for the next several days and nights.

The thirteen eggs would hatch between five and eight days later, and ornithologists from the Royal Society for the Protection of Birds, the country's biggest environmental charity, would introduce the newborn chicks to active nest sites on cliff ledges in northern Scotland. Eleven of the thirteen would fledge in the wild.

In Birmingham, McWilliam checked into an airport hotel and prepared for the next morning, when he would meet the egg thief.

THREE

THE INTERVIEW

Shortly before eleven o'clock in the morning on Tuesday, May 4, Andy McWilliam parked his Peugeot at the rear of the police headquarters in Solihull, a town in the West Midlands region southeast of Birmingham. A police sergeant buzzed him through a security gate at the back of the three-story concrete slab, and escorted him and two plainclothes detectives from the local Counter Terrorism Unit to the "custody suites" on the ground floor.

McWilliam and his fellow investigators entered a small, windowless interview room, furnished with a metal table and six chairs bolted to the floor as a precaution against outbursts from unruly detainees. A cassette recorder on the table would record four tapes—for the court, the police, and the solicitor, plus one backup—using a microphone mounted on the wall.

Accompanied by a solicitor provided by the court, Jeffrey Lendrum walked into the chamber. He had been brought in handcuffs from Birmingham International Airport to the custody suites the previous evening. The woman who'd been with him in the Emirates Lounge, his domestic partner and a South African citizen, had claimed to know nothing about the eggs on Lendrum's body. After strip-searching her and finding no incriminating evidence, the police had permitted her to board her afternoon flight to Dubai. "She was in a terrible state," Lendrum would say years later. "I regret that."

McWilliam studied the man. Dressed in jeans and a polo shirt, Lendrum was trim and good-looking, with large, deep-set eyes, vestiges of gray hair around an otherwise bald head, and an open and friendly face. He seemed in good shape, yet he didn't fit the image of a swaggering stuntman or adventurer. McWilliam could as easily picture him in a business suit as rappelling down a cliff.

The lead Counter Terrorism officer read Lendrum his rights and informed him that his statements were being recorded. As they had agreed earlier, McWilliam would let his colleague begin the interrogation; McWilliam, the wildlife expert, would take over when the moment seemed right.

"Okay, you were arrested yesterday," the agent began. "Why were you carrying the eggs strapped to your body?"

Lendrum repeated the story that he had told the airport police: he suffered from a chronic lower backache and his physiotherapist had instructed him to wear raw eggs strapped around his abdomen. It was an unusual remedy, he acknowledged, but nothing else had helped, so he'd decided to give it a try.

McWilliam, scribbling silently in a notepad, let Lendrum ramble on for several minutes. Then he jumped in.

"This is ridiculous," he said. "It's a cock-and-bull story. You and I both know exactly what kind of eggs you were carrying."

"They're duck eggs," Lendrum said. The solicitor sat beside Lendrum silently, jotting occasional notes, whispering into Lendrum's ear, but making no attempts to interrupt the questioning.

"They're peregrine falcon eggs," said McWilliam.

"Duck eggs," Lendrum insisted.

"They're peregrine falcon eggs," McWilliam repeated. Identifying himself as an investigative support officer with the National Wildlife Crime Unit, McWilliam described the marbleized browns and reds, the dark pigments produced by natural selection over the millennia to protect eggs from direct sunlight on the cliff ledges where peregrines nest.

Lendrum leaned back in his chair and went silent. McWilliam sensed what the suspect was probably thinking: the investigator across the table knew far more about birds of prey than he had expected.

"All right," Lendrum conceded. "They're peregrine falcon eggs. I've got an egg collection at home, and I was taking them back there."

"So they were for a collection, then?"

"Yes," Lendrum replied. Under McWilliam's gentle prodding, Lendrum talked of a boyhood spent climbing trees and rock faces near his Rhodesian home, of his longtime fascination with peregrines, eagles, and hawks. He described the weavers, rollers, and other passerines, or perching birds, that frequented the African bush. He had lived on and off for a decade in Towcester, a town in Northamptonshire in the Midlands, where his former wife and two stepdaughters still resided, but he always returned to Southern Africa, partly because of his love of the birds and other wildlife of the region.

"Hang on a minute," McWilliam said. "So you've lived in the United Kingdom, on and off, for many years?"

"That's right," Lendrum replied.

"But you can't live in this country and not know the legislation. It's inconceivable that you wouldn't know about the protections afforded these birds."

"I—I know that there are some laws," Lendrum said, appearing to sense a trap, "but I'm not familiar with the specifics." Besides, he went on, "I'm not quite sure what harm there is in what I did. The eggs that I collected were all dead."

"We had them all tested yesterday," McWilliam said. "They're alive."

"No," Lendrum replied.

"You know exactly what you were doing," the investigator said, exasperated by the smug denials. Lendrum had to have realized by now that McWilliam understood exactly what he'd done. "You strapped them to your body to get them through security because you didn't want them to be found, and you wanted to keep them warm."

"No, no," Lendrum protested.

"Let's cut the rubbish," McWilliam said. "You were taking these falcon eggs out live because they are destined for the falcon trade in Dubai."

"Dubai was just a stopover," Lendrum insisted. He preferred to travel from London to Johannesburg on Emirates using frequent-flyer miles, he explained, which made it far cheaper than a direct flight to South Africa.

McWilliam tried a new tack.

"So," he asked, "where did these eggs come from, Jeff?"

Lendrum said that he had taken them from four aeries in and around the Rhondda Valley, a rugged former coal mining region in the south of Wales. He had driven there on holiday in his car, he said, and had stumbled by chance across a dozen peregrine nests while hiking in the hills. His initial thought was that he might hatch them and breed them when he returned to Africa, but when he took them out of the vehicle at Birmingham Airport, he realized that they were dead.

So he wrapped them in socks to protect the shells, with the intention of "blowing" the dead embryos when he got home and mounting the eggs in his collection. He insisted that he hadn't realized he was breaking any laws.

"You parked your car at the airport?" McWilliam asked.

When Lendrum answered in the affirmative, McWilliam stopped the interview, ushered the two Counter Terrorism agents out of the building, and climbed back into his Peugeot.

"Let's go find that car," he said.

—

At Birmingham Airport, Counter Terrorism investigators typed Lendrum's name into a police database to obtain his registration information. The car in question was a 2008 gray Vauxhall Vectra Estate registered to his ex-wife's address in Towcester, with license plate number Y262KPP.

McWilliam and his two colleagues drove to long-term parking, a sprawling outdoor lot with a capacity of seven hundred vehicles. Dividing the lot, McWilliam and a second carload of agents drove up and down their allotted rows, seeking out the gray car. After twenty minutes, the other car radioed that they'd found the Vauxhall in spot C10. McWilliam had retrieved the key from Lendrum's personal effects before leaving the station. Now he inserted it in the door. It didn't turn.

"Smash open the window," McWilliam said.

An agent punched through the front passenger window with a tire jack. McWilliam opened the door, brushed the glass off the seat, and peered inside. Old folded maps of Wales and the Midlands and used coffee cups littered the musty interior. McWilliam opened the glove compartment. Inside, he discovered a handheld satellite navigation device. Then he walked to the rear. An officer popped the rear door using a lever beneath the steering column.

"Bloody hell," McWilliam said.

A large metal-and-yellow-plastic box bearing a label from British hatcher manufacturer Brinsea lay inside. McWilliam recognized it immediately as an egg incubator. An electric cable joined to a two-foot extension cord ran from the incubator through the space between the two backseats to the cigarette lighter on the dashboard. Beside the incubator was a three-foot-high blue canvas backpack filled with coiled climbing ropes, carabiners, and steel stakes. McWilliam photographed the evidence and returned to the interview room at police headquarters, where Lendrum was still waiting.

McWilliam laid the incubator, the ropes, and the other gear on the table.

"If you're just an egg collector, then how do you explain this?" McWilliam asked. "Why the hell do you have an incubator in your car?"

Lendrum shrugged. The incubator was intended for "hens in Zimbabwe." The eggs, he repeated, were for his collection in South Africa. Again he insisted that the embryos inside were no longer alive. He had worn them on his body to self-treat a bad back. He denied that the dyed red egg left behind in the Emirates shower room was a decoy.

McWilliam was used to dealing with liars, but this was a new level of willful deceit. Did Lendrum really expect him to believe such blatant prevarication? Was this some kind of casually sociopathic detachment from reality? Or had he gotten away with his crimes for so long that he'd come to believe he could talk his way out of anything?

"Bollocks," McWilliam said. "You know that peregrines are a protected species. You know you cannot legally export them without a permit."

"I didn't know that," Lendrum said.

"If you thought it was okay, then why did you conceal them? Why did you strap them to your body? All of your actions, the fact that you didn't declare them at any time to security, the fact that you were hiding them on your body, the evidence in the boot [the car's trunk], all of the evidence shows planning and preparation. Is there anything you want to say?"

Lendrum shook his head, and McWilliam terminated the interview. He saw nothing more to be gained from it.

=

The Crown Prosecution Service ordinarily has twenty-four hours following an arrest to charge a suspect with a crime, although the custody period can be extended for twelve more hours at the discretion of the police officer responsible for the prisoner. If the prosecution declines to charge the suspect by that deadline, he must be released immediately. If it decides to file charges, then it is up to a judge to set bail or to keep him in jail until trial. In this case, the police superintendent at Solihull had extended Lendrum's detention to thirty-six hours, and about eight hours remained on the "custody clock." McWilliam knew that most prosecutors in the United Kingdom had no familiarity with wildlife legislation, and it was impossible to predict what they would say about a batch of stolen eggs. If Lendrum walked out the door, McWilliam was certain that he would flee the country. Beneath the nonchalant demeanor, he sensed a career criminal who'd been undertaking this kind of operation for years—and would for decades more, despite this tussle with the law.

How had he financed his expedition to South Wales? Who had sent him there? How often had he made these trips? McWilliam wanted answers, and he knew he was running out of time.

FOUR

THE ART OF FALCONRY

In 1839, a twenty-two-year-old aspiring diplomat and amateur archaeologist named Austen Henry Layard quit his job as a clerk in his uncle's London law office and set out on what would become a decade-long journey across the Middle East. Arriving six years later at the Tigris River near Mosul in what is now Iraq, Layard excavated the ruins of Dur-Sharrukin, an Assyrian capital built between 720 and 700 B.C. There—amid temples emblazoned with cuneiform writings celebrating King Sargon II, the conqueror of Babylon, and giant statues of lamassus (winged creatures with the head of a man and body of a lion or a bull)—Layard unearthed a bas-relief that showed, he wrote, "a falconer bearing a hawk on his wrist." The bearded hunter holds thin straps made of leather, known as jesses, or *sbuq* in Arabic, between his thumb and index finger, with the ends tied around the raptor's feet. Layard's discovery, the earliest known representation of falconry, made a strong case that the sport had originated in the Arab world at least twenty-five hundred years before.

In its early days, long before the arrival of Islam in the Middle East, falconry served as a means of survival. Bedouins in the Arabian Desert trapped peregrines during the raptors' autumn migration from Europe or Central Asia to Africa. The nomads trained the birds to kill and return to the gauntlet worn on their human's fist, and to hunt hares or houbara bustards (large terrestrial birds) to supplement the Bedouins' meager diet of milk and dates and rice. It was an efficient way of putting food on the table, and it established a unique relationship between man and bird. "For the Bedouin the [falcon's] victory over its quarry was a feat of courage and strength in which they felt able to share," wrote Mark Allen, a noted Arabist and the onetime director of MI6's counterterrorism unit, in his 1980 book *Falconry in Arabia*. "In the [falcon's] graceful restraint at rest and her grim hardness in the field, the Bedouin saw qualities which were for him among the criteria for honor in a tribal society."

Arab traders likely introduced falconry to the West before the fall of the Roman Empire: in *Eucharisticos*, a confessional meditation written by the Macedonian Christian poet Paulinus of Pella in A.D. 458, the author recalls his adolescent wish to possess "a swift dog and a splendid hawk." But in medieval Europe, falconry was practiced differently than in the early Bedouin hunts: training and housing birds of prey was beyond the means of most manor-bound peasants, and forests were the protected domains of the nobility, so "hawking," as the sport also was known, became a leisure pursuit of monarchs and nobles, who organized lavish hunting parties on their estates. The aristocracy even established a pecking order, laid out in the *Book of Saint Albans* in 1486, for who could hunt with what. Only the king was entitled to a gyrfalcon, the world's most exotic raptor, brought by traders from frozen Nordic cliffs. A prince could use a "falcon gentle," or female peregrine, while a knight would have to make do with the slower but often equally agile saker. To a lady went a merlin, a small and sturdy falcon with a blocklike head. Lesser birds were designated for those common folk who did have the resources to hunt; these included the sparrow hawk for a priest, and the lowly kestrel for the "knave or servant" of a lord. Kings built elaborate mews on palace grounds, and lavished privileges on master falconers. The Laws of the Court under Hywel the Good, a tenth-century Welsh prince, stipulated that the royal falconer "is to have his horse in attendance, and his clothing three times in the year, his woolen clothing from the king, and his linen clothing from the queen, and his land free."

During falconry's boom times in the Middle Ages, relationships between Eastern and Western falconers flourished. In 1228 Frederick II of Hohenstaufen, the Holy Roman Emperor, hunted in the desert with Malik al-Kamil, the fourth Ayyubid sultan of Egypt, for three months during a lull in the Sixth Crusade. Twenty years later Emperor Frederick relied on the knowledge imparted to him by Syrian falconers whom he had brought back to Europe to write his classic work *De Arte Venandi cum Avibus* (*On the Art of Hunting with Birds*). By the seventeenth century, however, the proliferation of guns and, in England, the enclosure of land, rendered falconers an anachronism. No more than a few hundred falconers were left on the entire continent after the French Revolution and the Napoleonic Wars swept away the aristocracy.

And yet, as Austen Henry Layard made his way through the Tigris and Euphrates Valleys in 1845, he found that there, falconry was still appreciated as a form of art. In a caravansary (roadside inn) by the Euphrates, the archaeologist encountered Timour Mirza, an exiled Persian prince and the region's most famed falconer. Reclining on carpets spread on a platform, Mirza "was surrounded by hawks of various kinds standing on perches fixed into the ground," Layard would write in his 1853 memoir *Discoveries Among the Ruins of Nineveh and Babylon*, "and by numerous attendants, each bearing a falcon on his wrist." Layard noted the pageantry surrounding falconry and the esteem accorded the finest participants—and their birds. He admired such accoutrements as the raptor's hood, which temporarily blinded the bird, protecting its delicate optic nerves from a blitz of sensations and soothing its high-strung disposition. The hood "is generally made of colored leather, with . . . gold and variegated thread," Layard observed. "Tassels and ornaments are added, and the great chiefs frequently adorn a favourite bird with pearls and precious stones."

The bird that had come to command the greatest respect among falconers was the *shahin*, or peregrine falcon, a term derived from the Middle Persian word *šāhēn* (literally majestic or kingly). "Although the smallest in size," Layard explained to his readers, "it is esteemed for its courage and daring, and is constantly the theme of Persian verse." This raptor "strikes its quarry in the air and may be taught to attack even the largest eagle, which it will boldly seize, and, checking its flight, fall with it to the ground."

=

No consensus has ever been reached about the maximum speed of a peregrine as it stoops, or plummets, toward its prey. A BBC documentary pitted a peregrine named Lady against a free-falling skydiver equipped with a speedometer and a lure. The skydiver clocked in at 158 miles per hour. Lady, who hurtled past him, may have surpassed 180.

Perhaps the best accounts of falcons' hunting behavior come from

British writer J. A. Baker in his classic work *The Peregrine*. Baker, a nearsighted and arthritic clerk from Essex, tracked peregrines in the winter landscapes of his native East Anglia between 1954 and 1962. His observations are infused with a sense of the fragility of nature (the DDT poisonings were at their height), the beauty of the English countryside, and appreciation for the raptor's grace in flight. But over and over he returns in his writings to the stoop and the kill. "The peregrine swoops down toward his prey," he writes in *The Peregrine*. "As he descends, his legs are extended forward till the feet are underneath his breast . . . His extended toe . . . gashes into the back or breast of the bird, like a knife—If the prey is cleanly hit—and it's usually hit hard or missed altogether—it dies at once, either from shock or from the perforation of some vital organ." He describes with grisly admiration the raptor's "tomial tooth"—a sharp projection on the upper mandible that lets the bird snap the vertebrae of any prey that isn't killed instantly on the stoop. "The hawk breaks its neck with his bill, either while he is carrying it or immediately [when] he alights," he observed. "No flesh-eating creature is more efficient, or more merciful, than the peregrine."

To accomplish that—to target and then dive-bomb a wood pigeon or a grouse from five thousand feet at nearly two hundred miles an hour, and strike it dead with a single swipe of the foot—requires extraordinary physical abilities. The bird's large, well-developed chest muscles, connected to a broad breastbone and nourished by oxygen drawn in continuously by nine air sacs throughout the body, power its wings through high-speed flight. This hyperefficient respiratory and circulatory system also keeps the air flowing and the blood pumping as the peregrine descends at velocities that would render any other species unconscious. Light and hollow bones, long and stiff flight feathers, and streamlined wings keep air resistance to a minimum, while the extra-wide tail base supports powerful musculature to turn and brake while in hot pursuit. All this allows the bird to maximize its speed and flexibility. The bird's optic nerves, meanwhile, relay images to its brain ten times faster than those of a human, "so events in time that we perceive as a blur," Helen Macdonald, best known for her memoir *H Is for Hawk*, noted in an earlier study, *Falcon*, "like a dragonfly zipping past our eyes, are much slower to them."

Above all, peregrine falcons perceive the world with a vividness and depth that human beings can hardly appreciate. Photoreceptor cells cram into the falcon's fovea, the tiny pit located in the retina that handles the most important visual tasks. A human has about thirty thousand color-sensitive cones in the retina; a falcon has *one million*. With two foveae in each eye, one for depth and one for lateral perception, the falcon's eye functions simultaneously as both a macro lens and a zoom lens. Falcons can also perceive ultraviolet light, making colors stand out even more vividly and enabling the falcon to identify the shape and texture of plumage from as far as a mile away. Macdonald quoted Andy Bennett, a researcher in the field of avian vision, as saying that the difference between the eyesight of a human and that of a falcon is like the difference "between black-and-white and color television."

=

On October 16, 1931, south of the desert mountain known as Jebel Dukhan (Mountain of Smoke) in the island kingdom of Bahrain, the first oil spouted from a well drilled by the Bahrain Petroleum Company, a firm established two years earlier by Standard Oil of California. The well, which was soon pumping ninety-six hundred barrels a day, was the first to produce oil on the Arabian side of the Persian Gulf. Others quickly followed—in Qatar in 1935, Saudi Arabia and Kuwait in 1938, Abu Dhabi in 1958, and Oman in 1964.

The flood of petrodollars over the next decades turned Gulf societies upside down. The oil industry covered vast swaths of desert with wells, pipelines, refineries, access roads, and other infrastructure, creating a new urban population and erasing much of Bedouin society. Yet despite the upheaval, falconry remains fundamental to the culture of that part of the world. Falcons appear on corporate logos, banknotes, and the national emblem of the United Arab Emirates, a federation of seven Gulf sheikhdoms, the largest of which are Abu Dhabi and Dubai. The most extravagant new real estate project in Dubai is "Falconcity of Wonders," a 107-square-mile conglomeration of opulent hotels and residences, all laid out in the shape of a peregrine. And the sheikhs there have managed to retain fragments of a mostly vanished way of life. Wealthy falconers stock private reserves with prey such as captive-bred houbara bustards—having hunted the wild ones out of existence decades ago—and pack their falcons onto 747s and fly to leased hunting grounds in Central Asia and North Africa.

In 2002, Sheikh Hamdan bin Mohammed bin Rashid Al Maktoum, son and heir of Sheikh Mohammed bin Rashid Al Maktoum, the billionaire ruler of Dubai, introduced a new sport to the Arab world: falcon racing. While the crown prince had the luxury of hawking in his own private hunting grounds and on royal expeditions, he recognized that such opportunities were out of reach for the average Gulf citizen. Racing was Sheikh Hamdan's ambitious attempt to keep Emiratis connected to their heritage. The populist move also turned falconry into a multimillion-dollar global enterprise.

At the first falcon race organized by the crown prince in January 2002, several thousand participants—ranging from royal family members with an aviary full of falcons to ordinary citizens with a single bird—gathered beside a field of sand in Dubai to time their birds with stopwatches over a four-hundred-meter course. The falcons flew sequentially, to avoid catastrophic midair collisions, coaxed into action by a man positioned at the far end of the field swinging a *telwah*—a lure fashioned from a pair of bustard wings. A younger brother of Dubai's ruler trounced all other competitors with a peregrine that flew the course in sixteen seconds, or fifty miles an hour.

The races quickly caught on—and spawned a cottage industry. Royal families dispatched high-paid agents to purchase promising racers from breeders domestically and abroad, and set up desert training grounds where elite coaches could teach their falcons to fly in straight lines and stay low to the ground, even using light aircraft to drag feathered lures ahead of the birds at high speeds. Dieticians maintained the birds at racing weight, while veterinarians kept their feathers in perfect condition; a frayed or broken quill could be a significant disadvantage in a sport where a few tenths of a second can separate the top contestants in a heat. A champion falcon can compete for only three or four years before losing its edge, at which point the best are often retired to stud. (Rumors have persisted, but have never been proven, that older falcons are destroyed once they've passed their racing prime.) One of the greatest studs in racing history, Fast Lad, a sixteen-year-old gyrfalcon owned by Bryn Close—a breeder in Northern England for various Emirati royal families—has sired hundreds of winners in a dozen years.

Five years after bringing racing to Dubai, Crown Prince Hamdan introduced the Fazza ("Victory") Championships, a two-week competition with $8 million in prizes provided by his family. An Italian-designed system of laser beams that sensed exactly when a peregrine crossed the starting and finish lines ensured precision timing to the hundredth of a second. The crown prince created separate racing categories for sheikhs, professional falconers, and the public, with distinct heats for juvenile and adult birds, hybrids and purebreds, and males and females. In 2014 Sheikh Khalifa bin Zayed Al Nahyan, the ruler of Abu Dhabi and the fourth wealthiest monarch in the world, with a fortune estimated at $15 billion, created a tournament with even greater rewards. The President Cup, held each January at the Abu Dhabi Falconers Club and paid for by the Al Nahyan clan, offers a purse of $11 million. The prizes include sixty Nissan Patrol SUVs, dozens of cash awards of up to twenty-five thousand dirhams ($6,800), and—most important to status-obsessed royals—engraved golden trophies for the winners in the six championship events.

The President Cup is an exquisitely organized affair. In the huge spectators' tent at the edge of the desert racecourse, sheikhs and their entourages, draped in white gowns and keffiyehs, relax on ornate sofas and wing chairs, plucking grapes, apples, and oranges from porcelain bowls while observing the races through floor-to-ceiling windows or on closed-circuit television screens. Boys in white turbans circulate among the guests—mostly Emiratis, but also breeders from across the globe—pouring shots of bitter Arabic coffee from brass urns into white ceramic cups. Dozens of hooded falcons of different hues and sizes wait on wooden perches to be carried down a red carpet one by one to the starting gate, where an announcer whips up excitement with vehement exhortations and pleas to God. Dehooded and released from the trainer's wrist at a signal, most falcons hug the ground and fly on a straight trajectory across the four-hundred-meter-long field, but a few rise up as if preparing for the stoop, and, when I visited the President Cup in January 2018, one gyrfalcon belonging to Sheikh Mohammed, the ruler of Dubai, veered off toward a distant line of sand dunes, to the dismay of her supporters, before finding her way back to the course. She crossed the finish line with a time four seconds slower than the next-to-last bird.

The competition between the Al Maktoum and the Al Nahyan families, and to a lesser extent the ruling clans of other Gulf States, has fueled a quest for the fastest, hardiest, and most beautiful falcons in the world. The falcon market was "on a downward spiral before the races—breeders all around the world were struggling," Zimbabwean breeder Howard Waller told *Arabian Business* for a 2015 article entitled "Sheikh Hamdan's Bid to Revive the Glorious Arab Sport of Falconry." Now, he said, "it's become an international business opportunity—everybody's trying to get in." Waller quoted the top price for a captive-bred female peregrine from the United Kingdom as £70,000, up from just £1,500 a few years earlier. In 2013 a pure white gyrfalcon, the largest and most powerful species of the Falconidae family, had been sold to a royal in Doha, the capital of Qatar, for one million dirhams, or $272,000, "drawing gasps from breeders," according to the magazine. Crown Prince Hamdan matched that price four years later, a well-placed source in Abu Dhabi told me, for a captive-bred gyrfalcon-peregrine hybrid that had just swept to victory in four consecutive races in the President Cup. "Any strong falcon the Crown Prince hears about he buys," the source said. "For him, it is all about prestige."

=

By the twentieth century, Europeans had come to revile peregrines as pests and vermin. In June 1940 Great Britain's Air Ministry declared the peregrine a menace to the carrier pigeons that Royal Air Force pilots were releasing from cockpits to dispatch messages to contacts in Nazi-occupied Europe. The government authorized the shooting of hundreds of adult and juvenile birds and the killing of thousands of chicks and eggs in the nests.

The environmental consciousness that spread across Europe and the United States in the 1960s and 1970s helped revive an appreciation for birds of prey. These days some five thousand Americans and twenty-five thousand Britons participate in falconry, triple the number from five decades ago. The birders range from urban enthusiasts like Helen Macdonald, who trained a goshawk named Mabel in her home in Cambridge, to wealthy landowners who stage hunts on horseback each summer in the Northumberland countryside. One English writer called the revival a "back-to-nature quest," stemming from "a postindustrial society's hunger to reconnect with ancient traditions."

Near the Welsh village of Carmarthen, an English biologist, sportsman, and entrepreneur named Nick Fox has bred falcons for thirty years for Sheikh Mohammed bin Rashid Al Maktoum, the ruler of Dubai, an Anglophile who first traveled to the United Kingdom in 1966 to study English in Cambridge. In recent years he's been joined by other registered breeders in the United Kingdom, Ireland, France, Spain, Germany, the United States, and South Africa who now compete for shares of the fantastically lucrative Arab market; today, the majority of the twelve thousand captive-bred raptors exported from the West are destined for the United Arab Emirates. Fox also sells the richest Arabs a falconry flight-training device called the Robara, a remote-controlled machine, shaped like a houbara bustard, that can match the cruising speeds of falcons and act as the bait. In Dubai a venture partly owned by the Al Maktoum family takes Western tourists in hot-air balloons over the Arabian Desert to watch trained falcons fly and dive at five thousand feet.

This money-fueled globalization also has an underside: a thriving black market for wild birds of prey, driven by wealthy enthusiasts who believe that falcons stolen from nests are innately superior to those bred in captivity, and who are willing to break the law to get them. It's a shadowy world that would draw in a skilled climber, obsessive egg collector, footloose adventurer, and cunning manipulator, who had been heading for trouble since his boyhood in the Southern African bush half a century ago.

FIVE

RHODESIA

The boy was up to something, Pat Lorber was sure of it. From the moment she'd first noticed him carrying a fishing rod around the Hillside Dams, she could tell that he hadn't come there to fish. He was deep in the woods, nowhere near the water. And he was looking toward the treetops, where the nests were.

Lorber visited the Hillside Dams—a pair of man-made lakes in Bulawayo, the second largest city of Rhodesia (the Southern African country today known as Zimbabwe)—a couple of days a week to survey the birds during breeding season. The amateur ornithologist would leave her infant daughter with her mother or a caretaker to roam the footpaths for hours through forests and fields with a notebook and binoculars, compiling observations on nest building, breeding behavior, feeding methods, and birdcalls for articles she published frequently in a local journal or a South African birdwatchers' magazine. There were splendid sights at nearly every turn. African jacanas—chestnut-colored waders with black wingtips and a long black stripe sweeping across their white heads—probed for insects atop water lilies, using their enormous feet and claws to balance on the floating vegetation. Crimson-breasted shrikes, white-bellied sunbirds, scarlet-chested sunbirds, black-headed orioles, and fiery-necked nightjars, as brilliantly colorful as their names suggest, nested in the thick cover of acacias and leadwood trees. On that day, in late 1972, she had been studying the fork of a massive acacia where a spotted eagle owl, with prominent ear tufts and bright yellow eyes, laid its eggs each year. She was "hyperactive and aware," she remembers, when she noticed the boy peering into the trees.

Lorber ducked behind a rocky hill that rose over the forest. From her perch she watched the boy, a slightly built adolescent, expertly scale a leadwood tree and disappear amid the foliage. After fifteen minutes of probing the branches, he began his descent. As soon as his feet touched the ground, Lorber clambered down from the rocks.

"Hello," she said. "I'm Pat Lorber. Who are you?"

"I'm Jeffrey," he replied.

"What are you doing, Jeff?"

"Going to go fishing up at the dam," he said.

"You're not nest or egg collecting, are you?" she asked. Many local boys liked to clamber into trees and raid birds' nests after school, but this was the first time Lorber had ever encountered anyone threatening her work at the Hillside Dams, a government sanctuary where egg foraging was strictly forbidden.

"No," he said, "I just like to see what's in the nests."

"Now, here is the thing, Jeff," Lorber said. "I'm doing a survey where I'm trying to establish how many birds breed in this particular area. You're not going to be taking eggs, are you?"

"No, I don't collect eggs."

"Because a small and determined egg collector is going to muck up my figures."

"I'm not doing anything," the boy insisted. Then he scampered off.

That evening, the phone rang at Lorber's home.

"Jeffrey said you accused him of egg collecting while he was down at the Hillside Dams," said Peggy Lendrum, Jeffrey Lendrum's mother. Lorber knew her in passing as a teacher at the local high school, but they had never spoken and she was surprised the woman had managed to obtain her phone number. Peggy sounded defensive and aggressive. "I want you to know that Jeffrey is a very truthful boy," she said, "and if he says he's not egg collecting, he's not egg collecting."

"Okay, Peggy," Lorber said. "All right, then. 'Bye." She was certain that Jeffrey Lendrum had been lying, but she didn't want to make too much of it. The Lendrums were a respectable family. Hopefully the boy had learned his lesson.

=

It was Jeffrey Lendrum's father, Adrian, he would always say, who had sparked his interest in egg collecting. "My father was passionate about wildlife," the younger Lendrum would recall decades later, "not just birds, but beetles, butterflies, moths. He collected everything." When Jeffrey was eight years old, Adrian enlisted him to raid the nest of a groundscraper thrush, a small, black-and-white-speckled songbird that lays its tiny blue eggs in clutches of two to four, high in trees in cup-shaped nests often woven from spiders' webs. After Jeffrey had taken the eggs, Adrian taught him how to insert a pipette and "blow" the contents—expelling the live embryo so that it wouldn't rot inside the eggshell—and mount the empty shell in Adrian's modest egg collection, which contained about twenty specimens.

With his father's encouragement, Jeffrey Lendrum became a prolific nest raider, clambering perilously from tree limb to tree limb dozens of feet off the ground, combing through the foliage and grabbing colorful treasures. Lendrum had an instinctive sense of how to "read" a tree—calculating his route by the pattern of the branching, the brittleness of the wood, the width of the trunk and branches, even the quality of the bark. He prided himself on his intimate knowledge of the forest. "I've climbed to more nests than you probably had hot breakfasts," he would later say. And because most collecting was against the law, it required stealth and, sometimes, an ability to lie with a straight face. That day he was spotted by Lorber, Lendrum had been searching for the distinctive blue eggs of the redheaded weaver, a perching bird that builds nests out of leaf stalks, twigs, and tendrils in baobabs and other trees throughout Southern Africa.

Rhodesia had some of the strictest conservation legislation on the continent. The eggs of most small birds and common raptors could be taken from private land, but only if one had the landowner's written permission. The government banned collecting eggs in national parks, except with a hard-to-obtain permit for scientific research. It was illegal everywhere to take the eggs of several dozen "Specially Protected Species," including secretary birds, black pelicans, cranes, flamingos, and most raptors. African black eagles, martial eagles, bateleur eagles, brown snake eagles, black breasted snake eagles, Ovambo sparrow hawks, yellow-billed kites, black-shouldered kites, giant eagle owls, spotted eagle owls, tawny eagles, peregrine falcons, lanner falcons, and a dozen more birds of prey were very much sought-after by unscrupulous sportsmen, collectors, and traders; several of these species were unique to Southern Africa. The hunting, removal, and sale of these endangered animals was punishable by up to several years in prison. A handful of researchers and top falconers could get an exemption, but for everyone else, it was taboo.

Jeffrey Lendrum ignored all the prohibitions. He rode through the bush for miles each day on his bicycle, carrying a throw line with a heavy weight on one end to wrap around high branches and facilitate his ascent. He'd scan trees for bunches of sticks and developed a keen eye for following birds to their nests. And he came up with ingenious tricks for procuring eggs. Vernon Tarr, a neighbor in Bulawayo, remembers Lendrum's determination to sneak an egg away from a crowned eagle—one of Southern Africa's rarest raptors, a large and powerful bird with a russet-brown crest that has been known to seize small children in its huge talons. (In 1924, anthropologists in South Africa unearthed the skeleton of a toddler known as the "Taung Child," a humanoid that lived two million years ago; scientists would determine that a crowned eagle had swept up the child and taken it to its nest, where the raptor ripped out its eyes.) Lendrum would find a suitable tree, carry up "tons of sticks, and build a rudimentary nest there," Tarr says. "The next year the crowned eagles moved in." Lendrum would wait until the female laid her eggs in the aerie he had built, and then would climb into her nest and snatch them.

Howard Waller, one of Lendrum's closest boyhood friends, says that Lendrum was driven by an obsession that went far beyond that of a schoolboy hobbyist. Even then, stealing eggs was about more than just collecting; he had a real competitive streak. Waller remembers clambering into nests as an adolescent to take the live eggs of the common sparrow hawk. "I'd climb a tree and there would be a chicken egg in the nest with a sign on it saying, 'Too late sucker,'" he recalls.

=

The Lendrum family's route to Rhodesia had been a long one. Adrian Lendrum, a third-generation African with roots in Cork, Ireland, had been born in Kenya in the 1930s. (The word "Lendrum" is Celtic for "moor of the ridge.") His mother died just after his birth, leaving Adrian's father devastated, and with three young children to raise on his own. When Adrian was about three months old, he and his two older siblings left Kenya to live with their paternal grandparents in South Africa. Several years later, they were summoned back by their father, now remarried with stepchildren in Northern Rhodesia, a copper-rich and landlocked British protectorate in Southern Africa, just south of the Belgian Congo. Adrian attended school there, worked as a manager for the Rhokana Copper Mine, and met his wife, Peggy, also a third-generation African. Jeffrey, their oldest child, was born in October 1961 in Kitwe, the colony's second-largest city. It wouldn't be long, however, before Adrian Lendrum was moving on again.

In February 1960, British Prime Minister Harold Macmillan acknowledged, standing before the South African Parliament, that a black "national consciousness" was rising across the continent. Over the next four years, one British colony after another—Nigeria, Sierra Leone, Uganda, Tanganyika (modern-day Tanzania), Kenya—declared independence, along with the Belgian Congo and France's colonies in North, West, and Central Africa. Northern Rhodesia's turn came in 1964. Following nearly a decade of protest marches, strikes, and other civil disobedience, Britain's Colonial Office allowed an election early that year, with universal suffrage. A party led by a popular teacher and freedom fighter named Kenneth Kaunda won by a landslide, and what was once Northern Rhodesia became the independent black-ruled nation of Zambia.

Kaunda, who became Zambia's first president, soon declared his country a one-party state, and launched a massive scheme to nationalize land and private enterprises, which was when Adrian Lendrum started thinking about leaving the country. "He saw the way things were going in Zambia," says his younger son Richard, who was born in 1966. "He wanted something else." According to younger sister Paula, who was born in 1969, the immediate catalyst for the move was a robbery in Kitwe during which Peggy Lendrum was held at knifepoint.

In 1969, Adrian and his wife, Peggy, drove south from Kitwe with their children, across the massive Lake Kariba dam on the Zambezi River, to Southern Rhodesia, now known simply as Rhodesia, one of Africa's last holdouts of white-minority rule. Many of Rhodesia's 270,000 whites owned farms that had been in the family for two or three generations, and were terrified by what they saw happening around them. In 1965, the Rhodesian cabinet had unilaterally broken free of Great Britain and, in defiance of the international community, declared Rhodesia a sovereign state.

Situated on the Rhodesian Highveld, a vast stretch of savanna and bush-covered hills between the Zambezi and Limpopo Rivers, Bulawayo was a bustling colonial outpost, a factory town known for its furniture, clothing, and wooden construction parts, and the railhead for Southern Africa. About sixty thousand whites and several hundred thousand blacks lived in the city, their interactions limited by the white-supremacist politics of the era. The black population lived in crowded townships, while middle-class whites were all but guaranteed a big house, a garden, and servants. (Poorer whites, most of whom had come to Bulawayo to work for the railway, lived far more modestly.) White boys and girls learned British history and geography and played cricket, rugby, and field hockey on idyllic campuses carved out of the bush. For white adults, one's social life revolved around an academy of music, a theater club, a ballet society, a choral society, the Rotary Club, and the Bulawayo Club, a billiards-and-drinking establishment founded in the 1890s exclusively for men. The annual highlight was a parade down Abercorn Street, Bulawayo's main avenue, commemorating the Pioneer Column: a force of five hundred colonists and soldiers recruited by the mining magnate Cecil John Rhodes, that marched from South Africa through Matabeleland and Mashonaland in 1890 and established the first white settlements in what would become Southern Rhodesia. Just twenty miles down the road lay the Matobo National Park, carved in part from Rhodes's former cattle ranch, a sprawling reserve filled with big game and birds of prey.

The Lendrums moved into a handsome house in the leafy Hillside neighborhood on the eastern side of town, with a large garden filled with flowering trees and a live-in husband-and-wife team that worked as the family's gardener and domestic servant. After arriving in Bulawayo, Adrian landed a position as a human resources manager at Dunlop Tyres Africa, while Peggy taught at Girls' College, a private high school. Jeffrey attended a private elementary school, where he was well behaved but bored and easily distracted in class, preferring to roam the bush in search of birds and other wildlife with a handful of like-minded friends. The family was close, Richard says, but it was the older son, Jeffrey, with whom Adrian formed the deepest bond.

In early 1973, Adrian showed up with eleven-year-old Jeffrey at the monthly meeting of the Rhodesian Ornithological Society. Bird-watching was a popular pursuit in the young country, reflecting the pride that many of its privileged white citizens took in its game parks and rich wildlife. About thirty members were present the evening the Lendrums walked into the cozy basement lecture room of Bulawayo's Natural History Museum of Zimbabwe, opened in 1964 and considered one of the best in Southern Africa. The Lendrums, younger than almost all of the rest, exuded an energy and enthusiasm that drew a crowd as Adrian Lendrum recounted how an Ayres's hawk eagle, a fierce-looking bird mottled black and white, had roosted in his garden a year before. It was a thrilling sight, he said, and had sparked a fascination for birds of prey.

The father and son "were likable, smooth, gregarious, and chatty," says Pat Lorber, who was there that evening. She'd chalked up her encounter with the younger Lendrum the previous year to typical boyhood mischief and hadn't given him another thought. The Lendrums were asked to join a Saturday survey of waterbirds at the Aiselby Dam outside town, a reservoir rich with African pipits, sacred ibises, red-capped larks, African wattled lapwings, African purple swamp hens, ospreys, Temminck's coursers, and dozens of other species. The birders also encouraged the pair to come back to the museum for evening ornithological documentaries. Soon the group invited them to participate in its longest-running and most prestigious project: the African Black Eagle Survey, launched by a warden at Matobo National Park in the early 1960s. It was an invitation that all would come to regret.

=

Matobo is one of the African continent's geological oddities: a 165-square-mile field of granite domes, huge rolling rock slabs known as whalebacks, and blocks of broken granite piled one on top of the other as if some gargantuan toddler had used the boulders as playthings. The cooling and erosion of buried magma some two billion years ago formed the stony landscape. In between the striking rock formations, some of which rise to thirty-five hundred feet, lie swampy valleys, or *vleis*, fed by rainwater runoff and rich in acacias, mopanis, figs, euphorbias, and other vegetation. Thirty-two species of raptors—four hundred breeding pairs—nest in tall trees or on rock ledges, largely protected from baboons and other predators, subsisting on rock hyraxes and yellow-spotted hyraxes—small, furry mammals both known in Rhodesia as "dassies."

The black eagle has been one of the park's star attractions since tourists began visiting Matobo in the 1920s. Otherwise known as Verreaux's eagle, after French ornithologist Jules Verreaux, who brought back specimens to the National Academy of Sciences in Paris in the early nineteenth century, this coal-black raptor has fierce yellow eyes, a massive wingspan, and a telltale white V on its back. "They can fly in a gale of [one hundred miles] per hour," the South African raptor expert Rob Davies observed, "draw their wings in slightly and make progress into the eye of the wind, while other birds are being flung across the sky." Watching them fly alongside lesser eagle species was, he said, "like watching jet fighters escort a bomber." The raptors build massive stick nests on the ledges of cliff faces, often hundreds of feet above the ground, and frequently occupy them for decades. Some nests, augmented with twigs, grass, and other materials over the years, grow to twenty feet deep and ten feet wide. Survey participants had counted sixty pairs of black eagles in Matobo National Park—the highest concentration of the raptors in the world.

At the time that the Lendrums became involved, the survey leader was Valerie Gargett, a Quaker and former high school math teacher who had quit her job in 1969 to devote herself full-time to ornithology. Her many admirers had come to view her as a sort of Jane Goodall of the raptor world. A teetotaling vegetarian, whose years in the field had left her lean, suntanned, and supremely fit, Gargett spent many hours each week clambering up rock faces and perching on ledges to observe the life cycle of her beloved black eagles. Several of these wild raptors came to trust her and granted her extraordinary access. "Val could go put her hand gently under one particular eagle, feel how many eggs she had, then take the egg and weigh it," Lorber remembers. Vernon Tarr, the Lendrums' neighbor, once watched Gargett slip a thermometer between the eagle's breast feathers and her brood patch—a bare patch of skin filled with blood vessels that provides insulation for her chicks—to measure the incubation temperature. "The eagle didn't flinch," he says.

Gargett had assembled several dozen volunteers to help her follow the courtship of eagle pairs, their nest building and egg laying, and the incubation, hatching, and fledging of their young. "Do not stay at or near the nest for longer than five minutes to obtain the information," she instructed her assistants, who paired off and monitored two or three aeries per team during nesting season between January and April. "We are visitors to their world and respect their right to live undisturbed and uninfluenced by us." She urged volunteers, most of whom were not young, to keep in top condition. "It paid to be physically fit and if possible a little underweight, [as] it was sometimes necessary to pass through narrow cracks in the rocks, and even down short rock tunnels," Gargett wrote in her 1990 book *The Black Eagle*. "One member on the portly side became wedged in a crack and laughed at his own predicament, until he became so firmly fixed that nobody could move him. In those circumstances one simply had to wait for the victim to relax; struggling was useless."

When Jeffrey and Adrian Lendrum joined the group, Valerie and her husband, Eric, were delighted to have a vigorous, agile father and son to monitor some of the least accessible nest sites. Eric Gargett, a member of the Bulawayo city council and an experienced technical climber, taught Jeffrey the basics of rappelling, or abseiling, as it was called in Rhodesia: how to fix a secure belay at the top of a cliff, thread the line through the caribiners on his harness, tie the complex knots upon which his life depended, and maintain the proper stance as he launched from the top of the cliff and moved down and across the face. The younger Lendrum, a natural athlete, became a fearless rappeller, descending six-hundred-foot rock faces to perch on a narrow ledge beside an aerie. Sometimes his *shamwari* ("friend" in Shona, the dominant tribal language of Rhodesia) Howard Waller, an avid falconer, would join him. "Jeff was cocky, macho, and athletic, like his father," Lorber remembers. "Howard was the quiet, geeky one."

After two years Val Gargett entrusted Adrian and his son with a spin-off survey of the augur buzzard, a black raptor with a rust-colored tail that builds nests on ledges at the base of vertical cracks in cliffs, or at the intersection of trees and cliffs. Gargett had an endless appetite for data and often created new surveys to be carried out by other members of the society. "The Lendrums are so active, and so useful, and so nice," Gargett enthused to Lorber. "Adrian and Jeffrey will be perfect." Thirteen-year-old Jeffrey Lendrum was now struggling at the Christian Brothers College in Bulawayo, an all-boys day school staffed by lay teachers. Discipline was lax, Paula remembers, and her brother's difficulties focusing on classes and homework worsened. But his enthusiasm for the outdoors balanced out his lack of concentration in the classroom. Working on weekends and on holidays, the Lendrums located thirty aeries and surveyed the buzzards for hundreds of hours between 1975 and 1977. Hiking side by side for hours through the bush, climbing trees and cliffs, and sharing observations about the birds' behavior strengthened the father-son relationship. They noted the raptors' "kow-kow" courtship call and the "bombing-diving-and-stooping" and "spiraling-twisting-and-talon grasping" of the male's mating dance, as Adrian Lendrum described it in one report. They observed the bird's swoop from a perch and its plunge from a hover "that resembled a fast parachute drop" in pursuit of a rodent or an insect.

Three years later Adrian and Jeffrey took over a survey of the African hawk eagle, the park's second-most-prevalent bird of prey, which constructs large, heavy stick nests in tree forks. Gargett passed on to her protégés dozens of nest locations. Back in his element, Jeffrey—now lithe, strong, and brimming with a self-confidence in the outdoors that verged on brashness—scrambled to nests at the tops of euphorbias, ficuses, and brown ironwood, or *Homalium dentatum* trees, and though his father wasn't nearly the climber that Jeffrey was, he sometimes joined his son. "They would throw up a claw, and climb up the tree as high as they could," Lorber remembers. "It required a lot of skill, and involved some risk. This was derring-do stuff."

Adrian and his son didn't confine their contributions to the field. In their nine years working with Gargett and her team of volunteers, the Lendrums published a total of eighteen academic studies of hawk eagles, augur buzzards, crowned eagles, and other birds of prey, chiefly for *Ostrich*, a quarterly produced by the South African Ornithological Society. The pair also contributed to *Bokmakierie*, another South African magazine for bird-watchers. These were serious-minded and technical articles filled with exhaustive descriptions of clutch and egg sizes, the types of green foliage used in nests, the establishment of hunting territory, and, on a lurid note, examples of what Gargett called "Cain-and-Abel conflict"—the killing of one raptor sibling by the other shortly after hatching, usually by pecking it to death. Adrian Lendrum was the brains of the team, colleagues understood, while his son provided the derring-do.

Delighted by his development as an ornithologist, Gargett invited the elder Lendrum to join the Rhodesian Ornithological Society's steering committee, a select set of half a dozen individuals who met once a month to organize the bird-watching and film program for the next half year. She also took the Lendrums on field trips across Matobo, sharing the society's most closely guarded secrets: the exact locations of hundreds of nests.

=

In the late 1970s, as the Lendrums were surveying birds in Matobo, the Rhodesian Bush War crept up on Bulawayo. Rhodesia didn't have the brutal apartheid system of neighboring South Africa, but the country was riddled with injustices. The 1961 Constitution guaranteed that whites would hold fifty of the sixty-five seats in Parliament, even though they made up only 8 percent of the population. Other laws forced two-thirds of the country's black population to live in communally held Tribal Trust lands, which quickly became over-populated and overgrazed; banned black-opposition groups; and forbade speech and writing critical of Prime Minister Ian Smith. In 1972 the Zimbabwe People's Revolutionary Army, an Ndebele force in the south led by the trade union leader, politician, and activist Joshua

Nkomo, joined with Robert Mugabe's Zimbabwe African National Union guerrillas, most of whom belonged to Rhodesia's majority Shona tribe, to try to bring down the country's racist white-minority regime.

By 1978, 12,500 insurgents were fighting in Rhodesia. About 10,800 Rhodesian Army regulars and 40,000 white reservists opposed them. All white males between eighteen and sixty were obligated to train and serve part of the year in the reserve. Lorber's husband, a German national who wasn't even a Rhodesian citizen, volunteered to be a police reservist. Adrian Lendrum was drafted into service, too. "My dad used to go up on call-ups every six weeks to serve in the bush," Richard Lendrum recalled. "The war affected everyone."

At sixteen, in 1977, Jeffrey Lendrum transferred from Christian Brothers to Gifford High School, a boys-only, government-run institution with a reputation for strict discipline. But he failed most of his O levels—nationwide qualification exams in a variety of subjects—and left school in 1978, with no hope of continuing to college. That same year, as warfare intensified, he applied, at the age of seventeen, to join the Rhodesian Special Air Service (SAS) C Squadron, an elite unit originally formed during the Second World War. Lendrum has said that he spent about six months going through the unit's arduous selection process but was then felled by a hernia and never completed the training. His sister, Paula, remembers it differently. "Being a nonconformist [he] gave up," she says. He transferred to Internal Affairs, a unit responsible for guarding villages in the Rhodesian bush, a less-than-heroic posting that usually meant hunkering down with a rifle behind a pile of sandbags. Still, Lendrum claims that he saw some action, conducting "hot extractions" of troops under fire by military helicopter. "He saw some terrible things," says his friend Michelle

Conway, who grew up with the Lendrums in Bulawayo and later attended university in South Africa with Jeffrey's brother, Richard.

Today Lendrum's name adorns a "Wall of Shame" on the SAS C Squadron website, comprised of individuals who falsely claim to have served with the unit. "Some of these impostors are coming out with such ludicrous stories about their time spent in [C Squadron] that we have to expose them for the sad cases they are," the website says. "One thing you get to know about Jeff," says a friend of twenty years, "is that he likes to think that he's done everything and seen everything, and he has done a lot of things, but you got to take some of it with a pinch of salt."

In the last year of the war, Joshua Nkomo's guerrillas sought sanctuary in the rocky redoubts of the Matobo Hills just outside the national park. They buried land mines on roads, sabotaged water pumps, ambushed cars, and laid explosives on tracks. The Rhodesian Ornithological Society struggled to keep its projects going. Some volunteers dropped out. At her husband's insistence, Lorber never ventured into the field without stashing her nine-millimeter pistol under her seat. Gargett, who refused to carry a gun, made the twenty-mile journey to Matobo alone until her husband demanded that she either ride with him or find another armed escort.

As the war heated up, the Ornithological Society became an escape, a bit of normality in terrible times. Society members' opinions on the war ran across the spectrum, from hard-liners who backed Ian Smith and his Rhodesian Front and feared that black rule would lead to catastrophe, to liberals like Val and Eric Gargett, who wished for power-sharing and a more just society. Val Gargett had taught at a black high school before becoming a full-time ornithologist, and her husband had fought to improve health and education for black

Rhodesians while serving on Bulawayo's city council. But no matter their differences, all bird lovers flocked to the monthly meetings at the national museum to forget, briefly, the threat of being blown up by a land mine, ambushed by guerrillas—or jumpy government troops—or shot by a surface-to-air missile from out of the sky, as had happened to a mother and daughter the Lendrums knew.

It was around this time that Gargett began to notice disturbing things happening to her surveys in Matobo. The irregularities were small at first: a lanner falcon or snake eagle nest being monitored would suddenly turn up empty. Monkeys or other predators, people assumed, had eaten the eggs. Then the survey turned up an alarming rise in the number of "incomplete breeding cycles" among Gargett's black eagles. Breeding pairs built nests with sticks and lined them with greenery—the standard pre-laying ritual—but no eggs were ever seen by researchers. It could have been that the birds couldn't find enough to eat, which would have affected productivity. But scientists had determined that the park's dassie population had grown by 20 percent in recent years. The evidence pointed to sabotage or theft. And it seemed to be an inside job. "This had never happened before," Lorber remembers. "This was a small, tight community, threatened by a bush war, and you don't want internal strife. You are holding people together."

In the last weeks of 1979, with the war at a stalemate, Rhodesian Prime Minister Ian Smith entered into negotiations with the insurgents. The British government, led by Margaret Thatcher, brokered the talks in London. On December 12, the sides announced a ceasefire, and the following March, Robert Mugabe was elected the first president of Zimbabwe. Most blacks were jubilant. White reactions ranged from exhilaration to restrained optimism to a conviction that the country was about to descend into chaos. Pat Lorber tried to persuade her father and her husband, both of whom were strong Rhodesian Front supporters, that Mugabe intended to rule inclusively and transparently. But, unlike her friend and mentor Val Gargett, she also harbored doubts about the new state's viability.

Even as the fate of the new nation dominated thoughts and conversations, the inexplicable little troubles in Matobo continued. One day Adrian Lendrum joined Gargett to photograph a breeding pair of the rare Mackinder's eagle owl (*Bubo mackinderi*), one of the largest owls in Africa, a tawny brown bug-and-lizard-eater with massive talons and startlingly bright pumpkin-colored eyes. Only a single pair had ever been sighted in the park. Gargett carefully guarded the nest location, telling only Lendrum and a few other confidants. The nest had a clutch of two eggs inside it when Gargett and Lendrum visited. When Gargett returned alone to inspect the nest a week later, she was shocked to discover that the clutch was gone.

The Lendrums, meanwhile, were gaining more official responsibilities. In May 1982, the Department of National Parks and Wildlife Management issued the Lendrums a permit to place tracking tags on birds of prey in Matobo and in Hwange National Park, a fifty-six-hundred-square-mile reserve, two hundred miles northwest of Bulawayo, that was home to one of Southern Africa's largest populations of elephants. Jeffrey Lendrum, still living with his parents, was working as the manager of a local cannery, and he and his father now had carte blanche to roam both parks.

Later that same year Steve Edwards, a senior warden at Matobo, came across a spectacular find: a crowned eagle nest with a single egg—large, creamy white, with dark brown specks and blotches—perched in a high fork of a 120-foot-tall tree off one of the park roads.

The crowned eagle was, like the Mackinder's eagle owl, one of the rarest Southern African raptors; only three mating pairs had been counted in the park. Edwards, exhilarated by the discovery, headed back for another look two days later, the usual time it took for a crowned eagle to lay the second egg in its two-egg clutch. This time Edwards encountered Jeffrey Lendrum heading in the other direction.

"Have you just been to the crowned eagle nest?" Edwards asked him.

"Yes, and there are two eggs in there," Lendrum replied, adding, oddly, that the ranger now had no reason to check. Edwards clambered up the tree anyway and discovered that the nest was empty.

What the hell is going on here? he wondered. All but certain that Lendrum had stolen them, he would soon report to Val Gargett what he had seen.

Gargett had been wrestling with conflicted feelings about her protégés. She found it hard to imagine that the father and son she had watched grow into self-assured ornithologists might be engaged in anything unethical. She and her husband had mentored the Lendrums, spent many hours with them in the field, and come to view them almost as family; the possibility that they had betrayed the Gargetts' trust, lied to them, and corrupted their surveys was emotionally wrenching for her even to consider. Still, she began quietly increasing her visits to the aeries that the Lendrums had surveyed. At one African hawk eagle nest—where the Lendrums had reported that the eaglet had fledged—the surrounding rocks were missing the telltale "whitewash," or bird feces, that always accumulates as the chick grows older. She saw no indication that the eggs had ever hatched.

Gargett shared her suspicions about the Lendrums with Steve Edwards, and he agreed to initiate an investigation.

SIX

LIVERPOOL

Andy McWilliam fell into police work by a process of elimination. McWilliam's father had left school at fourteen following the death of his own father in his thirties from the lingering effects of a poison-gas attack in the trenches during World War I. After dropping out, the elder McWilliam had joined the British Merchant Navy, the national commercial fleet, and worked until retirement as a shipboard electrician. Growing up in the 1960s in Litherland, a working-class town in the Metropolitan Borough of Sefton, just north of Liverpool, and later in nearby Crosby, the young McWilliam had shown similar restlessness and no great enthusiasm for study. He couldn't wait to escape the classroom and join his friends on the rugby field or cricket ground. The only facts and figures that grabbed his attention were the wins and losses of the Everton Football Club, his family's favorite team for three generations.

Everton's archrival, Liverpool FC, had begun its rise to the championship of English football in the early 1960s, and matches between the two clubs were charged with tension. McWilliam watched them play from the standing-room-only tier at Goodison Park, Everton's home ground. On occasion he ventured into enemy territory, walking half a mile across Stanley Park, a 110-acre spread of lawns, flower gardens and lakes, to Liverpool's Anfield stadium. After every Liverpool goal, thousands of fans would break into spirited renditions of "She Loves You" and other hits by the hometown Beatles. The crowd would surge, and McWilliam would be right in the thick of it.

As a boy and into his adolescence, McWilliam watched two popular police procedurals each week on the BBC. *Z Cars*, a half-hour midweek drama set in the fictional town of Newton in northwest England, featured a rotating pair of patrolmen and a rousing theme song that Everton adopted as its anthem in 1963. On Saturdays came *Dixon of Dock Green*, centering around the relationship between a grizzled desk sergeant, Constable George Dixon, and a young detective, Andy Crawford, at a fictional station in London's East End. Each week the policemen cracked crimes ranging from missing persons cases to bank robberies to gangland killings. McWilliam loved everything about the dramas: the investigations, interrogations, banter between the police, and even Dixon's famous catchphrases that started and ended the program each Saturday night: "Evening all" and "Night all." Later, at Waterloo secondary school, McWilliam began searching regularly through the index card file at the Career Office for an occupation that matched his poor academic credentials. Great Britain's police forces in those years were desperate to fill their ranks, and paid little attention to test scores or grades. "I thought, *I can do this*," he recalls. The only other option, as he saw it, was joining the Merchant Navy like his father, which, considering his proclivity for seasickness, held little appeal.

In the summer of 1973, while waiting for the results of his O levels, he sat for the police exam to become a cadet in the Liverpool and Bootle Constabulary. It turned out to be more challenging than he had anticipated. "What is the Ku Klux Klan?" was one multiple-choice question. Flummoxed, he answered, "A Chinese political party." He failed the test. Then, as he pondered what possible career options he had left, his mother found an advertisement in the local newspaper, seeking recruits for the police in Surrey, a county in southeast England. The glossy brochure that the force sent him when he requested more information stressed "the active side of the job," he recalled, promising a heavy emphasis on sports and physical fitness. McWilliam decided to take the county's test. "They must have been really struggling to find recruits," he says, "because the questions were along the lines of, 'What is wet and puts out fires? And here's another clue: Ducks swim in it.'" This time, he passed.

Shortly after that, McWilliam received his O level results: he had failed six out of his eight exams, eking out passing grades in only mathematics and English. It was a dismal performance, but he consoled himself with the knowledge that he was already on his way to a career. In the fall, he took a part-time job in the toy section of Owen Owens, a Liverpool department store, waiting for his police training to begin at the start of the new year.

On the third of January, 1974, McWilliam's parents drove him down to the Hendon Police Cadet College in north London and dropped him and his single suitcase at the front gate of the urban complex. He was sixteen, the same age as most of his fellow students, facing his first extended period away from home, and he was terrified. A cadet in full regalia met McWilliam at the entrance and escorted him across the parade ground to a room with eight bunks in one of three concrete dormitories. Cadets rose at dawn, put on their uniforms, made their bedrolls, ate a quick breakfast, and then assembled on the field at seven-thirty. Inspection officers moved up and down the rows, searching for signs of sloppiness—"You, boots!"—and sentencing those who failed to "fourteen days' default" or "twenty-eight days' default"—two weeks or a month of extra predawn dress parades alongside other transgressors. McWilliam felt alone, friendless, and overwhelmed by regimented life. *What the hell am I doing here?* he thought. By the end of the second week, half the four hundred recruits had dropped out.

But McWilliam grew used to the military discipline and he came to feel at home in the academy. The course load was light. McWilliam spent a couple of hours each day learning about British common law—derived from tradition and precedent rather than from statutes—and took training in police tactics and martial arts. Since the era of Sir Robert Peel, a Conservative Party politician (and future prime minister) who founded London's Metropolitan Police in the 1820s, British law enforcement officers followed a policy of "policing by consent," in recognition that the power of the police rested on public approval of their behavior, not on force. McWilliam was regularly reminded that the key to good policing was public outreach, and learning how "to talk down a situation." British law enforcement officers proudly went about their duties unarmed, a policy that had earned the force respect around the world.

When he wasn't in class or marching on the parade ground, McWilliam was free to explore London's West End and other lively neighborhoods, and do what he enjoyed most—playing sports. He competed in rugby, football, and cricket. He race-walked and ran track. He developed a passion for weight lifting, impressing and amusing his peers with his intense competitive streak. Desperate to slim down to his weight class before one match, he donned two judo suits and ran dozens of laps around the gym. Then, bathed in sweat and in danger of overheating, he tore off his clothes and performed twenty sets of jumping jacks nude. As he swung his arms and legs feverishly to shed the final ounces, his eyes were drawn to a large picture window that looked out over the campus. A dozen cadets in a driver's education class had gathered on the pavement below, gaping and laughing at the naked, flailing figure. McWilliam nodded at them, grinned, and kept going.

McWilliam graduated from police college after one year, and then took a ten-week intensive training course in Kent. On the first of September, 1975, the British government, intent on increasing the number of police officers, lowered the minimum age from nineteen to eighteen and a half. McWilliam reached that age on the third of September, and joined the Surrey Police Force the same day—becoming the youngest policeman, by his reckoning, in the British Isles.

=

The Surrey command dispatched McWilliam to a precinct in Woking, a drab commuter town south of London, with a population of about sixty thousand. His first week, he learned the ropes with a veteran. Then he was told, "That's it, mate. You're on your own." Soon he was both walking the beat and patrolling the streets by car: a teenage cop, proudly wearing a blue uniform with shiny brass buttons and, while on foot, a tall rounded custodian helmet. He carried a pair of handcuffs and a twelve-inch wooden truncheon for protection. One evening a friend introduced him to an attractive and spirited eighteen-year-old named Linda Gilbart, who grimaced when he told her he worked as a cop.

"Don't you like the police?" he asked.

"No," she replied, explaining that she'd been arrested and fined at sixteen for riding a motorcycle with learner plates. Undaunted, he popped up the courage and asked her on a date. They spent the evening at a pub in Staines, an old market town alongside the River Thames.

McWilliam enjoyed being a constable in Surrey. But after three years of trying to afford housing in the London suburbs on £40 a month (£600 today, or about $780), he realized that he would never escape from financial worries as long as he lived there. McWilliam transferred back to Liverpool, to the Merseyside Police Force. He married Lin a few months later. He was happy to be back home among his fellow "Scousers," or born-and-bred Liverpudlians—a name deriving from "lobscouse," a cheap salted-lamb-onion-and-pepper stew that Liverpool seamen first ate about three hundred years ago.

In the late nineteenth century, when McWilliam's great-grandparents were growing up in Liverpool, the city had been one of the world's richest ports, described in an 1851 issue of *The Bankers' Magazine* as "the New York of Europe." McWilliam's maternal grandfather had been a merchant seaman in the early twentieth century; his paternal grandfather had joined the flood of young men who proudly left the port during the Great War for Continental Europe, where he inhaled the poison gas that would ultimately take his life. McWilliam's family was also present for the city's most traumatic chapter: a relentless eight-day aerial bombardment in May 1941 that became known as the Liverpool blitz. McWilliam's father, then an apprentice electrician, served fire-watch duty near the docks, dodging rats in total darkness, and was sheltering in a bomb-proof bunker in his front garden when the house across the street took a direct hit.

He was called up to serve the following year, and joined the Fleet Air Arm of the Royal Navy. McWilliam's mother, the daughter of the seaman, also survived the blitz, then entered the Women's Royal Naval Service in 1942 and left for a base in Scotland. (They would meet in Liverpool soon after the war.)

All told, the Luftwaffe bombed the docks and other parts of Merseyside eighty-eight times between August 1940 and January 1942, killing four thousand people, destroying ten thousand houses, and damaging a hundred eighty thousand more—the worst aerial bombardment suffered by any British city outside of London. Liverpool never recovered. Factories closed, trade moved to other ports, and the unemployment rate soared to among the highest in the country. The postwar government threw up shoddy council housing in the bombed-out districts but by the late 1970s, when McWilliam returned there from Surrey, an average of twelve thousand people each year fled the city, and a fifth of its land stood abandoned.

It wasn't long before McWilliam came face-to-face with his city's desperation in a once-grand neighborhood called Toxteth. During its commercial heyday, merchants and sea captains had built brick-and-stucco Georgian mansions along the portside quarter's boulevards and side streets. But most were subdivided or boarded up after the war. The houses "faced stretches of waste ground, where uncleared rubble from the war mixed with fly-tippings and dog shit," wrote Andy Beckett in *Promised You a Miracle*, a history of Britain in the early eighties. "Inhabited streets ended abruptly or degenerated into roofless shells . . . After dark, prostitutes used the shadows." Liverpool had long been one of the most racially diverse cities in England, with a large black population that dated to the 1730s, and a recent wave of Afro-Carribean and African immigrants. But largely black communities like Toxteth had suffered most from the city's post-war decline, and the police practice of stopping and searching black youths—known as the "sus" laws—had generated ill will. McWilliam rarely entered Toxteth, but from speaking to other policemen who patrolled there and simply living in Liverpool he knew that it was a neighborhood on the brink of an explosion.

In July 1981, three years after McWilliam's return, an unmarked police car was chasing a young motorbike-riding black man on Selbourne Street in the heart of Toxteth. The man lost his balance and fell. As the police moved in, apparently to arrest him, an angry crowd gathered and began throwing bricks and stones. The confrontation escalated into what would become a week of bloody street battles between the police and local residents, some of the worst riots in England's history.

McWilliam, a twenty-four-year-old who worked out of a station house eight miles north along the Mersey, was bused down to man the police line on Upper Parliament Street, ground zero in the urban war zone. He had a shield and a nightstick to defend himself; the rioters threw stones, chunks of pavement, and firebombs. The bobby helmets, made of molded cork, offered no protection from the barrage. A well-placed rock could drive the sharp metal badge straight through the cork, causing deep lacerations. A colleague beside McWilliam collapsed after he was hit in the head. Another suffered a fractured skull.

When they weren't hurling projectiles, the rioters stole cars and weighed the accelerators with rocks, so they could send them racing downhill at the police. They charged the lines with spear-like pieces of scaffolding, attacked fire engines, and hacked police vans with axes. McWilliam took a painful whack on the hip and had his helmet nearly

torn off by a well-placed stone, but otherwise he escaped the riot-
ing unscathed. Hundreds of officers, however, were injured. At the
time, McWilliam had no sympathy for the rioters—"It was us against
them," he would say—and after the violence subsided he mostly felt
grateful for the extra pay. He and Lin were hard up, and the overtime
meant that they could replace some windows in their home.

Soon after the Toxteth riots, McWilliam was called out to police another violent dispute. Prime Minister Margaret Thatcher had
ordered the shutdown of dozens of unproductive coal mines across
Great Britain, and the National Union of Mineworkers declared a
countrywide strike. Thatcher tried to reduce the unions' power by
protecting workers who chose to remain on the job, and McWilliam
was bused to bleak mining towns in Nottinghamshire and South
Yorkshire to stand between strikers and strikebreakers and prevent
the conflict from escalating into a bloody melee. He knew almost
nothing about the reasons for the strife. He was simply told, "You're
going to the Linby Colliery for a week." Thatcher made almost no
concessions, and after a yearlong standoff, the strike ended with
many coal mines shut for good, and Great Britain's once-powerful
unions badly weakened. Families in the old mining regions were
permanently divided. "There are fathers and sons who never spoke
again," McWilliam said.

==

But most of McWilliam's work was closer to home. Based at the
Crosby Police Station in Sefton, a fourteen-mile stretch of towns
along the Mersey Estuary near Liverpool, McWilliam arrested bur-
glars, thieves, and drug dealers, and executed search warrants against
the organized crime gangs that had seized control of the heroin trade.

By the mid-1980s they had flooded the streets with so much junk that Liverpool had become known as "Smack City." One drug baron, Colin "Smigger" Smith, amassed a fortune of £200 million; another, Curtis Warren, was reportedly even wealthier, earning a spot on the *Sunday Times*'s Rich List. Nearby Manchester Airport had become a transit point for drugs from Asia and North Africa, and McWilliam regularly provided relevant intelligence that he had gathered on the street.

One evening his colleagues in customs invited him to witness a multiple arrest based on information that he had supplied: three drug runners were about to land, carrying high-quality cannabis oil from Morocco. McWilliam watched real-time footage of the three stepping off the plane and going their separate ways, and he was waiting inside the customs office when one suspect was brought in for a search. The drug mule was grinning and laughing, playing pals with the agents. *He's a cocky little sod, acting like he's one step ahead of us*, McWilliam thought. The man looked McWilliam's uniform up and down and smirked. "All right, blue?" he said. "How you doin', blue?" Minutes later the customs men cut away the false sides of his suitcase, and pulled out dozens of pouches of cannabis oil. As the trafficker was handcuffed and led to a holding cell, McWilliam caught his eye and grinned. "How you doin', blue?" he asked, in a near-perfect imitation of the mule.

He worked night shifts and day shifts, in uniform and in street clothes, on the drug squad and the special crime unit. He cleaned up after suicides and investigated murders. He led a three-man team that broke up a ring responsible for an epidemic of bike thefts in Merseyside, arresting sixty-six people. He cultivated informants, and came to know almost all the local hoodlums, known in the lingo as "scrotes" and "scallies." The thugs got violent from time to time, but McWilliam, a rugby standout known on the pitch for both meting out and taking punishment, wasn't averse to—even welcomed—the occasional scrap.

Then, in 1984, he got into a scuffle that almost cost him his life. Serving on the plainclothes unit, driving "an old shat of a car" around Sefton, he received a radio dispatch about two men who had fled a stolen vehicle on foot and were reportedly armed. McWilliam and his partner spotted the suspects, who took off in two directions. McWilliam chased one to the end of a cul-de-sac, and pulled out his radio to call for assistance. The man hurled himself at McWilliam, knocking the radio from his hands and pinning him against a gate. One of his arms became trapped between rails. Immobilized, McWilliam thrashed as the assailant squeezed his forearm against his throat. He couldn't breathe, and realized with terror that he was blacking out. As he slipped into unconsciousness, McWilliam thought of the Scotland Yard investigator who'd been stabbed ten times, fatally, the year before, while staking out a suspect in a £26 million gold bullion and jewel heist. *John Fordham, John Fordham, John Fordham*, ran the voice in his head. *What must have been going through his mind?* A moment later, two constables arrived and pulled off the assailant. They stuck him in their van and drove away. McWilliam was left gasping on the ground.

McWilliam could have come in from the streets after a few years as a patrolman and settled into a comfortable desk job, but he had no desire to advance in his career. "You become detached" when you leave the beat, he would explain to friends, when asked why he never pressed to become a sergeant. "I've always provided for me family and paid the mortgage. I've never been that driven." His bosses questioned his absence of ambition at his annual job appraisal. "You've been at this station for fifteen years," they would say. "Why?" McWilliam would shrug. "I like it here," he replied. "I know everybody, and everybody knows me." Living in the area where he worked meant he was never far from the people who needed his help, or those who meant to do harm.

The proximity worked both ways. Sound asleep at home at two a.m. after an evening shift, he once awoke to furious banging on his front door. The assistant headmaster of a local school, an ex-neighbor whom he'd arrested years earlier for being drunk and disorderly, had decided to confront him. The schoolmaster, obviously intoxicated, grabbed McWilliam. "Listen here, you bastard," he began, before McWilliam sternly ordered him to leave the property. There were gratifying moments, too. Summoned to a wrecked car that had smashed into a tree, he discovered the driver unconscious, a hose leading from the exhaust pipe into the vehicle and an overdose of barbiturates in the man's system. McWilliam dragged the would-be suicide from the wreckage, roused him, and kept talking to him as he was rushed to the hospital. Three years later, when he answered a call about a burglary, he thought the victim looked familiar. "Do you remember me?" the caller asked. It was the man who'd attempted suicide, who wept as he thanked McWilliam for saving his life.

Still, the misery wore him down: Once, McWilliam broke into the house of a physician who'd been reported missing. The doctor's corpse was sprawled on his bed, soaked in blood. "Christ! This is murder," McWilliam exclaimed to his partner. Then he found a suicide note addressed to the doctor's son: the man had taken a knife, surgically cut a main artery, and lay down until he bled out. On another occasion, he inspected the corpse of a young hoodlum who'd been clubbed to death by a chain binder—a mace-like tool used to secure loads on trucks. The victim's skull was smashed in like a rotten fruit.

Then there was the woman strangled in her flat by a perennial sex offender nicknamed "Dirty Bertie." Dirty Bertie, whom McWilliam had often arrested and come to know well, lay in the next room, unconscious from an overdose he'd taken after killing her, and died a short time later. Beyond these quotidian horrors, there was the decomposed body in the trash, the mangled jumper on the railroad tracks. The worst were the crib deaths. He dealt with a few, the parents waking up and finding their baby motionless, unresponsive, for no understandable reason. For a man with a family, that was as bad as it got.

The athletic field provided McWilliam with a regular escape. Throughout the early eighties he ran track at the National Police Athletics Championships, one year winning silver medals in both the one-hundred- and two-hundred-meter dashes. For a decade and a half he competed every Saturday for the Merseyside Police Rugby Union team, which played an eighteen-match season in the North West Division 1 League, one of the top amateur associations in England. McWilliam starred as the team's inside center, a position that required both hard, head-on tackles and acrobatic passing. But in the mid-1990s, he started feeling his age. A painful tear in a stomach muscle needed surgery. Then it was a torn patellar tendon. He had a second operation to stitch it back together, returned to the field, and soon afterward took a hard hit to the face. He stayed in the match, with blood oozing from his nose, but when he stopped to clear his sinuses, something peculiar happened to his vision. "Suddenly," he recalled, "the opposition had twice as many players as they should have had." McWilliam had broken his cheekbone in four places, and blowing through his nose had dislodged his eye from its socket. After a third surgery, he packed it in for good. "This didn't pay the mortgage," he had to acknowledge. "Keeping at it didn't make any sense."

That's when he began to rediscover the local wildlife. McWilliam hadn't had a real brush with nature since he was six years old, when his grandmother had given him a copy of *The Observer's Book of British Birds*, a pocket guide by S. Vere Benson to the 236 species that inhabit the United Kingdom. The black-and-white photographs made it difficult to tell many species apart, and McWilliam had soon lost interest. But three decades later he began making weekend trips with his three young sons—ages ten, eight, and two—and six-year-old daughter to an adventure playground at the Martin Mere Wetland Centre in Lancashire County, a low-lying depression of open water, marsh, and grassland, gouged out by receding glaciers at the end of the last Ice Age. It wasn't long before McWilliam was venturing deeper into the reserve to watch birds. The children didn't join in that, although McWilliam sometimes brought his wife, Lin—or, as he liked to refer to her, "Mrs. McW."

He hiked along nature trails bordered by whorled caraway, golden dock, tubular water dropwort, early marsh orchids, purple ramping fumitory, and large-flowered hemp-nettle, peering through binoculars at the remarkable variety of avian life that gathered in the marshes and fields. He came to know several rangers who shared their expertise with him, and who would prove helpful in the next phase of his career. Weekend by weekend, McWilliam became a regular. In springtime, the wildflowers bloomed, and lapwings, redshanks, and other waders dove for fish in the marshes. Summer brought out the harrier hawks, merlins, buzzards, peregrine falcons, and other raptors, gliding on upward currents of warm air known as thermals and stooping in pursuit of their prey. In autumn, tens of thousands of pink-footed geese returned from Iceland, long, wavering V formations soaring inland from the coastal mudflats, filling the air with their cacophonous honks. During the winter, migrating families of whooper swans and widgeons engaged in boisterous, clamorous displays in the sky. McWilliam loved to plant himself in a blind beside two adjoining fields that were flooded with pumped-in water every September, attracting huge numbers of teals, pintails, shovelers, and mallards. By April, the fields began to dry, bringing in new populations of migrating snipes, black-tailed godwits, and dunlins.

McWilliam also discovered a sanctuary closer to home: the Seaforth Nature Reserve by the Liverpool docks at the mouth of the Mersey. He had played in the area as a schoolboy, when it was a no-man's-land of dunes, train tracks, and vacant lots at the end of the bus line. An ambitious harborside redevelopment project had transformed it into seventy-four acres of freshwater and saltwater lagoons, reedbeds, and rabbit-grazed grassland.

Many mornings and afternoons before his shift began, McWilliam would drive through the industrial-waste dump that bordered the reserve and quickly find himself in a different world. Walking along the water's edge, he took in the pleasant din of cackling gulls, whistling waders, and babbling ducks, amazed that such an Eden could be thriving at the edge of Liverpool. He cast his eye on oystercatchers, Canadian geese, ringed plovers, and more subspecies of gulls than he had ever known existed: black-headed, common, herring, lesser, great black-backed, Ross's, and Bonaparte's. Cormorants arrived by the hundreds, seeking shelter from storms on the Irish Sea. During the annual spring passage, from the final week of March to the first week of May, thousands of lesser gulls gathered in the lagoons en route to their breeding grounds in Finland. He came to know his fellow bird-watchers, and learned to recognize dozens of species and identify birdcalls.

It was around this time, shortly after McWilliam turned forty, that colleagues aware of his growing interest in ornithology asked McWilliam to look into some unusual cases relating to that field. Before long these investigations would come to redirect his police career—and lead to his encounter with the greatest falcon thief of all time.

SEVEN

THE TRIAL

At three o'clock in the afternoon on October 5, 1983, Christopher "Kit" Hustler, a young environmentalist at Hwange National Park, received a radio call at Main Camp from the Parks and Wildlife Management Authority headquarters in Harare, the capital of the new nation of Zimbabwe. (The country's name was derived from the term for "house of stones" in the language of the largest tribe, the Shona, referring to a complex of granite ruins dating to the eleventh century and situated in the hills near the southern town of Masvingo.) After a months-long probe of Adrian and Jeffrey Lendrum on suspicion of illegally taking the eggs of endangered species from national parks, officers were preparing to raid their house in Bulawayo. Investigators had secretly interviewed the Lendrums' housekeeper, who had described "a pair of live birds eggs" being kept inside the family's refrigerator. Headquarters in Harare believed that the suspects were "clever and devious enough to hide evidence from our people." The superintendent wanted a bird expert to accompany them.

"Leave as fast as you can," the superintendent instructed Hustler. "The raid won't happen until you get there."

It was dark by the time Hustler arrived in his ancient diesel-powered Land Rover in Hillside, the neighborhood of large homes and lush gardens on the city's eastern edge. Austin Ndlovu, the provincial warden of Matabeleland, was waiting with two field assistants. All three wore the parks department uniform of khaki shorts and a khaki shirt adorned with green and yellow epaulets. Hustler hung back while Ndlovu (the surname means "elephant" in the Ndebele language) climbed to the veranda and knocked on the front door.

The door opened a crack.

"Are you Adrian Lendrum?" Ndlovu asked.

"I am," a man replied.

Ndlovu held up a sheet of paper.

"We have a warrant to search your house."

Lendrum, a handsome, fit man in his late forties, opened the door wider and stood in the threshold, reading the document under the porch light. He handed it back to Ndlovu.

"Better come in, then," he said.

"We're here to inspect your eggs," Ndlovu explained.

Lendrum led the officers down an entrance hall. The family was in the middle of dinner. Peggy Lendrum and her two younger children observed the intrusion from the dining room in confusion, while Jeffrey got up to join his father. Decades later, Jeffrey Lendrum would claim that he and his father had been unaware that they had done anything wrong and that the raid had caught them by surprise. "We had no warning," he would say. "We were in disbelief, we were shocked, looking for words, wondering 'What the hell is going on?'"

Expecting to be taken to the refrigerator in the kitchen, Ndlovu was surprised when Adrian Lendrum instead escorted him and his team into a bedroom. While the younger Lendrum looked on,

Adrian pointed to a green wooden cabinet, five feet high, four feet across, and two feet deep. Ndlovu pulled open the drawers, one by one, revealing wooden display trays divided into compartments and covered by glass. Eggs, arranged like jewels on beds of cotton, filled each slot. There were opalescent green weaver eggs the size of marbles; the larger, custard-and-chocolate-blotched eggs of the nightjar; the purple-speckled eggs of the common bulbul, Zimbabwe's most widespread songbird; a clutch of crimson-breasted shrike eggs, with brown speckles on a cream background; and hundreds and hundreds of others. Several deeper drawers contained the eggs of the most endangered birds in Zimbabwe: African black eagles, peregrine falcons, tawny eagles, and white-backed vultures. Astonished by the find, Ndlovu counted three hundred clutches in all, or nearly a thousand eggs. Hustler walked into the room as the inspection was going on and identified himself as a Parks and Wildlife ornithologist. Adrian Lendrum looked at Hustler with relief.

"Thank God you're here," Lendrum said. "There seems to be a terrible mistake." Hustler sensed that they were attempting to "butter me up," he would say decades later, as though they expected him to be flattered that they didn't trust his colleagues. Lendrum explained that he and his son were trained ornithologists with good reputations. The eggs on display, he insisted, were "just a schoolboy collection."

It hardly looked that way to Hustler. The collection was the most extensive private one that he had ever seen. It confirmed the rumors he'd been hearing from people like park ranger Steve Edwards that the Lendrums were secretly amassing a large stash of eggs. Written on every egg in black Indian ink with a fine draftsman's pen was a "set mark"—a series of tiny numbers and letters, barely readable without a magnifying glass, that assigned codes to individual eggs and clutches ("c. 236") and sometimes identified the year they'd been taken. These codes could in turn be correlated with data cards to obtain more details.

"Have you got the standard?" Hustler asked Lendrum, using the hobbyist's lingo for the information index that always accompanied a collection.

Lendrum fetched boxes full of index cards. "All the information is in here," he said. "We're happy to provide that."

"In order to clear this up, I'm going to have to take the collection," Hustler told Lendrum. "And I'm going to have to take your data cards."

Hustler continued exploring the home. In the kitchen refrigerator—sitting inside a lidless Tupperware container on a shelf beside milk, cheese, and leftovers—were the objects that had catalyzed the raid on the Lendrums' house: two mottled brown and red eggs, slightly smaller than a chicken's. These eggs, unlike those in the bedroom, had neither set marks nor the telltale puncture mark made to push out the embryo before mounting the prize in a display case. Adrian Lendrum claimed these were eggs of a gymnogene, or African harrier hawk, an omnivorous gray raptor with double-jointed legs. They, too, were heading for his egg collection. "We just got them today, so we put them in the fridge to cool them down, while we ate dinner," he said. But Hustler was skeptical. They looked to him like peregrine falcon eggs, which were greatly sought-after by sportsmen around the world. Placing them in the refrigerator would keep them in a state of suspended animation (freshly laid fertile eggs can survive for more than a week in frigid conditions) until the Lendrums could sell them live on the underground market, a crime punishable under Rhodesia's 1975 Parks and Wildlife Act by a steep fine and sometimes a stretch in prison.

The Lendrums watched calmly as Hustler and the Parks and Wildlife officers carried the trays and the refrigerated eggs to their truck. Then the officers placed Jeffrey Lendrum under arrest and drove him to the Hillside Police Station, where he was booked on charges of possessing wildlife trophies without a license, and released on bail. Adrian would soon be charged as well.

=

The news of the Lendrums' arrests spread quickly through Bulawayo's bird-watching community. Pat Lorber had begun working five mornings a week as an administrator in the ornithology department at the Natural History Museum of Zimbabwe while her daughter and son attended school. She was sitting behind her desk in the "Bird Room" the next morning when Hustler walked in carrying a tray filled with eggs.

"What do you think this is?" he asked.

"An egg collection?" Lorber said.

"It belongs to the Lendrums," Hustler told her. Behind him trooped half a dozen uniformed Parks and Wildlife officers bearing twenty more trays of eggs. Lorber watched the procession with amazement. She had been been well aware that Jeffrey Lendrum had accumulated eggs in his youth, but had assumed he'd grown out of it. She and Hustler began to identify, one by one, the eight hundred shells mounted in the trays. Adrian Lendrum had made it easy for them. The collector had meticulously documented every one of his egg raids, noting the species, date, peculiar characteristics ("one single red blotch at sharp end"), and, if the egg had been taken inside Matobo National Park, the number of the nest, according to a map of the park that Val Gargett had distributed to her field teams. They found seven clutches of black eagle eggs, one crowned eagle egg, one brown snake eagle egg, three clutches of martial eagle eggs, as well as clutches of the eggs from fish eagles, peregrines, lanner falcons, black storks, white-backed vultures, buzzards, and tawny eagles. In all, the Lendrums had thirty-four clutches of Specially Protected Species—many, it appeared, seized from Matobo. It was an impressive collection, though the Natural History Museum's own—eight thousand clutches acquired over six decades from dozens of donors—dwarfed it.

Lorber compared the information with the nest record cards that the Lendrums had filled out for Gargett's surveys—all kept on file at the museum. Here Lendrum had meticulously described the chicks' supposed development: "chicks growing well," "flapping wings on edge of nest," "nest empty, left."

Every word was a lie.

Hustler called Gargett and broke the news. Gargett, always discreet, had at first kept her suspicions about the Lendrums largely to herself. But as her concerns had grown in recent months, she had confided in a few members of the Rhodesian Ornithological Society, now called BirdLife Zimbabwe. Several had reacted with skepticism. "Val is being over-the-top," one elderly falconer had complained to Hustler. Now, as she sifted through dozens of protected species in the Lendrums' collection, dismay and fury combined with a sense of vindication.

Gargett held up the egg of a Mackinder's eagle owl, one of the rarest birds in the world. She clearly remembered showing a Mackinder's nest with a clutch of two eggs to Adrian Lendrum in early August 1978. Both eggs had vanished without explanation, a lingering mystery that would now appear to be solved. According to his note card, Lendrum had taken the owl eggs from that nest on August 13, 1978.

=

The trial of Adrian and Jeffrey Lendrum opened in August 1984, nearly one year after their arrests, at the Magistrates Court, a four-story colonnaded and whitewashed edifice built in the 1930s on Fort Street in downtown Bulawayo. In the year since their arrest, the Lendrums had gone about their business as usual—Adrian working at Dunlop, his son in the cannery. The fifty-odd members of BirdLife Zimbabwe shunned them, but few others in Bulawayo knew about the case. To anyone who did inquire, Jeffrey would blame the trouble on a personal feud between his father and Gargett. Now that the trial was beginning, however, the *Chronicle*, Bulawayo's most popular daily newspaper, brought the story to a wider audience. A colleague at Girls' College, where Peggy Lendrum taught, recalled that fellow teachers were bemused but sympathetic. Most blamed the family's troubles on a "misunderstanding." It was a fantastical notion, they argued, that Peggy's husband could be stealing eggs from a research project that he served with such devotion and loyalty.

The state had charged the Lendrums with the illegal collection of seventy-nine clutches of eggs from a national park, the illegal possession of thirty-four clutches of eggs of Specially Protected Species, and submission of fraudulent records. "Adrian had thought he would bullshit his way out of it, and that it would all go away," Pat Lorber remembers. A few weeks into the trial, during a week-long recess, he would even prematurely celebrate his acquittal with a tea-and-cake party for his colleagues at Dunlop.

Clad in the business attire that he wore to his office job, Adrian

Lendrum sat beside his casually dressed twenty-two-year-old son in the first row of the gallery. Benches were filled with dozens of members of BirdLife Zimbabwe. Sunlight streamed through the north-facing windows and fans suspended from the high ceiling stirred the air. A framed photo of Robert Mugabe hung on a scuffed white wall.

The evidence that the Lendrums had committed a crime against endangered species was overwhelming. Lorber, Gargett, Hustler, and other experts explained the double sets of record cards and the phony data. Acquaintances described watching Jeffrey Lendrum ascending to the tops of trees in pursuit of protected species, and then trying to hide the eggs by stashing them in his clothing or in a bag. An acquaintance of Adrian Lendrum testified that, after his arrest, Lendrum had begged him to provide a phony statement to police that he had given Lendrum a large collection of eggs; he had refused.

Unlike the prosecutor, who was privately perplexed by the experts' equating egg theft wth elephant or rhino poaching, the magistrate—typically a judge who presides over a trial involving a less serious criminal offense than a murder, assault, or armed robbery—Giles Romilly, a respected holdover from the days of white-ruled Rhodesia and an avid outdoorsman, viewed the Lendrums' alleged offenses as serious crimes. At one point Romilly organized a field trip to inspect a black eagle aerie that the Lendrums were accused of robbing. The Matobo Hills were filled with Ndebele dissidents who had declared war on Mugabe the prior year following a series of politically motivated massacres and had vowed to kill government officials. Surrounded by armed guards, the magistrate inspected the nest, determined that the chicks had never hatched and so had likely been stolen—then got out of the park as quickly as he could.

On the witness stand, Adrian and Jeffrey Lendrum denied everything in self-assured but nonconfrontational tones. Jeffrey Lendrum swore that the few eggs he had taken from the national parks were dead, and demonstrated how he ran tests to determine if they were rotten by shaking them vigorously and listening for a particular sound, or by rolling them to see if they moved in an "irregular" manner. But Lorber and Hustler testified that such techniques were useless; shaking an egg as Lendrum described would kill the embryo. The Lendrums also attributed the false data on the nest record cards to their lack of scientific training, and not from any intention to commit fraud.

On October 1, six weeks after the trial began, the magistrate announced that he had reached a verdict. In a hushed courtroom, Romilly found both men guilty of theft and illegal possession. Adrian Lendrum was also convicted of fraud. "By their actions the accused have prejudiced an extensive research programme conducted by authorities over many years," Romilly said, according to the official transcript. "There was a trust placed in you by the Department of National Parks and Wildlife, your colleagues in the Ornithological Society and the museum staff [and] you abused this position."

The scale of the crime demanded the "maximum penalty," the magistrate said. Romilly imposed a $2,500 fine on the father and an equal amount on the son, confiscated their pickup truck, incubators, and egg collection, and sentenced each to four months in prison at hard labor, suspended for five years. If they managed to stay out of trouble during that period, they would serve no time at all. Parks and Wildlife had already barred them from Zimbabwe's national parks, a humiliation that, said Romilly, "will obviously bear very hard on you."

Pat Lorber was in the courtroom when the magistrate read aloud the judgment. Upon hearing the sentence, Adrian Lendrum's "face just fell," she said.

=

A year earlier the father and son had been Val Gargett's most accomplished protégés. Now they were pariahs. "People didn't want to have anything to do with them," Lorber says. Yet the verdict left conservationists dissatisfied. Kit Hustler was certain that the Lendrums were smuggling live eggs and chicks out of the country to buyers in Western Europe. The fresh peregrine eggs in the refrigerator had first raised his suspicions. Parks and Wildlife investigators had also found before the trial a five-egg incubator at the Lendrums' home and a belt with pouches that seemed custom-made for keeping eggs warm as they were being transported on foot—perhaps through airports. The most powerful evidence came from a statement provided in confidence by the family's maid, who had seen the younger Lendrum packing eggs into the pouch and taking them to the airport. "He would be gone for three days," she told the police, according to Hustler, who was closely involved in the investigation. Just before the trial, however, the maid recanted, afraid that she would lose her job if she testified in public against the Lendrums and perhaps remain unemployable. Romilly was left with only circumstantial evidence of the Lendrums' guilt—the incubator, the egg belt—neither of which was presented at their trial. It was not enough, he said, to convict them of trafficking and send them to prison.

Hustler's suspicions gained credibility a few days after the trial, when British police raided a farmhouse near Birmingham and arrested a man who had illegally imported both chicks and the fertile eggs of four martial eagles, three crowned eagles, and two black eagles from Zimbabwe, valued together at £10,000. Evidence that the police would never make public pointed to Adrian Lendrum as the source. (His son was apparently not implicated.) "British police asserted that they had enough evidence to arrest Lendrum should he set foot in Britain," reported the *Chronicle*.

In the end, Zimbabwean authorities again believed they lacked the proof—bank deposits or sworn testimony from buyers—that the Lendrums were profiting from their egg thefts. They never charged Adrian Lendrum, but the rumors of the Lendrums' involvement in a black market lingered. The March 1985 newsletter of the World Working Group on Birds of Prey and Owls, a pan-European network of enthusiasts and bird protectors, described the Lendrums as active bird-egg smugglers and explained that the trade "is organized internationally in a manner similar to international traffic in drugs." With ingenious new methods of keeping eggs protected in transit, and new tactics to hatch well-advanced embryos, unscrupulous elements in the tight-knit community of rare-bird collectors had begun spreading the word that raptors-in-the-shell could be had for the right price. The article estimated that the trade grossed a modest $3 million a year, with the most expensive raptor egg, that of a gyrfalcon, fetching $80,000 on the black market. For connoisseurs of birds of prey in search of the most beautiful and exotic specimens in the world, there would be no greater mark of prestige than flying an African black eagle—or even better, a rare crowned eagle—thousands of miles from the birds' native habitat.

Looking back two decades later, Peter Mundy, an ornithology professor at Bulawayo's National University of Science and Technology and a confidante of Val Gargett, would view the father and son as mutual enablers. Mundy had been friendly with Jeffrey and

Adrian Lendrum for years—attending evening gatherings with the father at the Ornithological Society, chatting with both of them amiably at the airport, a tire shop, and other spots around the city. But the trial and conviction of the Lendrums exposed a dark side that he had never seen. The younger Lendrum was "a very personable and likable young man, and terribly energetic," Mundy would write years later in *Honeyguide*, the quarterly magazine published by BirdLife Zimbabwe. "If only he had gone down the right path of scientific curiosity and endeavour, he could have contributed significantly . . . to ornithology at large. What went wrong? Perhaps the father's behavior influenced the son."

Over the course of the trial, Kit Hustler says, Jeffrey Lendrum demonstrated a "sense of entitlement" that might, he thought, have derived in part from growing up white and privileged in colonial Rhodesia. "He believed that it was his right to go into the game reserves and help himself," Hustler says. What Hustler didn't know at the time was that Jeffrey claimed to have been encouraged in these activities by corrupt Parks and Wildlife officials. From the time he was a teenager, Lendrum would say decades later, he was paid handsomely to snatch the chicks of black eagles, African hawk eagles, lanner falcons, and other Specially Protected Species. "They couldn't climb, so they came to me," he would say. The officials, he would claim, would then smuggle them to destinations overseas. Jeffrey Lendrum had never mentioned any of this on the witness stand; he would later explain that he had thought nobody would believe him.

=

Jeffrey Lendrum lit out for South Africa a few months after the trial, fleeing a criminal record and intent on starting a new life. Still deep in the apartheid era, led by the hard-line Afrikaner Prime Minister P. W. Botha, nicknamed "the Big Crocodile," the country was an easy place for a young white male who had flunked most of his O levels to find steady and well-paying work. He left behind bad feelings and at least one broken heart. Gargett never again spoke to the Lendrums, and never forgave them. Burdened with guilt for having trusted them, she left behind her beloved black eagle survey and moved to Australia, where her two children and grandchildren had settled.

Aggrieved conservationists in Bulawayo, still frustrated over their failure to convict the Lendrums on smuggling charges, were intent on dragging the younger Lendrum back to court. Eventually, Peter Mundy says, the South African police made a deal with Zimbabwean authorities to arrest Lendrum and swap him at the border for a couple of South African poachers in Zimbabwe's jails. A colleague of Mundy's even traveled to South Africa to search for the egg thief on behalf of the police, eventually tracking him to his boyhood friend Howard Waller's farmhouse in the veldt outside Johannesburg. But Lendrum caught wind of the plan, and, Mundy wrote in *Honeyguide*, "he slipped away in the gloom" and disappeared. Decades later, Lendrum would claim that the supposed extradition plan was a fiction. "The guy has been reading too many Tom Clancy novels," he would say.

Whatever happened, Zimbabwe's wildlife authorities soon lost interest in Lendrum. His ban from the parks expired after one year, and he began venturing back into the country. Soon he would have a new shopping list of Specially Protected Species and new clients—in the deserts of the Middle East.

EIGHT

THE COLLECTORS

Andy McWilliam's transformation into Great Britain's most prominent wildlife cop was hatched during a stage of profound restlessness. He was forty-one years old, working the night shift and fielding radio calls. While he still enjoyed being out on the streets and keeping connections to the community, he was tired of drug busts, burglaries, and violence, and impatient to try something new. One day, a fellow officer familiar with McWilliam's love of bird-watching passed to him the name of a thirty-year-old man in Merseyside who was secretly keeping a collection of bird eggs stolen from the wild. McWilliam obtained a search warrant from a West Midlands judge, entered the man's house, climbed to his attic, and seized three wooden boxes lined with cotton wool and filled with two hundred eggs—many of them from endangered species. The man claimed that he had inherited the collection from his dead brother, and got his mother to vouch for him. McWilliam arrested him anyway. He busted a second egg collector, thanks to a tip from a fellow birder, a few weeks later.

Shortly after the arrests, McWilliam reached out to Guy Shorrock, the senior investigations officer at the Royal Society for the

Protection of Birds (RSPB). Founded by the animal-rights activist Emily Williamson in Manchester in 1889, the society had begun in protest against the exotic feather trade. The hunt for colorful plumage to meet a new desire for feathered hats among fashion-conscious women in the United States and Europe had devastated the world's populations of ostriches, parrots, and great crested grebes. Since then, the RSPB had grown into the country's largest conservation group. It had two million members, owned two hundred nature reserves across Great Britain, and operated from a manor house on a forty-acre estate in the town of Sandy, north of London, that had once belonged to the Peel family—kin of the founder of London's Metropolitan Police. Shorrock was a member of a small team of full-time bird detectives at the private charity who kept a database on wildlife-crime offenders, and often joined forces with British police to solve bird-related crimes.

Shorrock was a wiry man with piercing blue eyes and sprinklings of gray-white hair. A biochemistry graduate and former Manchester police officer, he had a passion for chasing down wild-bird launderers; "pigeon fanciers" who poisoned or shot falcons, to stop them from preying on their flying pets; gamekeepers on hunting estates, who also viewed falcons as a threat; and, above all, egg collectors. "Their pointless pursuit of egg shells, for their own personal gratification, made them universally unpopular," Shorrock wrote in a blog post about a nationwide sweep he'd orchestrated to great public approval. "Each spring it seemed the phone was ringing every weekend with calls from around the country, particularly Scotland, about the sightings of possible suspects and their vehicles or the sad news that yet another nest had been raided." McWilliam asked Shorrock to keep his eye out for cases involving egg collectors in Merseyside.

As it happened, Shorrock had just opened a file on Dennis Green, a fifty-seven-year-old nature photographer, bird portraitist, and RSPB member, who lived quietly with his elderly mother in Liverpool. Green's name had turned up in the diary of another collector, and Shorrock suspected that he was hiding a large cache of eggs in his house. In April 1999, McWilliam obtained a search warrant, and he and Shorrock raided Green's small semi-detached home. A handsome man with bushy eyebrows and long strands of hair flowing from the back of his balding pate, Green first appeared shocked, then stood silently by as the investigators climbed up a narrow flight of stairs into a cramped loft jammed with the trophies of a lifetime of hoarding.

They sifted through stacks of football programs; moths mounted in display cases; autographs of British football players, television stars, and other celebrities; and taxidermied birds, including such rare species as hen harriers and short-eared owls. Then they began opening dozens of two-by-three-foot plywood boxes, each one screwed shut. Inside, McWilliam and Shorrock discovered hundreds of eggs. Hundreds more lay tucked inside plastic food containers, tins, and a forty-drawer display cabinet in Green's second-floor bedroom, half obscured behind many more stuffed birds. All told, Green had ninety-nine taxidermied specimens in the two rooms. McWilliam and Shorrock counted more than four thousand eggs— one of the biggest collections ever seized in Great Britain at the time. There were eggs of golden eagles, peregrine falcons, ospreys, and other species listed as "Schedule 1" under the 1981 Wildlife and Countryside Act—birds granted such a high level of protection that even "disturbing" them by approaching their nests is considered a crime. There were only 250 breeding pairs of golden eagles left in the United Kingdom, and McWilliam had found a dozen golden eagle eggs in Green's home.

Green insisted that it had all been "a misunderstanding." The eggs, he assured Shorrock and McWilliam, had been gathered by others before 1954, the year that Great Britain's Protection of Birds Act first made egg collecting a crime. He presented one thousand data record cards, all dating to the 1920s and 1930s, to support his claim. Analyses in a police lab, however, determined that the cards were forgeries, written by Green in ballpoint and felt-tipped pens, which hadn't gone on the market until decades later. Scribblings on two osprey eggs in Green's collection indicated that he had received them "as a gift" in 1991. Suspecting they had been snatched from the wild, Shorrock pored through hundreds of photographs of osprey nests in Scotland snapped that year by volunteer field monitors who kept tabs on eggs and recorded their characteristics in case they should be stolen. Two eggs bore the same unique red markings as the pair in Green's collection.

In Liverpool Magistrates Court later that year, Green accused Shorrock and McWilliam of behaving like "Nazi storm troopers" during the raid on his house. Shorrock presented to the magistrate a photo he had taken showing Green, McWilliam, and another police officer laughing over a joke in Green's living room.

"They don't look like Nazis," said the judge.

"But that was my nervous laugh," Green replied.

Green was found guilty of a dozen offenses, including illegal egg possession and possession of stuffed protected birds without a license. Then, citing Green's desperate finances—he survived on social welfare payments of £119 a week—the judge waived a fine, sentenced the photographer to a twelve-month conditional discharge—meaning he could avoid a guilty verdict unless he committed another offense within that time period—and confiscated both his egg collection and a handful of taxidermied birds. (Green claimed he had burned the rest of the birds in his garden; four years later he was discovered to have hidden the specimens in the home of a friend.) McWilliam had a T-shirt made up with the photo that Shorrock had taken and Green's "nervous laugh" quote, and sent the shirt to Shorrock as a souvenir.

=

Egg collectors hadn't always had such a dodgy reputation. In 1671, the writer John Evelyn, a contemporary of the famed Restoration-era diarist Samuel Pepys, visited Sir Thomas Browne, a distinguished physician, writer, and antiquary, at his home in Norwich, England. Evelyn remarked with wonder upon "a Cabinet of rarities, & that of the best collection, especially Medails, books, Plants, [and] natural things." Among Browne's "curiousities" was one of the world's first documented egg collections, a display "of the eggs of all foul and birds he could procure, that country (especially the promontorys of Norfolck) being . . . frequented with—cranes, storkes, eagles etc. and a variety of water-foule."

During the Victorian era, oology, as the study of eggs was known, became a distinct branch of ornithology. Wealthy sponsors such as Walter Rothschild, an heir to the Rothschild banking fortune and founder of a natural history museum at Tring, near London, dispatched collectors to sweep up specimens from the Amazon jungle, the Hawaiian Islands, Central Africa, Borneo, and other remote corners of the globe. "Acquisition in the name of national pride, meant that eggs and birds (in the form of study skins and skeletons), were accumulated on an unimaginable scale," wrote the British ornithologist Tim Birkhead in *The Most Perfect Thing* (the most perfect thing being, naturally, a bird's egg).

Oologists were often celebrated for their feats of bravery in the cause of scientific exploration. Charles Bendire, a German-born US Army officer, who collected eggs while based in a series of western forts after the Civil War, was snatching the egg of a zone-tailed hawk from a cottonwood tree in the Arizona desert in 1872 when Apache warriors on horseback attacked him. He placed the speckled orb between his teeth, shinnied down the tree, and made his escape. "As he rode headlong into camp, gasping and gagging, Bendire discovered that he couldn't spit the egg out," according to an admiring biographer. Soldiers pried open his mouth and removed the egg intact, in the process ripping out one of Bendire's teeth.

Other collectors lost more than denticulation: John C. Calhoon, from Taunton, Massachusetts, drew breathless newspaper coverage for his pursuit of ravens' eggs in the cliffs near St. John's, Newfoundland. "Daring Act of American Ornithologist at Birds Island," an 1889 headline proclaimed. "He scales Perpendicular Cliff Three Hundred Feet High. Shuddering Fishermen Lean on Their Oars and Witness the Dangerous Ascent." Two years later, Calhoon's strength gave out during a climb up from a raven's nest on those same cliffs, and he fell two hundred feet to his death. Gathering eggs during his Sierra Nevada honeymoon in 1901, Francis J. Britwell was blown from his perch atop a sixty-foot pine tree by a gust of wind, caught his neck in the loop of his safety rope, and strangled to death while his bride watched. Richardson P. Smithwick, the twenty-two-year-old scion of a family of North Carolina egg collectors, was smothered in a sand dune cave-in in southeastern Virginia in 1909 while raiding the nest of a belted kingfisher. The *Oologist*, a popular magazine for egg collectors in the United States, reported "the sad ending of an active, useful life. Mr. Smithwick was an active young worker in his chosen field of science."

A few oologists were, in fact, dedicated scientists: Edgar Chance, a Edwardian-era collector, devoted his life to observing the breeding habits of the common cuckoo and was the first ornithologist to document "brood parasitism"—laying eggs in the nest of another species and tricking the host bird into incubating them as her own. In 1911, three members of Robert Scott's doomed Antarctica expedition trekked seventy miles through blizzards and minus-eighty-degree-Fahrenheit temperatures to collect eggs from an emperor penguin colony. The explorers were out to prove a theory advanced by the nineteenth-century biologist Ernst Haeckel, that the development of an embryo from fertilization to gestation or hatching replicates the evolutionary stages of the same species. (Haeckel believed that grooves in the back of the human embryo's neck resembled gills, proving that man had a fishlike ancestor.) The Antarctic trio suspected that the penguin embryo would demonstrate that the bird had descended from reptiles. The eggs, alas, proved nothing. Most collectors, however, seemed driven by little more than what one Victorian observer called "a passion for beauty and a lust for curiousities."

The British curiosity seekers were by far the most prodigious. John Arthington Walpole-Bond, an Edwardian-era collector from Sussex, claimed to have seen in situ, or in their orginal place, the eggs of every species in the British Isles, and amassed a collection well into the thousands. "I have vivid memories of him striding along on the very brink of the Sussex cliffs," wrote one friend in his 1956 obituary, "and, in a high wind, stopping . . . to perch himself on the tip of a promontory in order to lean right over and clap his hands in an effort to put out a Peregrine"—that is, frighten the raptor away from the nest in order to seize her eggs. Francis Charles Robert Jourdain, an Oxford-educated minister, had a scar on his forehead from plunging off a cliff in pursuit of an eagle nest. He amassed 17,500 clutches, thought to be the largest collection of eggs in Western Europe. Tim Birkhead, in *The Most Perfect Thing*, speculates that many of these collectors felt an erotic attraction to their specimens. Cambridge University professor Alfred Newton, according to one contemporary, spent hours "ogling his eggs" and barred women from setting eyes on them. "Perhaps their wonderful curves trigger deep-rooted visual and tactile sensations among men," wrote Birkhead. "That may also be one reason Fabergé's eggs are so popular: an expensive nuptial gift that fuses sensuality of form with the ultimate symbol of fertility."

Newton and his fellow collectors eventually fell out of favor with other ornithologists and the British public. In the years after World War I a consensus was building that egg collecting had negligible scientific value and was threatening to drive some species to extinction. In 1922 the Royal Society for the Protection of Birds condemned egg collecting as a "distinct menace" to birds, and the British Ornithological Union, to which Rothschild, Chance, and Jourdain belonged, denounced the practice. The three oologists angrily split from the group and formed the British Oological Association, renamed the Jourdain Society after Jourdain's death in 1940. Its members gathered over dinners, often in evening dress, to show one another specimens and swap anecdotes about their adventures.

But the collectors were growing increasingly ostracized. "Are we English people so indifferent to the glorious heritage of birds that we will allow the selfish greed of individuals to denude our country of its rare birds?" wrote one enthusiast to *The Field*, a British ornithological journal, in 1935, reflecting the turning tide of public opinion. In 1952, the *Guardian*'s country diarist Harry Griffin scorned collectors as "the cloak-and-dagger men of the fells." Two years later the Protection of Birds Act made oology illegal. Undercover investigators from the Royal Society for the Protection of Birds bugged Jourdain members' hotel rooms and raided their dinners. Chris Mead, senior officer at the British Trust for Ornithology, claimed that the Jourdain Society provided a network for illegal collectors and had become the "pariah of the bird-watching world."

As a boy in Liverpool in the 1960s, Andy McWilliam had a few schoolmates whose fathers kept egg collections, and some of his friends made forays into the countryside to forage for themselves. But as an understanding of the dangers the hobby posed to nature spread, most collectors found other ways of passing the time. Still, some fanatics refused. After the Jourdain's secretary, James Whitaker, was found guilty of offenses under the 1981 Wildlife and Countryside Act—and had 148 illegally taken eggs seized (out of a collection numbering 2,895)—one Jourdain member likened the Royal Society for the Protection of Birds, which had gathered evidence for the arrest, to "little Hitlers."

=

Into the new millennium, hundreds of egg collectors across the British Isles continued to gather specimens on the sly. And Andy McWilliam was becoming one of their principal nemeses. In 2000 he was invited to participate in Operation Easter, a nationwide crackdown launched three years earlier by Guy Shorrock of the RSPB, and the Scottish police, that named 130 egg collectors as top-priority targets.

"It's very rare in the UK to have a national police operation of this kind," Alan Stewart, the police officer who started Operation Easter with Shorrock in the face of rampant nest robbing, and a man once described by the nature magazine *Scottish Field* as "Britain's foremost wildlife detective," told *The New Yorker* in 2012. "The others are for drug trafficking, human trafficking, and football hooliganism."

McWilliam began with a network of a dozen miscreants in Merseyside, many of whom ventured together on clandestine egg-hunting expeditions. The first target on his list was Carlton Julian D'Cruze, an unemployed cabinetmaker and longtime acquaintance of Dennis Green's, who had allegedly raided nests across the United Kingdom for years but had never been caught. Shorrock suspected that D'Cruze was keeping a huge stash of eggs hidden in a safe house somewhere in Liverpool. McWilliam shadowed D'Cruze, a moon-faced man with a shaved head and thin mustache and goatee. One evening he spotted the pickup truck of another Operation Easter suspect in D'Cruze's driveway. An inflatable dinghy lay in the truck bed. McWilliam was certain that they were preparing to drive to northern Scotland, one of D'Cruze's favorite nest-raiding spots. McWilliam accosted the men as they emerged from the house, but he had no evidence of a crime. The men grinned tauntingly as they drove off— but McWilliam may have had the last laugh. "I heard that when they reached wherever they were going, they couldn't blow up the dinghy because somebody had punctured it," McWilliam says coyly. "You can read into that whatever you want."

Soon after the driveway encounter, an informant told McWilliam that D'Cruze had moved—and had probably transferred his egg collection to his new residence. McWilliam obtained the address, secured a search warrant, and knocked on the front door. He waited, then knocked again. When a neighbor told McWilliam that D'Cruze was at home, the policeman kicked the door down and charged inside. McWilliam found D'Cruze on his knees in the second-floor bathroom, clad only in his underwear. He was frantically crushing eggs, tearing up data cards, and trying to flush the pieces down the toilet.

When Shorrock arrived from D'Cruze's mother's house—a second search warrant hadn't turned up anything—he shut off the water supply, took apart the toilet, and recovered the shredded note cards and egg fragments, which he laid out to dry. In the Royal Society for the Protection of Birds' laboratory outside London, Shorrock and other experts reassembled 138 eggs of peregrines, sea eagles, and ospreys. "We laid them out like a macabre jigsaw puzzle," he says.

They also had other evidence: McWilliam had seized 355 intact eggs that D'Cruze hadn't had time to crush and flush. D'Cruze pleaded guilty and was sentenced to six months in jail, making him only the second egg collector ever to serve time for his crime. In 2000 Parliament had amended the Wildlife and Countryside Act with the Countryside and Rights of Way Act, making egg collection punishable by a six-month jail term. Up until then, egg collectors could receive only a fine of £5,000 per egg, or about $7,500 at the time of the amendment. The highest penalty ever assessed had been £90,000, approximately $120,000, levied against Jamie and Lee McLaren, two brothers known to investigators as the "Abbott and Costello" of egg collecting, who had videotaped each other stealing seabird eggs in northern England.

=

After the D'Cruze conviction in 2002, the World Wildlife Fund honored McWilliam as its UK Law Enforcer of the Year. By now, with his supervisor's approval, McWilliam had scaled back his normal police duties and was taking on more and more wildlife-crime-related cases—investigations that nobody else in the department seemed to want and that often took him to far-flung corners of Merseyside. He cultivated informants in the underworld of badger baiters, who use dogs to corner and kill the burrowing omnivores for sport. He raided farms, served search warrants, seized graphic videos, and collected badger-blood splatter on clothing and in cars. The evidence he gathered helped to convict several notorious "terrier men," as the badger baiters call themselves, of animal cruelty under the Protection of Badgers Act of 1992. Some of the investigations he found hard to forget. McWilliam and his partner Steve Harris once raided the home of a suspected badger baiter near Liverpool, and found backyard kennels filled with dogs that had suffered terrible injuries—one with no nose, another missing its lower jaw—from savagely fighting the sharp-toothed burrowers.

Further searching turned up stacks of brochures in the backseat of the suspect's four-by-four, advertising free pest-extermination services. "I pass the brochures out in the countryside to people who have a fox problem," the man told the officers after his arrest. Foxes in rural areas often carry off poultry, piglets, lambs, and household pets, and can spread rabies, prompting farmers to hire pest control services to shoot them.

"Why don't you charge your clients a fee?" asked Harris.

"Because," the man replied calmly, "I fucking love killing animals."

Responding to complaints from animal welfare groups, McWilliam investigated the Southport Zoo, a decrepit Merseyside facility located beside the Pleasureland amusement park. He found wild cats—ocelots, servals, and snow leopards—pacing agitatedly in their enclosures next to a rickety wooden roller coaster, with carriages that clattered along the track every four minutes for ten hours a day during the summer. A solitary lioness spent most of her days confined in an indoor cell, while a pair of chimpanzee brothers lived separated and alone in barren, filthy cages. Disturbed by what he'd seen, McWilliam looked for a way to shut down the facility. In the end, he busted the owners for thirteen violations of Convention on International Trade in Endangered Species import regulations. The owners pled guilty, and authorities closed the zoo. To his discomfort, however, McWilliam "became a bit of a hero" to the animal rights protesters who'd demonstrated outside the zoo on weekends and bank holidays. "I wanted to distance myself from them," he recalls. He was a police officer, not an activist.

He investigated two real estate developers who had secretly dug up the riverside burrows of the water vole, a semi-aquatic rodent regarded as one of England's most endangered animals, to construct a drainage ditch for a housing complex. Relying on the account of a ninety-five-year-old witness who lived beside the reserve, McWilliam threatened the developers with arrest if they didn't come clean. In the end, McWilliam had them prosecuted for the reckless disturbance of a protected species, and they paid a significant fine. He carried out a sting operation on a local taxidermist who advertised stuffed rare birds and mammals in the classifieds of a Merseyside paper. Posing as a customer, he called the man. "Don't you need a CITES permit for that?" he asked, referring to the export and import documents issued by the Convention on International Trade in Endangered Species of Wild Flora and Fauna. "Nobody ever checks," the taxidermist replied. McWilliam made an appointment, brought along a search warrant, and arrested the man for import violations.

But it was the egg collectors who dominated his caseload. Working closely with Guy Shorrock from the Royal Society for the Protection of Birds, he deciphered encrypted notes and matched handwritten records to the bird charity's database of nest robberies, discrediting collectors' claims that they had acquired their collection at a garage sale or inherited it from family members. "The collectors couldn't bullshit him," says Steve Harris, who worked with McWilliam on many bird crime cases. McWilliam pored through eBay and other websites looking for suspicious purchases. One Liverpudlian had ordered large quantities of Bubble Wrap, plastic containers, egg box foam, and specialty books off the Internet; McWilliam got a search warrant while the suspect was out of the country, and found an egg-blowing kit—tiny files, drills, and pipettes—in his desk drawer and a thousand eggs in a specimen cabinet. He arrested him as soon as he returned to England.

He developed a network of tipsters, often cultivating the collectors' ex-girlfriends or collectors who had quarreled with their rivals. "Andy was a no-nonsense, old-fashioned bobby," said Shorrock. "He understood police work, he understood people." And he was discovering a web of hidden relationships. McWilliam turned up handwritten notes in D'Cruze's house that contained coded references to one Anthony Higham, a thirty-nine-year-old printing firm manager who had apparently been raiding nests across Great Britain. A source directed McWilliam to the likely location of Higham's collection: the home of an elderly woman who was a neighbor of Higham's ex-girlfriend. McWilliam obtained another search warrant, and knocked on the woman's door.

"Has Mr. Higham asked you to hide anything in your loft?" he asked.

"No," she replied, nervously.

She has "Yes" on her face, McWilliam thought.

McWilliam entered the house and, in a now-familiar routine, climbed to the attic and found boxes containing one thousand eggs, along with diaries and photographs documenting Higham's exploits. Higham had befriended the woman over several months and had asked her politely to store his cartons while being hazy on the details; she'd had no idea what was concealed inside them. After McWilliam arrested him, Higham, a broad-shouldered, clean-shaven man with trimmed blond hair and the slightly sagging physique of a former athlete, surrendered hundreds more eggs from another stash, including many from peregrines, ospreys, and golden eagles. As he handed them over, Higham looked at McWilliam wistfully. "They're beautiful, aren't they?" he said.

===

McWilliam struggled to understand the obsession. "It's the sixty-four-thousand-dollar question," he would tell Timothy Wheeler for the 2015 documentary *Poached*, which followed the lives of several egg collectors targeted by Operation Easter. "They blow the contents of the egg out and they keep a small piece of calcium which they can't put on display anywhere. They hide it away, and it's a mystery to me what they get out of it."

Some collectors had even narrowed their obsessions to a single species. D'Cruze focused compulsively on the chough, a crow-like bird found in Wales and Cornwall that lays cream-colored eggs with red markings, five to a clutch, on cliff ledges often hundreds of feet off the ground. Enticed by the nest sites' inaccessibility, D'Cruze had stolen twenty-eight chough clutches in his career. He had even written a lengthy manuscript about the eggs for a caliologists' series published by Oriel Stringer books, produced mostly by egg collectors for the benefit of other collectors and filled with clues about where to find nest sites. (Caliology is the study of bird's nests.) One book in the series, *The Osprey* by W. Pearson, guides collectors to eighty nesting sites in Great Britain, providing grid references and markers such as dead pine trees, Victorian-era monuments, and lochs. Pearson notes in his introduction that "the pseudo-protectionists were up in arms" after the publication of the series' first book, and "one society for the protection of birds tried to get a High Court injunction to get the book banned." The attempt failed.

Another collector McWilliam arrested had made his life's quest the tree pipit, a small songbird that lays its four to eight eggs in a ground nest, concealed in deep woodland or scrub. The man looked down on collectors who raided the nests of eagles and other raptors, he told McWilliam, because they were so large and conspicuous and, in his view, didn't present much of a challenge.

Anthony Higham admitted that he was "obsessed with the peregrine," while Derek Lee, a Manchester man whom McWilliam arrested in 2004, started at age sixteen and was led to increasingly rare specimens. Beginning with blackbirds and song thrushes, "I traveled elsewhere to pick up a kestrel or sparrowhawk egg," he told the *Guardian* in 2006. "Then the next challenge was the buzzard. Eventually I came across peregrines and red kites." The most tantalizing prize for many collectors, according to Guy Shorrock, is the egg of the greenshank, a large sandpiper with long green legs and gray plumage that inhabits the remote wetlands of northern Scotland. Laid in clutches of four in a depression in the ground and usually concealed among lichen, dwarf shrubs, and pine needles, the green-shank egg is almost impossible to find and represents, Shorrock says, "the pinnacle of egg collecting."

McWilliam noticed other common traits among the collectors. Several men styled themselves after their forerunners of a bygone age, back when oology was a respected pursuit. McWilliam found a handwritten thesaurus in D'Cruze's bedroom filled with turn-of-the-century terms that he used to make his diaries sound more like those of his Jourdain Society heroes. Higham fitted his home office with Victorian furniture, and, using John Walpole-Bond's diaries, retraced the famed collector's routes through the remote glens of northern Scotland. Higham undertook thirty-six treks, discovering sixty nests in many of the same spots where Walpole-Bond had found his. Matthew Gonshaw, among the most notorious egg collectors in British history, kept a photograph in his bedroom of Walpole-Bond. "In memory of Jock—The Man," Gonshaw had written on it, referring to Walpole-Bond by his nickname. In his long career, Gonshaw stole thousands of eggs, went to jail repeatedly, and was banned from Scotland for life.

All of the collectors relished the physical risks: the dangerous rappels down rock faces, the scrambles up trees, the crossings of turbulent waters. Climbing for peregrine eggs in a rock quarry in northern Wales in 1991, Higham had watched his partner, Dennis Hughes, slip and fall dozens of feet to his death. Instead of being traumatized by the accident, he wrote in his diary, "I was well and truly hooked." Higham came close to dying, too, after capsizing his dinghy while rowing to an island in a frigid loch. D'Cruze nearly froze to death one winter, he told McWilliam, while hunting for nests in northern Scotland and losing his way in the wilderness. Colin Watson, a maintenance man described in the media as "Britain's most ruthless egg collector," tumbled off a forty-foot larch tree in Yorkshire one May morning in 2006 while trying to raid a sparrow hawk nest. He suffered massive injuries and died at the scene. "Nest in Peace," declared the headline in the London *Daily Mirror*.

For many collectors, the cat-and-mouse game with the authorities was equally thrilling. Derek Lee posed as a bird-watcher and gleefully duped unsuspecting park rangers into leading him to nests. D'Cruze wrote field notes and letters filled with coded references to accomplices—one was "86," another "15"—and kept them in an envelope labeled "top secret." Several collectors whom McWilliam arrested had developed clever subterfuges, burying their caches in the ground or stashing them in the hollows of trees, then returning in the off-season to retrieve them, after the rangers and RSPB nest watchers had left. One of McWilliam's wildlife police colleagues arrested a master carpenter in Norfolk who had constructed secret compartments throughout his mobile home—hollow storage areas built inside seats and sofas, in which he had secreted thousands of eggs. Matthew Gonshaw hid the most prized eggs in his collection inside a hollowed-out bed frame.

The most exciting moment invariably came when the collector at last approached the object of desire. "The sight which met my eyes is one I shall treasure," wrote Higham about his first climb to a nest of osprey eggs, in 1992. As the female osprey flew off, "shouting" in agitation, Higham moved in. "Three richly marked eggs bedded in a cup of damp moss were visible in the twilight," he wrote. "I packed them into my gloves, then into my hat, carrying my haul in my teeth." In 1997 D'Cruze attempted to rob the nest of a white-tailed sea eagle, a large raptor that had been wiped out in Great Britain by hunters in the early twentieth century. An RSPB program had recently reintroduced a dozen breeding pairs to Scotland. D'Cruze traveled with an accomplice to the remote Isle of Mull in the Inner Hebrides, where a few pairs had taken up residence. "My body felt cold as there was quite a chill, so W and myself set a steady pace along the track towards the loch," began the harrowing account in his diary:

A hell of a walk in the dark and I slipped many times, but eventually we reached the wood around midnight—as quietly as possible W climbed the tree. When he was only half way, [the eagle] started screeching and clapping her wings up and down on the edge of the eyrie . . . W shouted to me that he could not get her off. I called up to him to remove a branch from the eyrie and ease her off. After a few minutes she decamped and W was able to reach in, only to find the eagle had broken the second egg and so we left it, hoping she would continue to incubate it. Both disappointed, we had a long walk back along the loch.

Such accounts reinforced McWilliam's view that egg collecting was an act of pure selfishness, an attack on the sanctity of the wild. As Holly Cale, the chief curator at Jemima Parry-Jones's International Centre for Birds of Prey, put it: "The [mother] bird's whole purpose of being is to procreate, to rear her young. She will be terribly distressed, traumatized by the loss, will vocalize about the fact that the eggs have gone, and sometimes she will come back to the nest, looking for the eggs." Birds can sometimes lay another clutch during the same breeding season if their first one fails, but producing calcium consumes a tremendous amount of the female's energy; usually the opportunity is lost until the next year.

But McWilliam wasn't incapable of feeling compassion for those he arrested. Many whom he came across were "loners and social misfits" in his eyes, who seemed to live for little else but their eggs. Dennis Green had resided with his mother in poverty until she died, then Scotch-taped a life-sized photo of her to the settee where she used to sit. Matthew Gonshaw was a recluse surviving on public assistance. He traveled to nest sites by public transport, and calculated down to the last pence the cost of every supply he would need in the field, according to *The New Yorker*, "from butter to packets of instant custard made by a company called Bird's."

Anthony Higham was a different sort. He had a solid job as the manager of a printing firm, a decent house, a long-term partner, and friends, and he was mortified that he had jeopardized everything to satisfy what he recognized as an addiction. "I can't believe that I'm going to prison, all for taking birds' eggs," he lamented to McWilliam in 2004, when the policeman visited him at his home in Merseyside, shortly before he began a four-month sentence. McWilliam, touched by Higham's genuine distress over what he had done, shared the perception of Timothy Wheeler, who likened the behavior of the egg collector to that of an alcohol or drug abuser. "They are somehow able to rationalize their behavior because the lust for the egg becomes more important to them than seeing that they're actually harming the very thing they love," Wheeler told the Audubon Society. Scientific research into what compels men like Anthony Higham has been thin, but a study of collectors of fossilized dinosaur eggs, published in the *Journal of Economic Psychology* in June 2011, hypothesized that the pursuit of eggs is a modern residue of a "signalling" strategy used by our ancestors to attract a mate through the acquistion of "rare and difficult to obtain . . . resources." Although such behavior has "low reproductive value today," it became hardwired into our genetic code through natural selection, the author suggests, and, for some anyway, is impossible to resist. The Anxiety and Depression Association of America drew a distinction between hoarding—which it linked to obsessive-compulsive disorder, attention-deficit/hyperactivity disorder, and depression—and the more refined and organized pursuit of collecting. For some egg collectors such as Dennis Green, however, who lived surrounded by useless mementos and seemed unable to throw anything away, the differences were clearly blurred.

McWilliam stayed in contact with Higham following his release on parole. Higham managed to get his old job back at the printing firm and had engaged a craftsman to make replicas of some eggs in his confiscated collection. "They're good, aren't they?" he told McWilliam, proudly showing him a peregrine egg made of plexiglass. *Oh my God*, McWilliam thought, saying nothing, but disturbed by the depth of Higham's obsession. Higham still loved walking in the wilderness, but he worried that his criminal record made him vulnerable to arrest. One day he went hiking on a mountain trail in North Wales and spotted a dead chough on the ground. The bird had half a dozen leg rings from scientific studies and a succession of owners, and Higham, fascinated by such arcania, could hardly resist retrieving the chough to study its history. He phoned McWilliam from the mountain. "If I pick this bloody thing up and get stopped, I'll be in trouble," he said. "What should I do?" McWilliam advised him not to lay his hands on it. Then he contacted a wildlife police colleague nearby, who met Higham on the trail, and took away the tiny corpse.

For other collectors, the stigma of incarceration did nothing to break the mesmerizing power of the egg. Gregory Peter Wheal, a roofer from Coventry in the West Midlands, was arrested ten times in a decade; he "just didn't seem to be able to stop," McWilliam said, even after serving a six-month prison sentence. After D'Cruze served five months in jail, McWilliam asked, "Is this going to be it? You going to quit?"

"You can never say never," D'Cruze replied.

—

Between 1999 and 2005 magistrates in the United Kingdom jailed eight egg collectors for their crimes; McWilliam arrested five of them. Anthony Higham served four months in prison and Carlton D'Cruze five. Dennis Green went to jail for four months in 2002 for "perversion of justice," after hiding dozens of illegal taxidermic trophies in D'Cruze's house and then lying to authorities about it. In 2004 McWilliam arrested John Latham, a cabinetmaker who had amassed 282 eggs in a three-month spree, including 14 from the rare kingfisher. That same year he apprehended Manicunian Derek Lee, who specialized in hard-to-find specimens. Then, thanks to Operation Easter's success and the imposition of jail sentences rather than fines, "egg collecting just fell off completely," says Guy Shorrock. "The major collectors stopped or died." While there are surely some big collections still hidden away in England, periodic amnesty programs have been successful at encouraging owners to turn them over to the police.

Yet despite a string of arrests and successful prosecutions, many of McWilliam's colleagues saw what he did as a bit of a joke. McWilliam and Harris would bring to the Crosby station a suspect they had just arrested for stealing rare birds or collecting endangered eggs, and other police officers would poke fun at them. "Put him before the beak," they would tell McWilliam—a British slang term for magistrate. Wildlife crime "was regarded as trivial," Harris says. But McWilliam shrugged off the mockery. After years of investigating egg enthusiasts—observing their idiosyncracies, familiarizing himself with their subterfuges, and grasping their obsessions—McWilliam understood the stakes of bird-related crime. And he would soon turn his skills to taking down the most formidable egg thief that he would ever encounter.

NINE

AFRICAXTREME

In the summer of 1998, Jeffrey Lendrum was thirty-six years old, recently divorced, and residing in Jukskei Park, a leafy middle-class neighborhood in northwest Johannesburg. Thirteen years had gone by since he'd left Bulawayo in disgrace, and he had built a new life for himself. He'd married a South African woman, who had a son with a previous partner, and though the relationship hadn't lasted and they'd had no children of their own, the two had stayed on good terms. She would still drop by Lendrum's house with her son for an occasional meal.

Lendrum now ran a one-man business called Wallace Distributors, procuring auto parts, mining equipment, and aircraft components and then driving them in his Toyota pickup truck to customers across the border in Zimbabwe. Strict limits imposed by the Mugabe regime on the flow of foreign currency in and out of Zimbabwe, along with high taxes and quotas on imports, had made it increasingly difficult to obtain spare parts through official channels. And Lendrum could get his hands on nearly anything: braided ropes for mine elevator shafts, engine blocks, chrome door-edge moldings. He seemed to be always on the road, driving as far north as the copper, tungsten, and nickel mines near Zambia, a fifteen-hundred-mile round trip.

Some years, during droughts, if he wasn't running other hustles, Lendrum would return to Zimbabwe to carry out mercy killings of elephants and other species on behalf of Parks and Wildlife. But he had, he would insist, abandoned his nest-raiding ways completely. "I had nothing to do with birds at all," he said. (Later, on a witness stand, he would modify that claim, admitting that he had continued to dabble in cliff climbing and nest raiding, legally "collecting black sparrowhawks for the Transvaal Falconry Club for their breeding program.")

Paul Mullin, a British businessman, met Lendrum that July after settling in Johannesburg as a senior manager for an American firm helping to roll out Internet access across southern Africa and the Middle East. Mullin's job was to advise state-owned telecommunications firms on installing servers and other hardware. Mullin was an army brat who claimed that his father had guarded Spandau Prison in Berlin when the Nazi war criminal Rudolf Hess was its sole inmate. He was a nomad who had traveled across Africa half a dozen times, a racing car enthusiast who self-published guidebooks each year to the Formula 1 Grand Prix season, and a spycraft aficionado who drove a Mitsubishi Pajero with the vanity license plate PCM 007.

Mullin's girlfriend, a former stripper at a nightclub called the House of Lords, who'd met Lendrum at work and sometimes paid him to be her driver, made the introduction. Lendrum invited Mullin to drop by his bungalow, a modest home that overlooked a garden bisected by the Jukskei River, a narrow, shallow stream that coursed over a bed of rocks. Over a round of beers, the men discovered that they shared an interest in fast cars and African safaris. Mullin found

Lendrum personable, garrulous, and passionate about his red Mini Cooper S. Before long they were getting together regularly for coffee or to take Lendrum's Mini Cooper out for 140-mile-per-hour spins at a Grand Prix–style racecourse outside Johannesburg. During their excursions, Lendrum bragged several times about his exploits as a member of the Special Air Service during the Rhodesian Bush War. Mullin says he knew it was "bollocks," but didn't let it get in the way of their developing friendship. A few months later Lendrum enlisted Mullin for a favor: to carry back from England a coil of walnut wood for the dashboard of a Jaguar E-type sports car that a friend was customizing in Bulawayo.

Lendrum was always looking for the next opportunity, and in early 1999 he made his friend a pitch. He had been struck by the curio shops he saw across South Africa, selling everything from novelty T-shirts to carved rhinos. There was even a large one at Johannesburg's international airport. "Wouldn't it be a good idea," he told Mullin, while eating oysters at an Ocean Basket seafood franchise in a Johannesburg shopping mall, "if we could bring African handicrafts into the UK and sell them?" Mullin thought that Lendrum might be on to something. "Let's give it a go," he said.

Mullin and Lendrum pooled their resources and came up with £15,000. They made a trial run to Zimbabwe, where they found reliable vendors and a company to clear everything with customs and ship the goods. Then they opened their first shop in Southampton, seventy miles south of London, where Mullin owned a house and where a former girlfriend and their five-year-old daughter still lived. Mullin hired his ex to work behind the counter, and decorated the store in African-bush-style, stringing a tented canopy from the ceiling, painting the walls in a zebra-skin pattern, and covering the

countertops with thatch. Mullin and Lendrum called their venture
AfricaXtreme.

The partners began traveling to Zimbabwe every month, on the
hunt for handicrafts. Mullin could make his own hours, and none of
his clients complained if he vanished for a week. He and Lendrum
would drive from Bulawayo north to Victoria Falls, and then back
south through Hwange National Park—a thousand-mile journey
that typically took them five days. After their first binge-buy to fill
the Southampton shop, an entrepreneur with a few dozen artisans
in her employ struck a deal with the partners to produce wooden
safari animals in bulk. Mullin and Lendrum paid cash and also
gave the carvers soap, sugar, mealy meal (a coarse flour made from
maize), clothing, and other necessities. Other dealers provided
them with ebony walking sticks, hippos and rhinos carved from
soapstone, leopards fashioned from the mottled dark green mineral
serpentine, herons and storks made of polished mukwa wood, teak-
wood side tables and fruit baskets, traditional drums, and carved
giraffes of all sizes, from two-inch miniatures to nearly life-sized
sculptures.

They packed their purchases into a trailer attached to Lendrum's
pickup truck and, back in Bulawayo, loaded everything into a container at the Southern Comfort Lodge—a thatched-roof retreat with
a pool filled with the skulls of culled elephants, owned by one of Lendrum's boyhood friends, a professional leopard hunter named Craig
Hunt. A shipping company fumigated the goods, transported them to
Durban, a South African port on the Indian Ocean, and put them on
a boat to London. Mullin collected the crafts and delivered them to
the store in Southampton. Mullin and Lendrum tried to avoid buying
mass-produced kitsch and sought out hand-carved works by skillful

artisans: in Cameroon Mullin found antique tribal masks in a street market that he bought for a pittance and sold in England for several hundred pounds apiece.

Lendrum was still bringing spare parts to his clients in Zimbabwe for Wallace Distributors, and Mullin often came along for the ride. To avoid the hours-long traffic jams at the Beit Bridge, the main crossing point between South Africa and Zimbabwe, Lendrum would pay someone at the front of the line two hundred rand (about $20) or give him case of Coke to trade places with him. Then he would chat up the Zimbabwean customs agents and slip them small gifts to wave him through the checkpoint. "If you're a border controller, and you're paid the equivalent of a month's salary to turn a blind eye, that will do it," Mullin says. Lendrum would make his deliveries, receive payment in cash, and play Zimbabwe's wildly fluctuating currency markets, trading rand, Zimbabwe dollars, and US dollars. Lendrum impressed Mullin as a relentless wheeler-dealer, willing, he said, "to do anything to make a quick buck."

The business spun off in new directions. A Harare craftsman sold them African heron and egret sculptures made of welded steel, three to four feet tall, which did so well in Southampton that they decided to manufacture their own. They imported welding machines from South Africa, set up a metalwork shop in Bulawayo, hired local craftsmen, and struck a deal with two chains of garden centers in the United Kingdom to export the steel birds in bulk. In Nairobi, they discovered an open-air crafts market and soon had a procession of carvers of ebony and kisii stone (an easily shaped, peach-colored soapstone found only near Lake Victoria) bringing their wares to their hotel room. They bought woven reed baskets in the wetlands of Botswana and wooden masks in Zambia. Lendrum knew how to bargain, had an eye for African arts, and chatted easily with the traders. As a boy, he'd picked up some isiNdebele, the Zulu-based language of southern Zimbabwe, and could converse in Fanagolo, a mix of Zulu, English, and Afrikaans that had become the lingua franca of Southern Africa's miners and other workers, who came from a collage of ethnic and linguistic groups. (Many white Rhodesians of a certain age learned to speak Fanagolo to communicate with their servants.)

When Lendrum claimed to be short on funds, Mullin assumed more and more of the financial risk. Mullin knew his business partner would probably never contribute his fair share, but he also understood that if he didn't keep providing the money the handicrafts would stop flowing and the venture would collapse. "There's something wrong with that guy," Mullin's ex—while still working behind the counter—warned him. "You can't trust him." By that point Mullin was in way too deep.

Their frantic pace led, on one occasion, to near-disaster. Mullin had bought a four-wheel-drive Mitsubishi Pajero, ideal for driving in the bush, and souped it up with a three-liter engine and a supercharger— an air compressor that feeds extra oxygen into the engine, greatly improving the car's performance. Racing up to Bulawayo from the Beit Bridge one scorching afternoon, he and Lendrum saw black smoke billowing out the side of the four-by-four, and a trail of black oil on the road. As they would later discover, one of the pistons had burned through, building up pressure in the crankcase and sending oil cascading over the engine manifold. When Mullin opened the hood to have a look, the influx of air ignited the oil. The pair managed to pull out their valuables just before flames destroyed the vehicle. They hitched a ride and left the Pajero smoldering on the road. Mullin bought a new Toyota Prado three-liter diesel four-by-four with the insurance money; this time he customized the license plate to read BOND.

=

As they traveled through the bush, Mullin began to see a different side of Lendrum. Often they would drive together into Matobo National Park and climb a sloping, lichen-covered rock face whose summit provided panoramic views of mist-shrouded pinnacles receding into distant hills. Hippos lolled in the reserve's rivers far below, their tiny ears and eyes protruding just above the waterline, while twelve-foot-long crocodiles basked in the sun on the sandbanks. Antelopes, zebras, warthogs, klipspringers, and baboons sometimes leapt across the roads as they approached. Scanning the sky over the craggy rock faces where African black eagles nested, Lendrum impressed his partner with his expertise about ornithology. He knew the scientific name of every bird, from the short-toed snake eagle (*Circaetus gallicus*) to the black stork (*Ciconia nigra*), from the white-necked raven (*Corvus albicollis*) to the mocking cliff chat (*Thamnolaea cinnamomeiventris*). He could glance at a raptor and instantly identify the creature's species and gender. "You could blindfold him and let him touch a dozen falcons and he could tell you which was which," Mullin says.

Lendrum took Mullin to the Chipangali Wildlife Orphanage outside Bulawayo, established in the early 1970s to rehabilitate creatures that had been abandoned or injured in the wild. Lendrum had often delivered wounded wildlife there and had become familiar with some of the animals' personalities. "Throw some meat in there and show my mate what he does," he instructed the caretaker of a male lion. The beast picked up the bloody slab and dunked it in a trough filled with water, daintily cleaning it with his paws as Lendrum and Mullin watched in amusement. Moving to a nearby cage holding a leopard, Lendrum urged his partner to "go up to the fence." As Mullin approached, the giant cat hurled himself against the barrier with a snarl, terrifying Mullin and sending Lendrum into paroxysms of laughter. When Lendrum beckoned to a vulture that he had rescued from the bush, the vulture, to Mullin's surprise, flew straight to him. "I've always rescued animals," Lendrum would say years later. "When I see a cow lying dead on the road in Africa, I will drag the cow off the road to save the vultures from being hit by trucks."

He showed equal compassion for other unloved species. During the Southern African winter, when temperatures can plummet to near-freezing and snakes slither across Zimbabwe's asphalt roads to absorb the warmth, Lendrum and Mullin would venture out in Lendrum's truck after dark. Headlights illuminating the way ahead, Lendrum might spot a puff adder—an aggressive snake whose cytotoxic bite can kill an adult human in twenty-four hours—screech to a stop, leap out of the truck, pin its head with a stick, and then pick it up by the neck and drop it safely into a cooler box. After accumulating a few snakes, Lendrum would release them all into a field. A YouTube video that Lendrum uploaded around this time shows him toying with an eight-foot-long Egyptian cobra: he dangles the snake by the tail, forces open its jaws, and displays its fangs before tossing it gently aside.

On another occasion, Lendrum rescued from the road a rhombic egg eater, a favorite of his: a slender nonpoisonous snake that climbs trees to raid birds' nests and feeds exclusively on eggs. Lendrum phoned Mullin in England.

"Do you want it?" he asked.

"Sure," Mullin said. Lendrum smuggled it in his pocket on a plane to Heathrow. Mullin gave it to his daughter, who named it Twinkle.

=

Despite all the energy that Mullin and Lendrum put into their project, AfricaXtreme struggled to turn a profit. The Southampton shop, situated on a main street, attracted a steady stream of curious passersby, but many came to browse, not to buy. The partners spent lavishly on print and radio advertising to get the word out. Throughout 2001 and into 2002, short spots would run ten times a day during rush hours on two local radio stations. Accompanied by elephant trumpets, monkey screeches, birdcalls, and beating drums, a sonorous-voiced announcer invited locals to come check out the exotic carvings and to "turn your garden into a tropical paradise with unique, handcrafted metal birds made from recycled metal from Southern Africa." But the blitz of publicity failed to whip up sales.

Still, the partners forged ahead. They opened a second shop in Towcester, an affluent town of twenty thousand in the East Midlands, where Mullin had several friends. They started a mail-order business. Mullin took advantage of his travels for the telecommunications firm to make solo buying excursions in Uganda, Zambia, Cameroon, and the Democratic Republic of Congo. Lendrum divided his time between the crafts business and Wallace Distributors. He continued to complain about money, but he had a new distraction: he had begun a relationship with a Frenchwoman of Algerian descent, who was married but separated from her English husband. She'd met Lendrum at a dance party in Towcester, and shared his enthusiasm for auto racing. Lendrum sold his house in South Africa, and moved to a one-bedroom apartment in Towcester—and then into the house where his girlfriend lived with her two young daughters. He also hired her to run his shop. During his trips to Zimbabwe he could talk about little else.

"I'm so in love," he would tell Mullin while lying in his bed in the chalet they shared at the Southern Comfort Lodge during their handicraft-buying trips in the bush. Mullin would roll his eyes.

"For fuck's sake, shut up," he would say.

=

Lendrum would always publicly insist that he had given up illegal nest robbing after leaving Zimbabwe in 1985. But in late 1999, Mullin began noticing something odd: cartons of hard-boiled eggs, dyed yellow, green, and brown, were turning up in the Bulawayo chalet. When Mullin asked Lendrum what he'd been up to, Lendrum replied that he had been driving into Matobo and snatching live raptor eggs for clients whom he wouldn't identify. He then filled the nests he robbed with hard-boiled replacements in the hope that the birds would reject the eggs as rotten and lay another clutch.

Lendrum loosened up and confided to Mullin that he also had more ambitious plans: he wanted to steal the eggs of exotic birds of prey from around the world and deliver them to wealthy falconers in the Middle East. Several months later, Lendrum left the handicraft business in Mullin's hands and traveled to northern Canada on what he called a "proof of concept" mission. His aim was to study the feasibility of bringing back the eggs of Arab falconers' favorite raptor, the gyrfalcon.

Financing the operation by himself, Lendrum flew for several days over cliffs and uninhabited tundra with a pilot in a chartered helicopter. "It's the most beautiful place in the world," he told Mullin when he got back. "In a week it changed from a place where you could land your helicopter on the frozen lakes to greenness and bears and all the rest of it. If you had come with me, you would have had such good fun." But, he reported with chagrin, he'd managed to spot just a single gyrfalcon and only one aerie. The guidebook that Lendrum had consulted claimed that gyrfalcons build south-facing nests; in fact, as he learned only toward the end of the trip, the aeries always face north, to avoid the prolonged exposure to sunlight that would melt the snow on cliff ledges and cause the eggs to rot from the moisture. He vowed to try again.

Lendrum talked of traveling to South America to raid the nest of a harpy eagle, named by the eighteenth-century naturalist Carl Linnaeus after the mythical harpy beast, the half-human, half-avian personification of storm-force winds in Greek mythology. The largest, strongest raptor in the rain forest and one of the world's most threatened birds, the harpy has slate-black upper feathers, a white breast, and a pale gray, double-crested head, and can grow to three feet tall and weigh as much as twenty-five pounds. Also high on his wish list were the eggs of the Eurasian eagle owl, a fast and powerful raptor with pumpkin-orange eyes and feathery ear tufts, which nests in rock crevices throughout much of Europe, Asia, and North Africa. But this was all just talk.

Then, one morning in early 2001, following another handicrafts-buying trip to Victoria Falls, Lendrum disappeared for several hours from the chalet at the Southern Comfort Lodge. When he returned he reached inside his backpack and set down three baby birds on his bed. The chicks had mottled black-and-white feathers, hooked beaks, and large yellow legs and black talons. They appeared to be one or two days old, and they were chirping and screeching at ear-piercing volume. They were lanner falcons, Lendrum told Mullin over the racket, a migratory raptor that is slightly smaller than the peregrine, with a propensity for hunting game by pursuing it horizontally, a technique known as the "chase and grab."

He told Mullin he planned to smuggle the babies to Dubai.

"What the fuck are you talking about?" Mullin asked.

"Don't worry," Lendrum assured him. He had a client—and a plan.

The next morning at dawn, Lendrum fashioned a nest made of towels and placed it at the bottom of his rucksack, then laid the three chicks inside. He placed the rucksack on the floor behind the driver's seat of his pickup truck, where it was cool and dark. The two men set forth on the thirteen-hour drive from Bulawayo to Johannesburg. Mullin wanted to see for himself if Lendrum could pull off the stunt and had invited himself along as far as London. On the road trip south Lendrum fed the birds every two hours with a blend of minced calf liver and raw egg yolk, placing the food into their beaks with a pair of tweezers. At the airport, Lendrum removed the birds from the rucksack to avoid the baggage scan machine, where their bones would be visible. Instead he put them carefully in the pockets of his fleece, and walked them through the metal detector. Lendrum fed them again in the shower room of the Virgin Atlantic business-class lounge, transferred them back to the rucksack, and, with Mullin, boarded a Virgin Atlantic flight to the UK. He stored the birds in the overhead compartment, and Lendrum and Mullin settled back in their business-class seats.

Then, in the middle of the night, Mullin awoke to a piercing noise emanating from directly above him.

Cheeep cheeep cheep. Cheeep cheeep cheeeeep.

"Jeff," he said, shaking Lendrum awake. "I can hear the children crying."

Lendrum listened. Then he burst out laughing.

"Go feed the fuckers," Mullin said.

Lendrum brought down the rucksack and a small plastic container filled with the yolk-and-liver mix, and carried all into the toilet. When he returned, the chicks had gone back to sleep. Soon Mullin fell asleep, too.

Then, two hours later, Mullin was jolted awake again:

Cheeeep. Cheeep. Cheeeep.

Lendrum again scooped up the birds and the mix and retreated to the lavatory.

The chicks woke up four more times in the course of the flight to London, but the white noise of the jet engine masked their hunger-driven screeches from the other passengers and crew, and Lendrum and his live contraband made it safely off the plane.

The two parted ways at Heathrow. "Make sure you look after the children," Mullin called, as Lendrum rushed to catch his flight to Dubai. Mullin soon heard from Lendrum that he had safely delivered all the chicks to his mystery client. (Years later, Lendrum would insist that Mullin's story was "a complete flight of fiction. Have you heard how noisy those birds are?" Mullin would stand by what he said.)

This sort of escapade, Mullin would come to realize, was Lendrum's oxygen. He wasn't doing it for the money—Mullin saw no evidence that Lendrum was cashing in, at least not yet. "He lived a very basic lifestyle," Mullin would remember, two decades later. "If he was making sixty thousand dollars out of each egg that hatched and became an adult, where was the big house, the big car? He did buy himself a new Toyota double-cab four-by-four, but he didn't make a lot." Perhaps, Mullin speculated, Lendrum was content to work for a relative pittance in return for the promise of adventure. He needed challenges, loved living on the edge—whether playing with deadly snakes, scaling the tallest cliffs and trees, or stealing the world's most endangered species. "It's always been about the thrill for Jeff," his boyhood friend Howard Waller would say. "He likes to beat the system. That's been his thing since he was a kid."

Now Lendrum's appetite for risk and his willingness to skirt the rules had pulled him into a global enterprise.

TEN

===

DUBAI

Centuries before Jeffrey Lendrum began raiding nests for wealthy Arab clients, trappers were shinnying up trees and scaling cliffs in avid pursuit of falcons. In 1247, Frederick II of Hohenstaufen, the Holy Roman Emperor, offered instructions to falconers on how to obtain chicks from the wild. "If the nest is in a tree, a man can climb up and, having put the young ones in a basket, carry them home," he advised in *On the Art of Hunting with Birds*, his classic work on falconry. If the aerie was built into the fissure of a high rock face, however, "a man is secured to the end of a rope and descends or is lowered from the rim of the mountain or cliff to the level of the hollow, and, entering, lifts the bird from the nest."

Adelard of Bath, a twelfth-century English natural philosopher, recommended capturing chicks "seven days after hatching" in the morning when their stomachs were empty and it was cool. Frederick II thought it better to leave the chicks in the nest as long as possible, "because the longer they are fed by their parents the better and stronger will be their limbs and pinions," he wrote, "and they are less likely to become screechers or gapers."

While Europeans raided nests, Arabs of the era (and for centuries afterward) trapped "passage" falcons: young birds that had left the nest for good. During the September-to-November migration of millions of birds from Eastern Europe and Central Asia to Africa, the trappers waited for the falcons (mostly peregrines, but also some sakers) in the Syrian Desert, the Tigris and Euphrates Valleys, and farther down the Arabian Peninsula. They would strap a pigeon to a *shabichet hehmama*, a lightweight wooden frame covered with a dozen nooses made from woven strands of camel hair, and then, as the falcon passed overhead, send the bird aloft. The raptor would zero in for the kill, ensnare a toe or two in a noose, and flutter down to earth.

Other trappers employed a lugger falcon, a sluggish raptor known as a *bizzuar* in Arabic. Partially blinded from a thread passed through each eyelid, the bird would be sent into the air clutching a decoy bundle of feathers called a *nigil*. The passage bird would attack the bundle, intent on wresting it from the weaker falcon, and, its foot caught in a hidden noose, fall to the ground.

The passage falcons, eighteen months old or younger, were ideal birds for falconry, wrote diplomat and Arabist Mark Allen in *Falconry in Arabia*, being far superior to both chicks snatched from their nests and mature raptors that had been trapped after their first migration. The juvenile passage falcon, with fully developed musculature and feathers and an ability to hunt inculcated by its parents, combines, Allen declared, "the [malleability] of youth with its capacity for adventure and carelessness of danger."

=

By the 1970s the trapping of wild falcons was dying out in much of the world. In 1973 the United States, which had lost about 90 percent of its peregrine population to DDT and other pesticides, passed the Endangered Species Act, making it illegal to acquire, deliver, hold, sell, or market falcons except for scientific purposes. That same year, eighty countries ratified the Convention on International Trade in Endangered Species of Wild Flora and Fauna (CITES). The treaty, which was eventually signed by 183 nations, designated twelve hundred species, including many birds of prey, as Appendix I—"threatened with extinction"—and prohibited trade of wild raptors except with hard-to-obtain licenses for research. In the decades since, the United Kingdom, Canada, Germany, Russia, Pakistan, the United Arab Emirates, and other countries in Europe, Asia, and South America have made illegal the trapping of almost all birds of prey.

The new restrictions forced falconers to seek alternatives to taking birds from the wilderness. There had already been experiments with captive breeding, or mating falcons in a controlled environment. Renz Waller, a German falconer and artist best known for his portrait of a white gyrfalcon owned by General Field Marshall Hermann Göring, Hitler's supreme commander of the Luftwaffe, had tried repeatedly, although with very limited success, to induce peregrines to breed in an aviary in the Nazis' falcon center in Riddagshausen in north-central Germany. Nazi leaders admired falconry in part because of its ties to medieval Teutonic knights, and Hermann Göring and SS chief Heinrich Himmler, both avid falconers, supported an expansive program of training raptors and teaching Nazis to hunt with the birds.

Waller's experiment ended abruptly in 1944 when an Allied bombardment burned his facility to the ground. Three decades later, the Midwest-based Raptor Research Foundation, the Canadian Fish and Wildlife Service, and Cornell University's Peregrine Fund relied on

Waller's notes in their attempts to breed peregrines in captivity for the purpose of repopulating the wild.

As Renz Waller had discovered, captive breeding turned out to be anything but easy. Raptors proved far more temperamental and sensitive to being cooped up than domestic fowl. Deprived of the acrobatic courtship flights, marked by loops, tight turns, and swooping dives, that served as an essential mating ritual in the wild, the birds usually refused to copulate. If they did, females would not sit on their fertilized eggs. Hatching falcon eggs in incubators was problematic, too. They often overheated, or weren't rotated at the proper intervals, preventing the embryo-nourishing albumen, or egg white, from spreading inside the shell. Moving an early embryo risked breaking the chalaza, the cord that anchors the yolk to the albumen, killing the chick-to-be; even tilting the egg at an incorrect angle could twist the cord and kill the embryo. Misjudging the humidity in the incubator could also prove fatal. High humidity would cause the egg to lose too much water between laying and hatching, leaving the chick too small and weak because of dehydration to break through the shell. Low humidity would result in a chick too large to maneuver inside the shell, and so it would be unable to peck its way out of its tiny enclosure.

Ornithological researcher Heinz K. Meng at the State University of New York at New Paltz succeeded in breeding the first pair of peregrines in North American captivity in 1971. He lent the birds to Tom Cade, the founder of the Peregrine Fund, who helped the couple—and two other pairs—produce twenty falcon chicks in 1973. Across the world, breeders were learning how to select compatible pairs, construct congenial nests, induce the birds to mate, perfect artificial incubation, get parents or surrogates to rear the incubator-hatched chicks, and encourage birds to lay a second clutch of eggs to increase the number of young. As the handful of breeding programs became more successful, "the whole thing snowballed," says Jemima Parry-Jones, who'd started breeding birds of prey in the early 1970s at her raptor center in rural Gloucestershire. Arab devotees of falconry, flush with oil wealth and prohibited by international law from obtaining wild birds, began buying captive-bred birds in the United States and Europe, creating a commercial market. By the early 1980s breeding programs had produced thousands of raptors of a dozen species, including two thousand peregrine falcons.

=

In 1968, Great Britain, after 150 years of controlling the armies and foreign policy of seven coastal sheikhdoms at the southeast end of the Arabian Peninsula, announced that it was granting them complete independence. Weeks later, at a desert oasis, Sheikh Zayed bin Sultan Al Nahyan, the ruler of Abu Dhabi, met with the leader of Dubai, Sheikh Rashid bin Mohammed Al Maktoum, and agreed to try to unite the sheikhdoms into a new federation. On December 2, 1971, Abu Dhabi and Dubai joined Sharjah, Ajman, Umm Al Quwain, and Fujairah in creating the United Arab Emirates. (The seventh sheikhdom, Ras Al Khaimah, joined a year later.) The UAE would be a constitutional monarchy, with laws enacted by a Federal Supreme Council made up of the seven dynastic rulers of the individual emirates. Whoever was the sheikh of Abu Dhabi would serve as president; the sheikh of Dubai would be prime minister.

Sheikh Zayed, a powerfully built figure with a lean and weather-beaten face and a sternly charismatic presence, became the United Arab Emirates' first ruler. An ardent falconer, he considered the sport an essential part of the new nation's cultural identity, and set out to introduce captive breeding to the Arabian Peninsula by luring Western experts to run the programs. In the mid-1970s, Sheikh Zayed invited a prominent English falconer named Roger Upton to join him on a hunt in the Arabian Desert. The pair rode camels in a wilderness area about an hour from Abu Dhabi, then a small town on an island in the Persian Gulf; with half a dozen falcons, they brought down bustards throughout the day. Upton and Sheikh Zayed became close friends, and Upton stayed on to breed falcons for him.

Then, in the late 1980s, in a turn of events that would prove fateful for Jeffrey Lendrum, Howard Waller, Lendrum's boyhood companion (no relation to Renz Waller), who was then breeding falcons commercially in South Africa, heard through friends about potentially lucrative falcon-related opportunities in the United Arab Emirates. Waller had begun hunting with falcons and hawks as a boy in Bulawayo. "I remember being nine years old and walking down a dirt road when a sparrow hawk came up and caught a small bird right in front of me," Waller would recall. "I thought, 'Wow,' and that's where it started." (Falcons, belonging to the *falco* genus, are long-winged birds that hunt in open areas and kill their prey with their curved, notched beaks; hawks, which belong to the *accipiter* genus, have shorter, rounded wings and hunt in woodlands, seizing their quarry with their talons.) Lendrum would say years later that his initial encounters with Waller, who had been a part of the same adolescent gang of wildlife enthusiasts, had not been auspicious. "We actually hated each other at first," Lendrum would recall. "I thought he was a bit of a know-it-all, and I suppose I was a know-it-all, but eventually we became friends."

Around 1988, Waller was invited to visit a new breeding program that a Canadian former colleague had started in Dubai. When

Waller arrived, captive breeding programs were still trying to get off the ground, and wealthy Arabs remained dependent on wild falcons for hunting. Smugglers brought birds overland through Pakistan or Iran, and then ferried them across the Strait of Hormuz to the Arabian Peninsula. Waller ventured into the Arabian Desert during the annual bird migration, and encountered trappers hiding among the dunes. But bird populations in Europe had thinned over the past decades, largely because of rampant poaching in the Balkans and other countries directly on the southern migration route; fewer raptors were flying over the desert. And the Emirates had become a signatory to the Convention on International Trade in Endangered Species of Wild Flora and Fauna. The government announced its intention to crack down on wild taking, and many falconers agreed to play by the new rules.

In Dubai, Waller was later introduced to Sheikh Butti bin Juma Al Maktoum, an insurance and construction magnate then in his thirties, and a dedicated falconer and conservationist. An intense, energetic, and deeply knowledgeable figure with an aquiline nose, arched brows, and a trim mustache, Sheikh Butti was also the first cousin of Sheikh Mohammed bin Rashid Al Maktoum, Dubai's crown prince. Impressed by the Al Maktoum family's wealth, and by their devotion to falconry, Waller recognized a unique opportunity. "I said that I'd like to come out and start breeding for [Butti]," Waller says, "and he said yes."

Soon Waller, who was married, with two young children, opened falcon pens at Sheikh Butti's desert palace, on the edge of an eighty-seven-square mile camel farm that Butti's cousin, Sheikh Mohammed, would later purchase and turn into a wildlife refuge called the Dubai Desert Conservation Reserve. Waller was on his way to becoming one of the most successful breeders in the Emirates—and the world.

=

Waller's move to Dubai came at a time when falconry on the Arabian Peninsula was running up against the consequences of environmental recklessness. For centuries falconers had hunted, without limit, the Arabian Desert's population of houbara bustards (*Chlamydotis undulata*), ungainly turkey-sized birds known for flamboyantly flaring their white chest feathers, running around in circles at high speed, and emitting booming calls to impress a potential mate. When under attack, they vomit a slimy secretion that can paralyze a bird of prey. British travel writer Wilfred Thesiger had seen bustards everywhere during a hunting trip he took with Sheikh Zayed, already the ruler of Abu Dhabi, in the desert dunes of the Empty Quarter during the winter of 1949. In his book *Arabian Sands*, Thesiger captured the excitement of that hunt and of the battle to the death between pursuer and quarry that had transfixed Bedouin for millennia. "Suddenly an Arab on the left of the line signaled to us that he had found fresh tracks," he wrote:

> A falconer unhooded his bird and raised it in the air, then it was off flying a few feet above the ground; the bustard was climbing now but the peregrine was fast overhauling it . . . then someone shouted, "it's down!" and we were racing across the sands . . . We came upon the peregrine in a hollow, plucking at the lifeless bustard—Zayid pointed to some oily splashes on the ground and said, "Do you see that muck? The hubara squirts it at its attacker. If it gets into the *shahin*'s eyes it blinds it temporarily. Anyway if it

gets on to its feathers it makes a filthy mess of them, and you cannot use the bird again that day."

A decade or so later, Sheikh Butti, his father, and other members of the royal family of Dubai would take four-wheel-drive vehicles down sand tracks in the Arabian Desert and use falcons and salukis (hunting dogs also known as African greyhounds) to hunt for hares, bustards, kairowans (mid-sized birds), wolves, and rheem gazelles (miniature antelopes that stand only two and a half feet tall). "What I remember most is the fact that other than our vehicles there were no other car tracks in the desert. It was pristine," Sheikh Butti said in a 2011 interview with *Wildlife Middle East*. In this world of harsh sunlight and heavy silences, he recalled collecting truffles in the desert in February following drenching autumnal rains, and getting lost at night "and being navigated by an old Bedouin who took us safely out using only his knowledge of the vegetation and the wind direction pattern of the dunes."

But the landscape of Dubai was already changing. Sheikh Butti's uncle, Sheikh Rashid bin Mohammed Al Maktoum, a semiliterate visionary who spoke only Arabic and displayed the ascetic habits of his Bedouin ancestors, ordered Dubai's creek dredged in 1961, making the city the most accessible port in the Middle East. He brought electricity, running water, and telephones, built the first luxury hotels and dry docks, and turned Dubai into an international shipping center. The Al Maktoum family continued to build over the next four decades, expanding the airport and transforming Dubai into a giant shopping arcade and tourist magnet. They financed ambitious construction projects such as Dubai Internet City, a sleek campus of low-slung glass-and-concrete buildings and palm-fringed lawns with 1.5 million square feet of commercial office space designated for high-tech companies such as Microsoft and Oracle, and the Burj Al Arab, a 590-foot-high, sail-shaped hotel on an artificial island in the Persian Gulf. The building boom ripped up the desert and depleted the bustards' habitat. Thousands of workers "would go out onto the huge gravel plains, collect rocks, clean them, and load them onto trucks," remembered Howard Waller, who had watched the desert be torn up to supply building materials for the expanding municipality. "Amongst the rocks were the beetles, lizards, and other prey which the bustards had fed on." Four-wheel-drive vehicles had already replaced camels, allowing hunters to travel longer distances, and now the Arabs used shotguns as well as falcons to hunt down bustards in their increasingly constricted territory. Before long, hunters would wipe out the bustard on the Arabian Peninsula.

The billionaire sheikhs of the Emirates, Qatar, and other Arab countries, faced with the disappearance of their favorite prey, began to look for hunting opportunities overseas. The Al Nahyans, the Al Maktoums, and other wealthy Arabs leased vast tracts of desert in Uzbekistan, Kazakhstan, Afghanistan, Pakistan, Algeria, Morocco, Iraq, and other countries that still had healthy houbara bustard populations. Every fall they packed hundreds of falcons onto private jets and then spent a week or more hunting from mobile tent camps in the bush, preparing feasts each night with the prey that their falcons had killed. These lavish seven- or even ten-day expeditions, usually involving a caravan of four-by-fours and dozens of falconers, veterinarians, drivers, cooks, and other support staff, fueled a sense of competition as well as camaraderie among the sheikhs. It helped feed the demand for ever bigger, faster, and more powerful falcons.

By the new millennium, these trips would become shadowed by

legitimate concerns from conservation groups that argued they were threatening the houbara bustard with global extinction. One Saudi prince's party reportedly killed twelve hundred bustards during a weeklong falcon hunt in Pakistan—where the birds migrate during the late fall and winter breeding season—despite having a permit to kill just one hundred. (In 2015, Pakistan's Supreme Court would rule that no further hunting licenses for bustards could be issued.) For the most part, however, "They don't care in these places," I was told by one trainer who hunts in Uzbekistan every October and in Algeria in November with Dubai's crown prince, Hamdan bin Mohammed bin Rashid Al Maktoum, and his father, Sheikh Mohammed, who became Dubai's ruler in 2006. The hunts also channel millions of dollars into unstable areas, something that would have calamitous consequences in November 2015, when a heavily armed, Iran-backed Shia militia would seize twenty-six members of a Qatari royal hunting party in Iraq's southern desert. Only after sixteen months of negotiations and a ransom payment of $1 billion were the royals released.

The increasing sensitivity to environmental protection, along with fears of a scenario like the Iraq kidnapping, were among the reasons that Crown Prince Hamdan would introduce falcon racing to the Emirates.

=

In the early 1980s, in his search for bigger, more powerful, and more beautiful birds, Sheikh Butti became one of the first Arabs to import a gyrfalcon to the Middle East. The world's largest species of falcon— and "a killing machine without equal," as the British falconer Emma Ford wrote in a 1999 book on the birds—gyrfalcons almost exclusively inhabit zones of ice floes and frozen tundra, stretching from Alaska and northern Canada through Greenland, Norway, and Lapland, to Siberia. Viking settlers in northern Scotland called them "geirfugel," from the epithet *geir*, meaning "spear." The scientific name is *Falco rusticolus*, or "country dweller." Roosting in rock crevices sheltered from blizzards and gale-force winds, they can survive for weeks on icebergs in the open ocean and circle the skies for hours in search of prey—including lemmings, voles, seabirds, and ptarmigans (game birds of the grouse family). Powerful musculature and circulatory and respiratory systems as hyperefficient as those of the peregrine falcon allow the raptors to outlast their quarry in exhausting horizontal pursuits or dive-bomb them like a missile. T. Edward Nickens described the gyrfalcon in *Audubon* magazine as "a predatorial mash-up of Muhammad Ali and Floyd Mayweather, speedy and large enough to kill a fleeing Pin-tailed Duck in midair but agile enough to snatch a Lapland Longspur off a tundra tussock."

Beginning in the medieval era, trappers embarked on expeditions to the Arctic to bring back gyrfalcons for European and Mongolian monarchs. These journeys, writes Ford, "required such courage and single-mindedness that they beggar belief." Many trappers froze to death, while others disappeared forever into glacial crevasses or tumbled fatally off cliffs. For the nobility, gyrfalcons—and white gyrfalcons in particular—became unsurpassed symbols of wealth and prestige. In 1396, Turkish soldiers captured Jean de Nevers, the future Duke of Burgundy, during the Battle of Nicopolis in Greece; the Ottoman Sultan refused increasing offers of ransom, setting de Nevers free only after he agreed to hand over the ultimate prize: twelve white gyrs. Ivan the Terrible, the Russian czar, dispached his first envoy to England in 1550 with "a large and faire white Jewrfawcan" as a gift to Henry VIII's daughter, the future Elizabeth I. And in the mid–nineteenth century, Husan-Dawlah Mirza, a claimant to the Persian throne, wrote about a white gyrfalcon that had been brought from Russia and presented to his father, the Shah. Kept on a damp bed of pebbles and sand near Tehran, "she feels the heat greatly," Mirza observed, "so that she has to be well supplied with ice and snow." He watched with awe each time the gyrfalcon was sent out to hunt and dived headlong to earth in pursuit of her prey. "All I know," he declared, "is that neither I, nor has the oldest falconer of Persia, ever seen a falcon like it."

Butti's pure white gyrfalcon dazzled everyone in the sheikh's circle. But almost all feared that the bird—which he had obtained from a breeder in Germany—would drop dead of exhaustion in the desert heat, or succumb to local pathogens. Not to mention that no one had the skills to train it. But under Sheikh Butti's intuitive and attentive care, the gyrfalcon, named Hasheem ("Generosity"), became a skilled hunter—its talents easily visible during the sheikh's early-morning training sessions in the desert and on his annual fall hunts overseas. Emma Ford's *Gyrfalcon*, the classic text about the raptor, contains a photo of Sheikh Butti proudly holding a huge gyr on his *manqalah*, a muff-like cylinder of canvas or carpet, worn on the falconer's wrist instead of a glove. Members of Sheikh Butti's circle, as well as other enthusiasts on the Arabian Peninsula, began to import gyrfalcons, too.

=

Howard Waller's setup in Dubai exceeded anything he could have imagined back in South Africa. He established his base on the palace's expansive grounds, a serene retreat one hour east of central Dubai that offered views of the urban skyline on clear mornings. He'd venture into the desert before dawn to observe the training of the birds, sharing observations with Sheikh Butti about falcon lineages, injuries, past performances, and horizontal and vertical speeds. His employer would become a confidant and a soul mate. "Almost like a long-married couple, they eagerly anticipate each other's answers and communicate using a shorthand inscrutable to nearly everyone else," wrote Peter Gwin in an October 2018 profile of the two falconers in *National Geographic*: "'The gray whose father was the one we hunted with two years ago. . . . The gyr with the broken tail feather that we fixed.'" Waller could often be found on the palace grounds alone or with the sheikh, inspecting the aviaries that were home to several hundred falcons or visiting the kitchens where butchers prepared hundreds of quail and pigeons for daily feedings.

Encouraged by the sheikh, Waller introduced gyrfalcons to his breeding pens—purchased, he says, legally in the United States. From them he bred both pure gyrs and hybrids that, it was hoped, would combine the strongest qualities of different species. He crossed gyrfalcons with saker falcons (*Falco cherrug*), hardy flyers that are born and fledge in the arid zones of Mongolia and Central Asia, to create "turbo sakers"—big, fast-diving birds that thrive in a desert climate and are more aggressive than pure sakers. He also crossbred gyrfalcons and peregrines, which proved equally popular with Arab hunters. Over time Waller and Sheikh Butti would put together what the *National Geographic* described as "arguably . . . one of the most exquisite collections of falcons ever assembled."

To get their birds to build up wing strength, Waller and Sheikh Butti introduced "hack pens" to Dubai—enormous indoor bird gymnasiums—and equipped them with multimillion-dollar air-conditioning systems so that the birds wouldn't be exposed to the 130-degree summer heat. To keep his gyrfalcons healthy during the molting season that typically lasts from March until the end of September, when the Arctic birds shed their forty-four wing and twelve tail feathers and grow new ones, and are especially sensitive to desert temperatures, Waller introduced air-conditioned "moulting chambers," which led to higher survival rates and became a standard for raising gyrs in the Middle East.

When the birds got sick, they were taken to a falcon hospital in Dubai built by one of Sheikh Butti's uncles. The facility had dozens of air-conditioned rooms, an intensive care unit and an opthalmology department, the latest model X-ray machines, heart monitors and endoscopy instruments, a full range of antibiotics and other drugs, and a team of international veterinarians who treated everything from aspergillosis (a lung infection caused by a fungus) to bumblefoot (a bacterial disease causing lesions of the spurs of the feet) to damaged feathers.

Back in Sheikh Butti's desert palace, Waller was also conducting research into artifical insemination. From the time the chicks were just a few days old, he spent hours each day with his baby males in their breeding pens, talking to them, singing to them, playing with them, and eventually inducing them to regard him as a sexual partner. (Birds don't instinctively identify with their own species upon hatching, and can be taught to bond sexually with a human—a process known as "imprinting"—rather than another bird.) Waller would wear a tight-fitting hat resembling a honeycomb that the copulating male—known as a "hat bird"—would leap on top of, ejaculating into a hole. Waller would then collect the semen in a capillary tube and drop the liquid into a female.

During the breeding season that runs from March to May, when lengthening days and warmer temperatures trigger the hormonal changes that initiate the reproductive cycle, egg cells grow, and pass down to the mouth of the female's oviduct, awaiting fertilization. "I put my hands on her back, she lifts her back up, I bend her tail to the side, and I slip the semen into her cloaca," the bird's reproductive orifice, Waller explained to me. Waller and I were speaking in Inverness, Scotland, where Sheikh Butti had moved the bulk of his breeding operations in 2013; raptors breed more easily in a cold and windy climate. Waller now spends most of the year on the windswept, rocky moor with his second wife and their two children. "If the female is sucking [the semen] in well, chances are very good that it will fertilize the egg." The egg then condenses into a protective but permeable layer of calcium surrounding a yolk, which will develop into a chick in about a month. Most breeders have one or two reliable semen producers; Waller always had more than a dozen—and dozens of breeding females.

As Waller had discovered, artificial insemination was the only way to create hybrids because, as with almost all birds, interspecies mating among peregrines, sakers, and gyrfalcons is extremely rare in the wild. (One 1963 study estimated that only one in fifty thousand wild birds is a hybrid.) Insemination was also the only effective method to bring together the sperm and ova of desirable birds of the same species that didn't get along. "You can't just put a male and female together and say they're going to breed," Waller explained. "Falcons are like humans, they fall in love." Incubating the eggs proved to be another challenge. Natural hatching is impossible for falcons in the desert, because the females refuse to sit on their eggs in an inhospitable and unfamiliar environment. But incubating artificially requires constant monitoring: tracking weight reduction due to water loss, maintaining the exact ambient temperature to keep the developing embryo warm . . . Waller estimated his hatch rate from incubators in the early days was far below 50 percent, although that improved over the years.

Waller and Sheikh Butti boasted that their prolific production of captive-bred falcons was benefiting global conservation by eliminating the need for wild taking. "I am a falconer, but my desire is to protect the wild populations of falcons," Butti declared in a 2011 interview. He gave away falcons to family members and close friends, and maintained a loyal clientele of affluent Emirati enthusiasts. "The local falconers are very happy with the hunting quality of the birds I produce," he said.

Sheikh Butti's reputation as a wildlife conservationist preceded him. In the 1990s he'd opened the Sheikh Butti bin Juma Al Maktoum Wildlife Centre, a thirty-seven-acre walled zoo in the center of Dubai where he bred endangered animals. The project was the consummation of a fascination with animal husbandry that had begun when he was five years old and his father brought home baby hares, hedgehogs, and gazelles to live in the family compound in Jumeirah, a wealthy seaside neighborhood in Dubai. "There was one mountain gazelle I remember in particular that had been hand-reared and would follow us around the garden," Butti recalled.

In his zoo, he resuscitated species that had nearly vanished from the Arabian Peninsula—the Arabian oryx, the sand gazelle, the Rüppell's fox—as well as threatened African species, such as the black hippotragus, Cape giraffe, gerenuk (a long-necked antelope found in Somalia and other arid zones of the Horn of Africa), Speke's gazelle, bontebok (a medium-sized, brown antelope indigenous to Southern Africa), and Grant's gazelle. Butti's desert palace had a large aviary with doves, Somali guinea fowl, gray-crowned cranes, 250 flamingos, and (Butti's special pride) northern bald ibises—magnificently ungainly specimens listed by conservation groups as "critically endangered," with ruffled black feathers, a bare red face, and a long, curved red bill. Sheikh Butti even reared a female cheetah that he mated with a male from a wildlife center in the Emirate of Sharjah. The pair produced six cubs, the first cheetahs born in the Arabian Peninsula in decades.

But his main passion was falcons.

=

In the late 1990s, just as AfricaXtreme was getting off the ground, Waller invited Jeffrey Lendrum to come visit him at Sheikh Butti's desert palace. The friends had remained close in Lendrum's early years in South Africa, but had fallen out of touch during the mid-1990s. Lendrum was busy with his spare-parts trafficking schemes and Waller was dealing with some personal trouble. "Howard and his wife were going through a divorce, and I had kept out of the way," Lendrum would say. Now Waller missed his old *shamwari*.

Lendrum was impressed by the opulence of the palace, the attention lavished on the falcons, and his friend's success. Waller introduced Lendrum to Sheikh Butti—whom Lendrum would describe blandly as "a very nice guy"—and took him to see the Al Maktoums' veterinary hospital. But he laid down one strict rule: Lendrum could not accompany him as he collected semen in the breeding pens. "The birds would get stressed if they saw a stranger," Lendrum would recall. "Howard was the only one allowed in." When Lendrum returned to South Africa, he gushed to Mullin that "you wouldn't believe the job that Howard has." The medical care for falcons in Dubai was better than that available to humans, he said, and the hack pens on Sheikh Butti's property were "the size of three football fields."

One day, Lendrum alleges, Waller took him aside and made a stunning proposal: he asked Lendrum to work for him as a trapper in the wilderness. With his skill as a climber and his experience moving goods across borders, Lendrum would be the ideal partner in a covert plan to strengthen his stable with feral birds. Waller wanted Lendrum to provide wild falcon eggs, rather than live birds, Lendrum says, because they could be carried across borders undetected.

Lendrum claims he told Waller that it wasn't a promising idea. "It's ninety-nine percent unlikely that it would work," is the way that Lendrum says he put it. The length of time the eggs would be out of the nest—dozens of hours from door to door—"was just too long." He would have to keep the eggs warm, probably by wearing them strapped to his body, which just wasn't practical. And he questioned why Waller would need wild raptor eggs anyway, given the number of captive-bred chicks he was producing each season. "The time I went there, there were about one hundred babies," he would say. "What the hell was he going to do with one hundred babies?" After this discussion, Lendrum says Waller dropped the subject.

Years later Waller would not deny that such a conversation took place, but he described it as idle chatter. "Lendrum and I may have discussed the idea, or Lendrum may have come to me with it, but nothing ever happened," Waller would insist. Lendrum returned to South Africa, and they remained in periodic touch.

=

Lendrum and Waller would hardly have been the first Western birders to contemplate conducting sketchy business in the Middle East. In 1981, a few years after new regulations in the United States and Canada banned trapping and trading birds of prey, the US Fish and Wildlife Service recruited John Jeffrey McPartlin, a hunter, falconer, and convicted wild bird dealer from Great Falls, Montana, to assist them in a sting called Operation Falcon. It was the first attempt by law enforcement authorities to prove that a raptor underground linked Western smugglers with wealthy clients in the Middle East. After a three-year investigation, three hundred federal, state, and provincial agents swooped down on falconers and breeders in fourteen states and four Canadian provinces who had purchased wild gyrfalcons from McPartlin. Thirty people were arrested, dozens more interrogated, and one hundred birds seized. Fish and Wildlife Service agents claimed that the royal family of Saudi Arabia had acquired wild birds of prey illegally from some of these individuals, and might have used diplomatic privileges to sneak the birds past customs.

But although Operation Falcon officers described a "worldwide, multi-million dollar illegal black market in birds of prey," the sting failed to pin down anything concrete. (The only organization conclusively determined to have been involved in the trapping and selling of wild falcons was the Fish and Wildlife Service, which had permitted the seizure of fifty gyrfalcons from the wild to use in the sting operation.) The Saudi Arabian suspects hired a Washington, DC, lawyer who vigorously denied all the allegations. In the end, no Saudis were convicted of crimes, most buyers pleaded guilty only to misdemeanors, and Operation Falcon was widely attacked as a waste of government resources. One defense attorney claimed that McPartlin's sting was a classic case of entrapment. Offering to sell breeders pure white gyrfalcons was "like having someone bring Marilyn Monroe by and asking if she can spend the night," he said.

Nearly a decade after Operation Falcon, an investigative series on the British ITV nework aired "The Bird Bandits," a half-hour exposé of the Arab connection. The host, Roger Cook, promised to provide "evidence of an organized and vastly profitable trade in endangered birds of prey." Guided by an investigator from the Royal Society for the Protection of Birds, Cook's producer staked out a peregrine nest in northern Scotland, and caught on camera an egg thief, Steven McDonald, rappelling down a rock face and making off with a clutch. Cook dressed up as an Arab sheikh, with fake beard and mustache, keffiyeh, and robes, and—using a hidden camera—filmed himself meeting with a European smuggler who promised to deliver to him peregrines stolen from Scottish nests. "Many Arabs still believe that wild birds have superior speed and killing power, and Scotland . . . is the source of the most highly prized," Cook claimed in his narration. "The young birds are then passed into the system, and a variety of middlemen, in [Great Britain], France, Belgium, and Germany," arrange for their passage to the Middle East. The average price paid by Arabs for a wild peregrine, Cook claimed, was £15,000, then equal to about $25,000.

The falconry community vehemently disputed the program's contentions. The Hawk Board, an association of British falconers, charged that the producers had spent weeks in the Gulf "trying desperately" to locate a sheikh interested in buying a Scottish peregrine—and failed. The board insisted that the prices presented in the show were wildly exaggerated, that no market existed in the Middle East for British peregrines, either wild or captive-bred, and that eggs, chicks, and nestlings that had not yet developed into mature flyers had no value to the Arab falconer.

Perhaps it was true that sheikhs weren't purchasing many falcons stolen from Scotland, but, following the collapse of the Soviet Union, a huge black market trade sprang up in sakers and peregrines from the Kamchatka Peninsula and the Altai Mountains. In 2006, the World Wildlife Fund office in Vladivostok reported a "catastrophic drop" in the number of saker falcons in Russia, from sixty thousand to two thousand pairs in twenty years. The Middle East Falcon Research Group, an Abu Dhabi–based veterinary and ornithological institute, identified the perpetrators as Syrian and Lebanese students studying at Russian universities, including one Syrian gang that had captured fifty sakers before its leader was arrested, convicted, and sentenced to three and a half years in prison. A network of Russian coconspirators, from railway personnel to airline baggage handlers, moved the birds through the Russian interior, placing them on flights to Moscow, Novosibirsk, Yekaterinburg, and Irkutsk, before transferring them to Azerbaijan, Armenia, and other neighboring countries. From there, according to an article in the journal *Contemporary Justice Review*, they were smuggled into the Middle East. Traffickers wrapped the falcons in cloth and squeezed them into tubes, hiding them in sports bags, under fruit, and in diplomatic packages. "Eyes can be sewn shut, supposedly to reduce nervousness, and once swaddled they can be packed into rigid suitcases with holes drilled in them," the article reported. Many of the birds suffocated en route. Others died from high temperatures, stress, and lack of food and water.

Other investigations seconded that captured falcons were headed to the Middle East. The British newspaper the *Telegraph* reported that in October 2004, police had intercepted a commercial aircraft carrying 127 sakers shortly before it left a military air base in Kyrgyzstan. The falcons, estimated to have a black market value of £2.6 million, then worth approximately $4.7 million, were heading for Syria. In the same *Telegraph* article, a zoologist in the Mongolian capital Ulan Bator described how falcons were trapped using pigeons fitted with plastic noose traps as bait. "There were several Arabs and their Mongolian trappers careering all over the steppe in a Land Cruiser," the zoologist said. "Every time they spotted a falcon, they leapt out and released about twenty pigeons in different directions. It was crazy." In October 2013, the *Express Tribune*, a Pakistani newspaper, reported that the wildlife authorities had raided a falcon-hunting camp near the Khyber Pass and confiscated pigeons intended as bait to catch sakers and peregrines. A forest officer told the newspaper that most of the sakers "are netted in Afghanistan, China and Russia," and then transported to Peshawar for sale to visiting Arab sheikhs.

One licensed breeder in Europe who does frequent business with royal families in the Middle East confirmed to me that the trade is flourishing, although talking about it is taboo. "There's huge, huge money in wild falcons," the breeder told me, with the most sought-after bird, the "ultra-white" gyrfalcon, fetching $270,000 to $400,000 in the Arab world. During a recent trip to a sheikh's palace, his meeting was interrupted by the arrival of trapper-smugglers carrying gyrfalcons from eastern Russia. "They'd been hooded, and they were in a horrible state. [The smugglers] had driven them three thousand miles," he said. The breeder confirmed that the underground involves royals in such falconry-obsessed countries as the United Arab Emirates, Bahrain, Qatar, Kuwait, and, increasingly, Saudi Arabia, which remains one of the last countries in the region to permit wild falcon trapping within its borders.

In 2012, after years of illegal smuggling of saker falcons from Central Asia, the bird was declared "globally endangered" by the

Switzerland-based International Union for Conservation of Nature. Six years later the Convention on Migratory Species established a Saker Falcon Task Force, comprising forty specialists from twenty countries, to monitor the raptor and save it from extinction. By many accounts, the Emirates has successfully cracked down on bird smuggling. According to a 2017 report by the nonprofit Center for Advanced Defense Studies, the country had the highest number of bird-trafficking seizures in the world between 2009 and 2016. (The majority of the raptors were heading for Dubai.) But it is vastly more difficult to stop a skilled smuggler from sneaking eggs across a border than to prevent the smuggling of chicks or adolescent birds—and, once wild falcons or eggs have entered the Emirates, Convention on Endangered Species rules are still so loosely enforced that, as the European breeder put it, "laundering illegal birds into the system is easy."

=

The genetic superiority of falcons procured from the wild has been an article of faith among many Arab hunters since captive-breeding programs took hold decades ago. Only the toughest, strongest, and fastest birds survive in nature, the argument goes, and these genes are passed down through the generations. Yet Jemima Parry-Jones, who breeds raptors in Gloucestershire, insists that "anyone who believes that a peregrine egg from a wild nest is more viable, stronger, and healthier than a good bird bred in a captive situation is mistaken. You might as well say, 'Wild horses are better than specially bred race horses,' which is rubbish."

Nick Fox, the longtime breeder of falcons for the ruler of Dubai, says that Arab falconers want wild eggs primarily for a different reason: because they introduce new bloodlines into captive breeding programs. It is a widely held assumption that small populations of captive raptor species become vulnerable to "genetic decay" and need periodic reinvigoration from the wild. "Inbreeding has reduced survivability," says Fox, who started a breeding program thirty-five years ago with six New Zealand falcons and, unable to import more due to trade restrictions, watched the quality of the descendants gradually deteriorate over the decades. Toby Bradshaw, the chairman of the biology department at the University of Washington in Seattle, and an avid falconer, argued in a 2009 academic paper published on his departmental website that the "regular infusion of genes from wild populations [is] necessary" to keep captive-bred falcons from losing the "wild qualities"—speed, power, and hunting instinct— that expert falconers seek. "This is a strong argument for maintaining a modest wild take for propagation purposes even in countries where a falconry take is not allowed," Bradshaw maintained.

Jeffrey Lendrum had his own opinions about Arabs' affinity for wild birds. "The thing they would worry about is that so many birds are being interbred, they don't know what they've got anymore," he would explain. "A gyrfalcon could be one-quarter peregrine. A lot of these guys think, 'It's better to get something from the wild [so] we'll know what we've got.'" That may well have been the thinking of Lendrum's Emirates-based contacts when they sent him off for what would be the most ambitious wild take of his lifetime. He had a blank check, the full confidence of his sponsors, and a plan to capture the most prized falcon of them all.

ELEVEN

OPERATION CHILLY

On the early evening of June 10, 2001, Jeffrey Lendrum sat in the front passenger seat of a Bell JetRanger 406 helicopter, gazing through the window at the vast wilderness of northeastern Quebec. The sun was still high in the subarctic sky, and the temperature hovered just above freezing. As the helicopter traveled north, marshy valleys filled with forests of black spruce and larch gave way to near-treeless tundra still dappled with snow. Black bears and wolves loped along the boggy terrain. The chopper descended toward Kuujjuaq, an Inuit community of 2,500 that had served as a fur-trading post for the Hudson's Bay Company in the mid–nineteenth century. A few hundred bungalows lay in neat rows beside a boulder-strewn beach facing the Koksoak River, the longest waterway in Quebec's Nunavik territory, comprising the northern third of the province, an area larger than California. Ungava Bay, an icy basin at the mouth of the Koksoak just below Baffin Island and the Hudson Strait, lay about thirty-five miles to the north.

The pilot set down the helicopter gently at Kuujjuaq Airport, a single rutted tarmac runway. Then the pilot, Lendrum, and a third passenger, Paul Mullin, presented their passports to an official in a turquoise-painted corrugated-metal shed. They caught a waiting taxi to the Auberge Kuujjuaq Inn, a rustic two-story structure overlooking the river.

The men had booked rooms for a week. If anyone asked, they would say they were documentary filmmakers for *National Geographic* who had come to northern Canada to gather nature footage for the society's archives. But they were there for a different purpose: to steal the eggs of wild birds of prey. Four months earlier, in England, Lendrum had approached his business partner with a proposition. He was organizing his second trip to the Canadian subarctic, one of the prime habitats of the gyrfalcon. It'd been two years since he and Mullin had flown together from Johannesburg to London with the lanner falcon chicks concealed in Lendrum's carry-on bag. Now he invited his friend to tag along again.

"It's going to be the adventure of a lifetime," Lendrum promised. And all of their expenses would be covered.

Lendrum would later insist that the mission was just a sightseeing trip—"a dream on my bucket list"—financed by the sale of a house he owned in England. But Lendrum, who was sharing his girlfriend's home in Towcester, didn't own a house, Mullin maintains. Months earlier, Mullin says, Lendrum had met with Howard Waller in Dubai, and asked him to put up expenses for what he presented as the ultimate wild take. "The gyrfalcons are like bluebottle flies up there. They're all over the place," Lendrum assured Waller, according to Mullin—though his mission in 2000 had been something of a bust.

In Dubai Lendrum received $100,000 in hundred-dollar bills. Lendrum hid the cash on his body to avoid currency-reporting requirements, and then headed to Dubai International Airport for the flight home. Waller insists that Mullin's story is a fabrication. "Because we grew up together it's always assumed that it's me" who financed Lendrum's schemes, Waller said with a sigh when I pressed him on his role in Lendrum's egg-thieving adventures. He claimed that after each one of Lendrum's arrests he had tried to discourage his longtime friend from raiding nests and smuggling eggs. "I told him, 'Stop what you're doing, every time you do this it falls back on me,'" he said. "I told him this a long time ago." Lendrum, like Waller, denies Mullin's assertion that Waller commissioned him to obtain gyrfalcons in Canada. But when confronted with Waller's claims, Lendrum would call his old friend "a complete liar," insist that "he never rebuked me," and accuse him of acquiring rare wild birds, including gyrs, from all over the world. "He's trying to cover his own ass," says Lendrum, who claims he stole black sparrow hawk eggs from nests for Waller in South Africa in the 1980s. "When Howard finds himself backed into a corner, he shouts and he gets abusive." Waller denies that he ever asked Lendrum to steal wild raptors for him in South Africa or anywhere else.

—

Canada outlawed the wild harvesting of gyrfalcons in 1976—not that this stopped men like Lendrum. David Anderson, the director of the Gyrfalcon Conservation Project, says that pure white gyrs attract so much black market money that if he or his researchers spied one in the field, they kept the sighting a secret. The birds' hues run from black to brown to gray, but it's always the whites that disappear from their nests. "They are the biggest, baddest, meanest, prettiest falcons," he says. "It's not surprising at all that this mystique exists."

The black market trade isn't the only threat to the gyr's survival.

Scientists are finding increasing doses of mercury, DDE, aldrin, chlorinated hydrocarbons, polychlorinated biphenyls, and other toxic substances in birds and eggs as far north as Greenland and northern Norway, putting birds that eat other birds at a particular risk. And the warming of the Arctic's summers is causing migratory peregrines to expand their territory—seizing the nests of gyrfalcons and competing with them for scarce food and territory. Kurt Burnham, a raptor expert at the High Arctic Institute in Orion, Illinois, predicted in a 2016 article in the *Atlantic* that the intensifying battle between gyrs and peregrines would likely cause "one of them to go extinct in the area" by 2030.

The birds' difficult lives in the wild provided Lendrum with an argument for why removing eggs from their nests didn't present an ethical problem. He described to Mullin the satisfaction he'd feel knowing that he had "rescued" birds from increasingly uninhabitable environments and delivered them to a pampered life in the care of devoted Arab falconers—a life of generous feedings, plenty of room to fly, and state-of-the-art medical care.

Lendrum recruited a friend from his childhood to serve as his pilot in the far north. The son of a Special Forces operative in the Rhodesian Bush War, the pilot had flown helicopters for logging and power companies in Alaska and Canada, laying down pylons in the wilderness, and now conducted rescues for a sheriff's department in Northern California. "[I am a] utility bush pilot with over 16,000 hours spent freezing in Alaska to cooking in the [Papua New Guinea] jungle and everywhere in between," he wrote on his LinkedIn profile, "Africa, Australia, Venezuela, Hawaii and all over the Pacific—settling in California for the privilege to fly a Huey." Working for the sheriff's department, he had flown injured hikers and their rescuers on the end of a one-hundred-foot fixed line, a feat that required extraordinary concentration and precision maneuvering. These were the same skills the pilot would require on his clandestine new mission.

Lendrum chartered the Bell JetRanger 406, a robust, versatile machine on which the pilot had done much of his training, from Cherokee Helicopter Services in Pennsylvania. He arranged for the chopper to be delivered to Montréal-Dorval International Airport. In Montreal, Mullin, Lendrum, and the pilot loaded the helicopter with equipment that they had picked up mostly on a shopping spree in London, financed, according to Mullin, by the cash advance. They had titanium-threaded Arctic jackets, snow pants, and liners, ropes, generators, three GPS devices, harnesses, survival kits (containing knives, snares, a compass, a saw, waterproof matches, candles, fishing lines and hooks), mobile incubators, lights, boots, and dozens of jerricans filled with jet fuel. They also had a professional-quality Canon XL 10 video camera with multiple lenses, which they would use to support their *National Geographic* cover story; Mullin planned to shoot footage of gyrfalcons and peddle the video to nature-documentary companies when he got back home. The spycraft aficionado was still driving his Toyota Prada with BOND license plates, and he invented a code name for their mission: Operation Chilly. They hadn't told their wives, partners, friends, business associates, or anyone else about their plans.

The men were in a boisterous mood as they prepared to set off in the early morning of June 10 on the long journey north to Kuujjuaq, a nine-hundred mile, twelve-hour flight, with scheduled refueling stops in Quebec City and a series of old French trading posts, mining towns, and lumber settlements: Saguenay, Baie-Comeau, Labrador City, Schefferville . . . Gyrfalcon egg-hatching season runs from mid-May to mid-June. They were heading to the subarctic right on time.

Mullin broke out the video camera and filmed the pilot and Lendrum placing the last gear inside the JetRanger's cargo hold.

In the video, the pilot, a strapping blond-haired man wearing a pair of Ray-Bans, looks directly at the camera and grins.

"Look at us," he says. "We're fucking criminals."

Lendrum gives the thumbs-up.

=

The morning of June 11 dawned cold and clear in Kuujjuaq. The pilot guided the fully loaded helicopter west out of the Inuit village, leaving all traces of a human presence behind. They flew for half an hour over pale green and russet hills dotted with patches of ice and snow, and rivers choked with ice floes. Mullin, in the backseat, followed the route on a NATO topographical map that he had procured in London, and pointed excitedly to a pod of white beluga whales frolicking in an icy river. At last they arrived at a palisade that plunged at a near-ninety-degree angle to a body of water labeled Basalt Lake. The helicopter soared over sheets of ice, small breaks providing glimpses of the crystalline blue water underneath.

Lendrum, in the front, peered out the window, searching the sky. After several passes over the lake, the pilot set the chopper down on firm ground high above the water and the three men climbed out of the craft. The tundra abounded with lichens, tussock sedge, Arctic poppies, dwarf heath shrubs, scrub birch, and willows. It was the most unspoiled corner of the world that Mullin had ever seen. Then, suddenly came a screech through the silence. A pair of peregrines soared overhead, emitting high-pitched warning cries. An aerie was nearby.

"They're beautiful," Lendrum said. Mullin had his video camera out again. "Look at this male."

Even at a distance of several hundred feet, Lendrum could discern the difference in size between the two birds. Female peregrine falcons are about one-third larger than their mates, a phenomenon known as "reversed-size sexual dimorphism" and unique to owls, eagles, hawks, and falcons. Some evolutionary scientists theorize that because male raptors engage in territorial duels in midair, natural selection favors the smallest, lightest, and most agile of them. Others have posited that females need to be stronger because they are responsible for guarding the nest and protecting the eggs against predators, while males can remain focused on hunting prey.

"*That* is a fucking noise," the pilot said in the video, laughing. "See Lendrum fucking smiling now."

"It's fucking nice," Lendrum replied.

Then he picked out a speck of white on the horizon and knew—instantly, from half a mile away—that it was the raptor he had come to the end of the earth for: the elusive gyrfalcon, the bird of kings. Above the lake, the trio watched, enthralled, as the bird approached its aerie. "Here it comes on the right," the pilot could be heard exclaiming on the video. "She's coming in, coming in, staying on the ridgeline," he narrated like a sports announcer. "Here she comes, over the ridge now, traversing." The gyrfalcon settled on a ledge. "Beautiful," the pilot said, continuing to observe the gyrfalcon. "We're on."

It was a white gyr—meaning that if its breeding partner was also white, the chances were excellent that the chicks would be that color as well. Still, you could never be sure: a scientific study in the Koryak Mountains of far eastern Siberia had turned up a nest in which a pair of white gyrfalcons had produced gray chicks. And if a white gyrfalcon mated with a gray, black, orange, or other morph, there was no telling what the pair would produce. Sometimes one clutch could contain birds of three or four different hues. But Lendrum was optimistic.

The pilot and Lendrum fastened a one-hundred-foot static line to the helicopter skids, with the free end of the rope hanging down. Wearing leather boots, snow pants, gloves, and a green parka against the subarctic chill, Lendrum slipped a nylon safety harness around his legs and waist. He threaded the rope through a caribiner on his belt and secured it with a single figure-eight knot and a safety knot. The pilot lifted off slowly, making sure that the downwash from the rotors didn't tangle the rope. The slack tightened and Lendrum began to rise in a seated position into the azure sky.

Soon he was dangling seven hundred feet over the water. A video that Mullin shot of the moment would be seized by Great Britain's National Wildlife Crime Unit nine years later and broadcast around the world: Lendrum swayed calmly in the breeze, framed against water and sky both dazzlingly blue. One hand grasped a padded green cooler bag, large enough to fit four cans of beer, while the other held the rope. Nothing but two well-tied knots stood between him and oblivion, yet he seemed utterly self-assured. (Mullin didn't know how many times, if any, Lendrum had pulled off this stunt before, but he was so adept at climbing trees and scaling cliffs that "dangling from a helicopter would have been a piece of piss" for him, Mullin says.)

The Bell JetRanger hovered close to the rock wall, almost stationary, rotors spinning. The pilot masterfully manipulated the cyclic stick, collective lever, and anti-torque pedals to keep the machine virtually still. One tiny slip would have sheared off the blades and sent both pilot and thief plummeting to their deaths.

Lendrum turned toward the ledge. The female gyrfalcon circled overhead, distressed, as Lendrum inched closer to the aerie, an odoriferous heap splattered with whitewash, or bird feces, ptarmigan feathers, and other remains. "The nest was . . . the most filthy mess . . . covered with a thick layer of old wings and other debris, mostly of puffins and black guillemots, and simply hopping with little black flea-like creatures," a one-eyed, one-armed naturalist named Ernest Vesey wrote in his 1938 memoir *In Search of the Gyr-Falcon*, about his own aerie raid in northwestern Iceland. More than a century before Vesey's expedition, American ornithologist John James Audubon left a similar account of finding the nest of white gyrfalcons on the southern coast of Labrador, not far from Kuujjuaq. "The nest of these hawks was placed on the rocks, about fifty feet from their summit, and more than a hundred feet from their base," he wrote. "It was composed of sticks, sea-weeds, and mosses, about two feet in diameter, and almost flat. About its edges were strewed the remains of their food, and beneath, on the margin of the stream, lay a quantity of wings of the *Uria Troile*, *Mormon arcticus*, and *Tetrao Saliceti*, together with large pellets comprised of fur, bones, and various substances."

Inches from the aerie, Lendrum reached out and grabbed his prize: four large cream-colored eggs, with reddish brown freckles. Charles Bendire, the American oologist who escaped death at the hands of Apache Indians while snatching the eggs of a zone-tailed hawk, described gyrfalcon eggs vividly in an 1892 report from the field:

> The ground color, when distinctly visible . . . is creamy white. This is usually hidden by a pale cinnamon rufous suffusion . . . The eggs are closely spotted and blotched with small, irregular markings of dark reddish brown, brick red, ochraceous rufous, and tawny. Some specimens show scarcely any trace of markings, the egg being of near uniform color throughout . . . In shape they vary from ovate to rounded ovate. The shells of these eggs feel rough to the touch, are irregularly granulated, and without luster.

Lendrum placed the eggs in the cooler bag, and gave a hand signal. The pilot pulled away from the cliff, lifted into the sky, and deposited Lendrum gently on the tundra, before touching down nearby.

Later that day Mullin would slip into the harness and dangle from the helicopter just for the experience. He realized, terrified, that he had no control over his movements. "You're dependent on air flow, downwash, you're spinning left, and you're spinning right," he recalled. Hanging from the line made him appreciate Lendrum's athleticism even more.

Over the next few hours the pilot, Lendrum, and Mullin covered hundreds of square miles of gyrfalcon-rich territory, becoming steadily more proficient at spotting gyrs and their nests. The pilot circled high above the cliffs, zeroing in on a soaring bird and following it along the rock wall until its whitewash-splattered aerie came into view. Then he'd set down the helicopter in a meadow atop the cliff. If Lendrum thought the rock face was scalable, he fixed a rope, rappelled to the aerie, snatched the eggs, and climbed back up, with the cooler bag dangling from his belt. Sometimes the pilot managed to find flat ground at the base of the cliff where he could land his helicopter, and picked up Lendrum at the bottom, sparing him the arduous ascent back to the summit. Usually, however, the water reached to the very edge of the cliffs, making landing impossible. Three times that day, the rock face proved too steep to manage, and Lendrum approached the nest at the end of the fixed line suspended from the helicopter.

After each heist they flew on for another four or five miles—the limits of each gyr's territory—and renewed their search. Mullin observed the hunt from the backseat of the JetRanger, marveling at the birds' elegance and at the dramatic landscapes. "A lake, a mountain and the sea beyond," wrote Ronald Stevens in his 1956 book *The Taming of Genghis*, in which he traps a gyrfalcon chick in Iceland and teaches it to hunt. "The sky so blue in the transient smiles of an Arctic summer, so leaden and lowering at most other times. Against this background Genghis had his home."

Remarkably the trio made no attempt to hide their activities, apparently assuming that authorities would never obtain the visual and audio record. "Are you down?" shouted the pilot from the top of a cliff in one video sequence. A male gyrfalcon circled above, calling out in agitation. "Are you in the right spot?"

"Yeah, I'm here," Lendrum replied. "I may not have enough rope."

"I'll belay you down, keep going," his partner said. "We'll meet you at the bottom."

"I'll be fine," Lendrum said, as he clambered out of sight to snatch the eggs from the aerie.

The men showed no particular sensitivity to other species they encountered on their felonious romp. Halfway through the day, the pilot spotted a herd of caribou and chased it by helicopter across the tundra. Mullin filmed the beasts as they stampeded in terror, some of them slipping on the slick ground or toppling over into pools of water. They pursued a herd of musk oxen next—great shaggy beasts that look like a cross between a buffalo and a yak. Then the pilot and Lendrum headed off for some more aerial reconnaissance, leaving Mullin to explore the cliffs on his own. Unarmed and wary of encountering polar bears, he cautiously clambered up the rocks to an aerie where four unattended, pure-white gyrfalcon chicks, days old, chirped helplessly at him and huddled in fear.

Many years later, Mullin would try to rationalize his role in what he would forever refer to as a "black op." He pointed out that he had never raided a nest nor touched a gyrfalcon egg; that was all "Lendrum's business," not his. "He was always protective of the eggs," Mullin remembered. "I wasn't even allowed to hold one to feel what it was like." He repeated Lendrum's argument that stealing eggs was an unorthodox conservation method—"rescuing" the raptors from probable death. (There's some truth to Lendrum's reasoning. About 60 percent of gyrfalcons in the wild don't survive past their first year.) And he emphasized that the trip had been motivated by a lust for adventure, not greed. All he was getting was a vacation, all expenses paid. The real payoff—between $70,000 and $100,000 per white gyrfalcon egg, he had been told—would come long after Mullin had moved on.

Yet the phony identities, the secrecy (Mullin had kept his South African girlfriend in the dark about the trip), and the possibility of arrest had a powerful appeal. Like Lendrum, there were days he enjoyed being an outlaw.

=

On that first full day in northern Canada, Mullin says Lendrum climbed into six nests and took eight gyrfalcon eggs. Back at the hotel, he placed the trophies inside two incubators stored in a suitcase. The next morning the accomplices went up in the helicopter again. Over four days Lendrum invaded nineteen nests, found clutches in twelve, and stole twenty-seven eggs, a far greater haul, says Mullin, than any one of them had dreamed possible. Although Lendrum had announced to Mullin a plan to replace the live eggs with hard-boiled chicken eggs—with the hope that the breeding pair would reject them as rotten and lay a new clutch—Mullin admitted, "We never bothered to do that."

Lendrum wrapped the eggs in woolen socks and stored them in his hand luggage for the twelve-hour helicopter flight back to Montreal. At every refueling stop he took them out and shone a flashlight on them—a process known as "candling"—to make certain, through the glow of the light against the thin eggshell, that the embryos' hearts were still pumping. From Montreal, the pilot flew back to Northern California and returned to his job in the sheriff's department, telling nobody about what he had been up to in Nunavik. Mullin and Lendrum caught a British Airways flight to Heathrow with the twenty-seven eggs concealed in Lendrum's carry-on bag. There they parted ways. Mullin headed to Johannesburg, Lendrum to Dubai. Lendrum reported that he had delivered all the eggs alive to his sponsor.

"It was a total success," he announced.

It was such a triumph that Lendrum was already thinking ahead to the next year's trip. They would leave for Kuujjuaq a few weeks earlier, he told Mullin, when not as many chicks would have hatched and there would be even more eggs for them to steal. Lendrum had decided that he would hire a pilot and helicopter from a company in Kuujjuaq, rather than bring his boyhood friend back from California. He was financing this next venture himself, and he wanted to keep costs to a minimum. Mullin felt uneasy about inviting outsiders into their scheme, but Lendrum brushed off his concerns. It was the prelude to a disastrous series of events that would come to haunt Mullin for the next two decades.

TWELVE

BUSTED

They couldn't see a goddamned thing.

Paul Mullin trudged through knee-deep snow on a ridgeline high above a frozen lake, lugging his video camera, his face hidden behind a woolen ski mask. He wore a heavy down parka, fur-lined boots, and fur-lined gloves, the best he could find in London, but his fingers were so cold that he could barely feel them. When he went to urinate, the stream froze on impact. Every breath he took felt like a knife thrust in his lungs.

He was perched atop a cliff forty miles west of Kuujjuaq, the tiny Inuit settlement on the Koksoak River that he was visiting for the second time in a year; the tumbling snow had diminished visibility to a few yards. He and his partner, Jeffrey Lendrum, had instructed the helicopter pilot to leave them there, in the middle of the wilderness, with a promise that he would come back to fetch them in ninety minutes. They were shooting a documentary for *National Geographic*, they had told him, lying. If the helicopter stayed at the scene, the pilot would have to keep the engine running to avoid ice buildup, and the rotor noise would scare off the birds.

Mullin hadn't been keen on the plan. What if the pilot got way-laid somehow? They had no way of reaching him, no satellite phone, no cell phone signal, no emergency kit, a single Mars bar apiece if they got hungry, and no weapon for protection against polar bears or other predators, except for a twenty-two-inch Buck knife that Mullin had strapped to his leg.

What the hell had Lendrum been thinking?

It had been Lendrum's idea to arrive in Canada in early May, cal-culating that fewer eggs would have hatched but those would be far enough along to survive a journey to Dubai. He hadn't anticipated that four weeks might make all the difference in the subarctic between spring thaw and whiteout, between forty degrees Fahrenheit and ten below. The weather had been so bad they'd managed just a single flight during their first three days in Kuujjuaq, raiding three nests and stealing five eggs. They'd spent the rest of the time tooling around the frozen Koksoak River on snowmobiles.

While immersed in these thoughts, Mullin heard the *whup whup whup* of a rotor. Through the fog and the snow, he could just make out the ghostly outlines of the helicopter. The AStar 350 touched down on the frozen ground fifty yards from them, and Lendrum and Mullin climbed aboard. But rather than order the pilot to return to Kuujjuaq, Lendrum instructed him to drop them off at another lookout point farther west. The pilot, an Inuit from Kuujjuaq named Pete Duncan, steered the chopper through the snowstorm with fierce concentration. Mullin, in the front seat, would remember being mes-merized by "the *Star Wars* effect" of the flakes hurtling against the windshield.

"This is getting too much, man," Duncan muttered, looking for a place to land.

Duncan was the cofounder, vice president, and chief pilot of Nunavik Rotors, an all-Aboriginal-owned division of Air Inuit, the biggest commercial airline in Quebec's far north. He'd flown hundreds of sightseeing expeditions deep into the Nunavik outback—and conducted a fair share of search-and-rescue missions. The Kuujjuaq native had saved a tourist whose snowmobile had run out of fuel and who had wandered on foot, disoriented, deeper into the wilderness and pulled out five people stranded on an ice floe after a boating accident. He'd also taken hunters, fishermen, adventure tourists, and photographers into the Torngat Range—3,750 square miles of polar-bear-infested tundra and glaciated mountains stretching north from Saglek Fjord to the northern tip of Labrador.

But in his twenty years of running the airline Duncan had never encountered any clients like the two he was flying with today. He'd recognized the shorter one with the South African accent immediately: the man had hired a helicopter and pilot from Nunavik Rotors back in 2000, flying over rock walls for what he had claimed was a reconnaissance trip for a nature film. At the end of the mission, the South African had surprised Duncan by asking whether he could buy the helicopter. "I'm planning to come back for a few years in a row," he'd explained. "I'll just need it for May and June, and for the rest of the year you can do what you want with it." The fellow had even offered a large sum of cash, but Duncan, suspicious, had turned him down.

He'd seen the South African again the following June, although they hadn't spoken at all. On that trip the man had brought his own helicopter from the States, and a pilot and an English friend had joined him. Now, eleven months later, the South African and the

Englishman had returned to Kuujjuaq, claiming to be gathering more documentary footage. Duncan didn't believe them for a minute. The Englishman behaved as if he'd never shot video before; Duncan wondered whether the camera even held a battery. And when the "film crew" repeatedly had him drop them on a ridge and pick them up an hour later to take them to a new location, he was sure they were up to something shady. "Any wildlife photographer who's serious would ask to be dropped off at sunrise and picked up at sunset," Duncan would say years later. "Who in the hell sits around on a mountain and asks me to go back in town and return in a couple of hours? These guys had something to hide."

After his first day in the field with the suspect documentarians, Duncan stopped by the Kuujjuaq headquarters of Quebec's wildlife protection agency, to look up his old friend Dave Watt.

"There's something fishy about these two," he told Watt, a veteran law enforcement officer. "I'll be finished with them on May 11." He asked his friend to wait until they'd paid him for his last day of work before he closed in.

Early the next morning, during a break in the weather, while Mullin and Lendrum were charging around on snowmobiles, Watt and Vallée Saunders, another wildlife protection officer, retraced the route that the two alleged filmmakers had taken with Duncan the day before. As they flew low in a police helicopter over the frozen tundra, they could spot the men's footprints in the virgin snow along the ridgeline, clearly leading to ledges where gyrfalcons and peregrines nested. Circling in for a closer look, Watt and Saunders saw that several clutches at fresh aeries appeared to be missing.

"These guys are stealing eggs," Watt told Saunders, and Saunders agreed.

The officers contacted their superiors at the head office in Chibougamau, a logging and mining town in central Quebec, and requested a search warrant. Late in the afternoon of May 11, Watt, Saunders, and two officers from the Quebec Provincial Police drove across town to the Auberge Kuujjuaq Inn, where Mullin and Lendrum were settling down after a brutal day of egg snatching in a blizzard.

=

Stretched out on their backs on twin beds, too tired to remove their boots and gaiters, the two egg thieves luxuriated in the warmth of their hotel room. Twenty minutes earlier, Duncan had dropped off the pair in front of the inn and received his $5,000 payment, in cash, for eight hours of flying plus fuel costs. Duncan had known the police were planning a raid that evening, but hadn't given anything away. Now, as Watt and his fellow officers closed in, the men talked obliviously about the subzero temperatures, the sealskin gloves Duncan had lent Mullin to prevent frostbite, and their plans to leave the following day.

Conditions had been so awful today that Lendrum had rappelled down to only a single gyrfalcon nest in the snow and retrieved two eggs, giving them a total of seven for a week's work. Though just a quarter of the previous year's haul, "it was enough to turn a decent profit," Mullin would later say. (Mullin understood that he wouldn't be sharing in the profits; he had simply been hungry for another adventure.) Those eggs were now keeping warm in a portable incubator plugged into a wall socket. Ropes, carabiners, climbing harnesses, and egg boxes lay scattered about the room.

At five o'clock, someone knocked on the door. Mullin and Lendrum looked at each other.

It must be the police, Mullin thought, his heartbeat quickening. "This is it, Jeff," he said.

"Okay," Lendrum replied with resignation.

Mullin swung his legs around, stood up, and opened the door. Saunders, Watt, and the two Quebecois police officers burst into the room.

"Are you Paul Mullin and Jeffrey Lendrum?" asked Watt.

The men nodded.

"Stand to one side," he said.

Lendrum and Mullin watched silently as the officers removed the film from Mullin's video camera and seized the climbing equipment, GPS devices, and mobile telephones. They opened carry-on bags, unplugged and removed the incubators, and peered at the creamy white-and-yellow eggs being kept warm inside.

"Have you been stealing eggs?" asked Watt.

"No, no, I've been filming," insisted Mullin, gamely explaining that he was gathering "exclusive footage" about gyrfalcons for *National Geographic*. The four officers ordered Lendrum and Mullin outside, led each to the back of a separate four-by-four, and drove them across Kuujjuaq toward wildlife protection agency headquarters.

Lendrum and Mullin stared out the windows as they passed long rows of single- and two-story bungalows encrusted with snow and ice. They had agreed that if they were caught, they would stick to their cover story. The officers escorted them into the Wildlife Protection Services building and down a fluorescent-lit corridor, into separate rooms. Asked what he and his partner were doing with seven gyrfalcon eggs in a heated incubator in their hotel room, Mullin, who was still carrying the twenty-two-inch Buck knife strapped to his leg, professed ignorance.

Lendrum was a bit more voluble. He had taken a break from gathering *National Geographic* footage, he explained, to retrieve a few "addled" specimens from nest sites to perform postmortems to investigate possible pesticide poisoning. He planned to weigh and measure the eggs, just as the British ornithologist Derek Ratcliffe had done to examine the effects of DDT in rural England in the 1960s. He also intended, he insisted, to put the clutch back on the ledges the following day.

Watt, however, had found a laptop containing a record of expenses from the pair's trip the year before—including a $30,000 helicopter rental and thousands of dollars for plane tickets between London and Philadelphia, and Philadelphia and Montreal. Lendrum and Mullin were, he was sure, well-financed international wildlife smugglers, who intended to profit from selling the live eggs of one of Quebec's most endangered species. If it were his decision, Watt would have had them tried on wildlife trafficking charges, an offense that potentially carried a $1 million fine and a five-year jail term in Canada. But Watt knew that he lacked indisputable evidence—boarding a flight with the contraband, for example—that the two men intended to smuggle the gyrfalcon eggs abroad. Instead he conferred with the provincial prosecutor in Chibougamau, then came back to Lendrum and Mullin with an offer:

"You can either plead guilty and pay a fine, or we'll lock you up and Monday you'll go to court," Watt told them.

"How much?" Mullin asked.

"Seven thousand two hundred and fifty dollars," said Watt. It was the highest penalty possible under Canadian wildlife legislation.

"I need to speak to my partner," said Mullin.

Half an hour later Mullin and Lendrum pleaded guilty to twelve charges of illegal hunting and wild egg possession. The men paid their fine with US dollars. After the money changed hands, the police drove them through the darkened streets and deposited them in front of their hotel.

"Be on the first plane out of here tomorrow," Watt advised, "and don't come back to Canada."

Wildlife authorities transported the eggs to a birds-of-prey recovery center near Montreal, where only one hatched; the others had apparently died of shock from being ripped out of their nests and jostled by either the thieves or the police. Dave Watt would claim that Lendrum had turned up the heat in the incubator either in the hotel room or during a brief period when he was close to the hatcher at headquarters after his arrest. "He wanted to destroy the evidence," Watt would say. But Mullin insists that Lendrum would never deliberately kill a bird of prey under any circumstance. "He would risk his own life to save them," Mullin says.

=

Mullin and Lendrum, shaken by the arrest, speculated about who had turned them in. On the flight back to Montreal, Mullin hypothesized that a room cleaner might have rummaged through their equipment while they were out. But the most likely culprit, he believed, was the pilot. "He was the weakest link in this whole damned thing," he told Lendrum. "We shouldn't have done it this way." For his part, Lendrum suggested that his old friend Howard Waller might well have betrayed them "out of jealousy." Up to that point, Mullin had assumed that Waller may have been on the receiving end of the eggs. Lendrum, who had been guarded with Mullin about his clientele this time, now implied that he was freelancing for wealthy backers in the United Arab Emirates.

The first article about the pair appeared four days later on the front page of the *Nunatsiaq News*, a northeastern Quebec weekly. The antics of the globe-trotting criminals stood out amid the vocational school graduations, airport renovations, and other small-town events that typically filled the paper. "Poachers Fined for Illegal Possession of Falcon Eggs," the article was headlined: "Two men masquerading as nature photographers, one from South Africa and the other from Britain, were caught red-handed in Kuujjuaq last week with a cache of falcon eggs worth thousands of dollars on the international black market." In the article Guy Tremblay of the Quebec wildlife protection agency noted, "Kuujjuaq isn't a big place and word traveled fast. People found their activity strange." He estimated the black market value of each gyrfalcon egg at $30,000, theorized that the thieves "were linked to some organization," and said that the Quebec government planned "to alert federal officials to the men's identity so they can't try to enter Canada at some later date."

Toronto's *National Post* picked up the story on May 18. "Poached Eggs Seized from Fake Film Crew," the headline declared. "Wildlife Officials Confiscate Incubator to Thwart Falcon Trade." A spokesman for Canada's Ministry of the Environment and Fauna told the paper, "Nobody goes to Kuujjuaq to collect eggs to make an omelette. Clearly, they had another goal in mind." Canadian TV news ran a brief report about the arrests. Mullin and Lendrum later appeared at number fifty-seven in the rankings of the world's one hundred top birds-of-prey smugglers on the website of savethefalcons.org, an obscure conservation group run by an American raptor biologist. But after this flurry of attention, the story disappeared. The public shaming that Mullin had feared never happened. None of his friends or relatives ever learned about what had occurred during that bizarre week in Kuujjuaq.

Still, Mullin's brush with the authorities chastened him. He legally changed his name and received a fresh passport under his new identity. He had occasional business in Canada and took Tremblay's warning seriously; the last thing he wanted was to find himself turned back at the Canadian border. And he vowed never to accompany Lendrum on another egg stealing mission. It had been fun, but he should have known there would be consequences. Lendrum was too much of a risk-taker.

Lendrum, too, seemed spooked by the arrest. "That was it," he told Mullin when they returned to England. "The show's over." He would scale down his global wanderings for a while, mostly staying put in England with his French-Algerian girlfriend, and focus on running AfricaXtreme. But Lendrum was not a person who could sit still for long—especially when so many wild falcons were nesting just a short drive away.

THIRTEEN

THE UNIT

By 2002, the year Jeffrey Lendrum was arrested in northern Canada for stealing wild gyrfalcon eggs, British lawmakers were starting to become serious about fighting wildlife crime. Just fifteen years earlier, the only institutions investigating such offenses were private animal-welfare charities like the Royal Society for the Protection of Birds. Guy Shorrock at the RSPB had even mounted private criminal prosecutions against falcon poisoners and other animal abusers—applying for summonses, taking evidence, and hiring attorneys—because no law enforcement agency seemed willing to take them on. Only a few police forces had a dedicated wildlife officer, and the stiffest penalty one could receive for poaching, smuggling, or harming animals was a small fine.

Now about half of the forty-three police forces in England and Wales employed full-time wildlife cops. Some had two. The 2000 Countryside and Rights of Way Act had imposed jail sentences for wildlife offenses, including two years for the taking, sale, or killing of protected birds. (In 2005 Parliament would raise the maximum penalty to five years.) And Richard Brunstrom, the chief constable

of North Wales and one of Britain's most high-profile law enforcement figures, had proposed creating an intelligence team dedicated to
tracking down wildlife criminals.

Brunstrom, a longtime colleague of Andy McWilliam's—they
had met at a conference when Brunstrom was the national police
"lead," or specialist in a chiefs' committee, on wildlife crime—took
an aggressive and often controversial approach to police work. He
had once cracked down on public urination by having officers haul
buckets and mops on patrol and order offenders to clean up their
messes or face arrest. In his zeal to stop speeders, he'd proposed
tripling roadside cameras and hiding traffic cops behind billboards
and bushes, leading British tabloids to dub him the "Mad Mullah
of the Traffic Taliban." He filmed himself being stunned by a fifty-
thousand-volt taser to prove that it wasn't lethal. (Footage on the
department's website showed him crying out as his legs buckled.) He
climbed scaffolding and broke into his own office late one night to
expose security lapses within the police department.

Brunstrom was also a conservationist with a degree in zool-
ogy from Bangor University in North Wales; he'd advanced halfway through a Ph.D. in the subject before joining the police. So he
grasped the growing threat of wildlife crime and the sophistication
of some of its perpetrators. The trade went far beyond the familiar
smuggling of elephant ivory and rhino horn from African game parks
to the Far East. It involved hundreds of protected species, global networks, and often-violent perpetrators. It extended from East Java,
where smugglers were wiping out the island's population of yellow-
crested cockatoos; to the Brazilian Amazon, where a British pet shop
owner would be caught with one thousand rare spiders (including
tarantulas) hidden in his suitcases; to Guyana, where traffickers se-

dated chestnut-bellied seed finches with rum, stuffed them inside hair curlers, and shipped them illegally to New York City, where local impresarios staged contests pitting caged finches against each other to see which one could reach fifty whistles the fastest.

The National Wildlife Crime Intelligence Unit, as the National Wildlife Crime Unit's precursor was called, started operations in London in 2002. The *Independent* reported that the new unit would "use investigative tactics similar to those deployed against drug barons, such as undercover operations and bugging suspects," to combat what was estimated as a "£5 billion a year illegal business." But Brunstrom's vision was ahead of its time: the unit had a minuscule budget and just three detectives, whom local forces largely ignored. By McWilliam's estimate, the unit sent out 250 requests for action in three years; police responded to just 30. McWilliam, who was still specializing in wildlife crime for the Merseyside Police Force, was involved in a handful, including a case that concerned Liverpool shops that sold Chinese "health tonics" manufactured from the bones of leopards, tigers, and other endangered mammals. But he was the exception. "Most officers would say, 'We've got drugs, we've got serious crimes, what are they going on about?'" McWilliam says. In 2005, the unit's parent organization, the National Criminal Intelligence Service, merged with a new group, the Serious Organised Crime Agency, and the National Wildlife Crime Intelligence Unit, never seen as particularly effective, was phased out of existence.

=

McWilliam often felt like he was fighting for a cause few cared about, but occasionally he received a reminder that some people were taking notice. In 2004 the BBC came to Merseyside to capture a day in the life of Great Britain's most prominent wildlife cop. McWilliam warned the producer that his daily routine was often uneventful, and suggested they restage some of his more dramatic arrests. While riding in a bus with his wife a few weeks before, McWilliam had witnessed a youth kicking to death a small songbird called a mistle thrush, as the bird tried to protect her young. McWilliam had leapt off the bus and arrested the killer, carried the corpse to a vet to verify the cause of death, and then stashed the thrush in a freezer at the police station to use as evidence.

Minutes before the BBC crew arrived to stage the reenactment, McWilliam remembered that he had forgotten to remove the bird from the freezer the night before. He quietly carried the rock-solid corpse upstairs to the deserted canteen, placed it on a plate, slid it into the microwave, and turned the setting to defrost.

Midway through the seven-minute thawing, a policewoman entered the kitchen to heat a bowl of oatmeal. McWilliam stood beside her, nervously making small talk. When the microwave pinged, McWilliam reached in and removed the plate. The policewoman stared at the dead thrush.

"Don't knock it until you've tried one," he told her. "Have you seen the salt and pepper?"

After that, McWilliam recalled, the colleague gave him a wide berth.

=

The failure of the National Wildlife Crime Intelligence Unit to find support from local police only hardened Richard Brunstrom's resolve to create an effective environmental crime force. In 2005 he lobbied the Home Office—the British equivalent of some combination of the US Departments of Justice and Homeland Security, responsible for immigration, domestic security, and law and order— to fund a more hands-on outfit comprised of specialists who would roam the country, providing guidance and support to local forces. As Brunstrom envisioned it, the new National Wildlife Crime Unit ("Intelligence" had been dropped from the name) would have a staff of seven: two field investigators, a senior intelligence officer, two analysts, an administrator, and the unit's head. To avoid ruffling the feathers of turf-conscious police, all field investigators would be retired wildlife officers and would have no authority to make arrests. In 2006, the Home Office and the Department for Environment, Food & Rural Affairs allocated £450,000 for the NWCU's first year of operations.

McWilliam got a phone call from Chris Kerr, the first head of unit, that summer. Kerr was a longtime wildlife cop whom McWilliam had come to know through the National Conference of Wildlife Enforcers, an annual gathering of police investigators and conservation groups where he'd also encountered Brunstrom.

"Have you thought about applying?" Kerr asked him.

McWilliam hadn't, but after thirty-one years with the police he was again ready for a change. The Merseyside force was in the middle of reorganization. McWilliam had been reassigned against his wishes from the Crosby Police Station, where he had worked for the past three decades, to a new station filled with officers he didn't know. He cringed at the posters emblazoned with soaring eagles and motivational slogans that papered the station's sterile walls. McWilliam had nurtured friendships with many people in and around Crosby, passing out his phone number to hundreds and becoming a real member of the community. "Suddenly I was moved to a station with senior officers who didn't have a clue," he would say. "All the experience that people had built up, they didn't seem to give a toss about."

McWilliam had some reservations about the new position. He was not especially fond of traveling, and working for the National Wildlife Crime Unit would require being on the road for three, sometimes four days a week. The unit's very existence was precarious, dependent on a renewal of its funding every year. But his wife, Lin, was encouraging. "Give it a go," she said. McWilliam had a pro forma interview, and Kerr offered him the job. In July 2006, he retired from the police force and a month later signed a twelve-month contract as a field investigator.

On October 5, Biodiversity Minister Barry Gardiner inaugurated the National Wildlife Crime Unit at Dynamic Earth, an environmental education-and-entertainment center in Edinburgh. Gardiner railed against "people who think it is acceptable to kill endangered animals because their fur is a fashion statement, or steal a rare bird's egg because it's one that they don't yet have in their collection." He declared, as McWilliam looked on, "We are talking about something on a par with drug trafficking and people trafficking, with the same nasty people involved."

=

The National Wildlife Crime Unit commenced operations from a backwater: North Berwick, a picturesque Scottish fishing village of four thousand people on the southern shore of the Firth of Forth. The hamlet was perhaps best known for having the world's largest colony of northern gannets, white seabirds related to boobies. The deputy constable of the local Lothian and Borders Police Force had donated for the squad the top floor of a small police station. "The

[Home Office] didn't want the unit to be London-centric," explained Alan Roberts, a retired detective and bird expert from East Anglia who had worked on Operation Easter and joined the NWCU as an investigative support officer at the same time as McWilliam. "There was always that suggestion that if it's based in London that's all they care about."

Soon the NWCU relocated to a more convenient headquarters in two large adjoining rooms on the third floor of a police station in Stirling, just outside Edinburgh, where the unit head, his administrators, and his intelligence team based themselves. McWilliam and Roberts worked from home but traveled throughout the country, joining cops on investigations and sharing their expertise in complex wildlife legislation. Both men had studied the Control of Trade in Endangered Species (Enforcement) Regulations of 1997, for example, legislation enacted by the European Union that categorized thirty-six thousand species according to three levels of protection and gave the police the power to take punitive action against wildlife smugglers and traders. The regulations covered everything from the proper labeling of crocodile skins and caviar containers to the eight species of pangolins (spiny anteaters found in Africa and Southeast Asia) and nine species of howler and spider monkeys that could not be traded for any purpose but scientific research. The regulations were essential tools for the wildlife cop, telling him what activities were worth investigating, what permits were required for which animal, and what crimes, if any, had been committed. McWilliam took the north of Britain, Roberts the south, though they sometimes overlapped. The unit soon added two more investigators responsible for policing Wales and Scotland.

It wasn't long before raw intelligence came flowing in—300 to

350 reports a month from local police departments, wildlife protection agencies, and concerned citizens. McWilliam chased poaching gangs that roamed the countryside in four-by-fours, armed with guns, crossbows, night-vision goggles, dogs, snares, and poisons, killing deer, hares, and other mammals for thrill or for profit. He investigated raptor persecutions: the shooting, poisoning, and trapping of peregrine falcons and other protected birds of prey by disgruntled farmers or by gamekeepers on hunting estates in Scotland and northern England. "Those killing birds of prey are typically serial offenders, just like egg thieves," wrote Guy Shorrock in his blog for the Royal Society for the Protection of Birds. "We have received detailed reports of gamekeepers that have apparently killed hundreds of raptors during their career" to prevent the birds from eating their pheasants and grouse and so threatening their livelihood. McWilliam helped put several of the more prolific falcon killers behind bars.

Occasionally he was drawn into more esoteric offenses. One of Richard Brunstrom's signature initiatives had been Operation Bat, launched in 2004 to protect the nocturnal mammals from lumberjacks and developers. Following Brunstrom's lead, McWilliam arrested a commercial builder who had deliberately destroyed the roosts of a brown long-eared bat (*Plecotus auritus*), which often secretes itself in roof spaces and chimneys, and is listed as threatened under the Endangered Species Act. And he busted a farmer who had dredged up a riverbed filled with freshwater pearl mussels—another high-priority endangered species.

McWilliam did some of his most important work sitting in front of his home computer. After a stuffed orangutan sold on the British black market for £16,000 in 1993, prices for taxidermied rare animals—Philippine eagles, Siberian tigers, stuffed Palawan peacock-pheasants, blue-naped parrots, ring-tailed lemurs, golden lion tamarins—had soared. McWilliam scoured eBay, Alibaba, Bird-trader, Preloved, and other e-commerce websites that allowed users to trade live and stuffed animals and animal parts. He identified suspicious sales, obtained court orders forcing the websites to turn over trading records, and then, armed with a search warrant, joined the police in arresting suspected traffickers and buyers.

There was the curio dealer selling "antique ivory carvings" on eBay, which carbon dating proved had been made from an elephant killed illegally in the 1980s. This was a decade after the Convention on International Trade in Endangered Species banned the trafficking of ivory taken from Asian elephants after 1975 and from African elephants after 1976. There was the collector with a degenerative eye disease who had created a bucket list of wildlife trophies to acquire before he lost his sight. First on the list: the skull of a mountain gorilla from central Africa, one of the most endangered animals in the world. The man contacted a Cameroonian trader through Alibaba, obtained a photo of an ape's newly severed head, and was sent the trophy in the mail. When police searched the man's garage, they discovered the skull, still covered with bits of flesh. "It still smelled bad," remembers McWilliam's colleague Alan Roberts. The Cameroon dealer had pulled a bait and switch, delivering a chimpanzee head instead, but the species is also listed as Appendix I, accorded the highest level of protection, and the buyer was arrested for CITES violations.

The National Wildlife Crime Unit followed the activities of a dodgy couple who ran a pet shop in West Yorkshire, buying and selling exotic animal skulls from Indonesia, South Africa, and other countries on the side. One of the couple's major buyers was a man named Alan Dudley, a father of three who inspected Jaguar Land

Rovers for a living. When the investigators entered Dudley's storage room in his house in Coventry, they found two thousand skulls—including that of a howler monkey from Ecuador, a penguin, a loggerhead turtle, a chimpanzee, a giraffe, a hippo, a Goeldi's marmoset from Bolivia, and even a Great Dane. In addition to buying the grisly mementos online, some of them illegally, Dudley made use of contracts he had with zoos and academic institutions to "clean up" the carcasses of dead animals and return the skeletons for research and display. (He evidently held back some of the skulls for his personal collection.) Convicted of seven counts of violating CITES regulations, Dudley was given a fifty-week suspended sentence, a three-month dusk-to-dawn curfew, and a £1,000 fine, on top of £3,000 in court costs. The judge spoke of an "academic zeal" that had "crossed the line into unlawful obsession."

Soon the evidence room at the Stirling headquarters spilled over with ocelot and leopard skins, monkey skulls, elephant tusks, rare butterflies, stuffed badgers, taxidermied birds of prey, and other contraband. McWilliam dubbed the odoriferous chamber the Room of Death. But the animals that crossed his path in the line of duty weren't all deceased. Wildlife charities across the United Kingdom began writing to McWilliam with requests for assistance in keeping at-risk species alive. Froglife UK sought his help protecting Britain's endangered amphibians and reptiles. Buglife wanted support for the Ladybird Spider Project, the Narrow-Headed Ant Project, the Shrill Carder Bee Project, and other campaigns to bring threatened insects "back from the brink" by introducing new populations into carefully managed habitats. Plantlife UK sought to save from extinction the pasqueflower, the sand lizard, the Duke of Burgundy butterfly, and other fragile flora and fauna. McWilliam was a sympathetic listener, but he could offer little concrete assistance since such problems lay well outside his portfolio. "There's not a lot of bug crime or frog crime," he said dryly.

=

In 1984, Alec Jeffreys, a geneticist at Great Britain's Leicester University, produced the world's first DNA profile, revolutionizing crime scene analysis. Jeffreys extracted DNA from cells, used an enzyme to slice up the strands, mounted the fragments in gel, and then introduced radioactive "tracers" that attached to specific sequences of proteins and other genetic material. When Jeffreys exposed the irradiated DNA fragments to X-ray film, the exposure produced a unique pattern of more than thirty stripes, resembling a universal bar code. Two years later, DNA collected from semen stains on the bodies of two teenagers who had been raped and murdered in a small village in Leicestershire secured the first conviction using genetic profiling, and exonerated an innocent man implicated in the killings. Soon the RSPB's Guy Shorrock began promoting it as a tool to combat falcon laundering.

Because captive breeding had a successful hatching rate of just 33 percent, unscrupulous breeders often found it far more cost-effective to illegally snatch nearly hatched eggs or chicks from the wilderness and then pass them off as having been hatched legally in their breeding centers. The Wildlife and Countryside Act of 1981 required that nine species of birds of prey bred in captivity, known as Schedule 4 birds—honey buzzards, golden eagles, white-tailed eagles, peregrines, ospreys, merlins, Montagu's harriers, marsh harriers, and goshawks—be fitted with permanent identification rings on their legs when they were two weeks old or younger. Captive-bred birds of prey also had to have a registration certificate approved by the

Convention on International Trade in Endangered Species, known as an Article 10. But breeders found it easy to launder wild birds into the system, usually by mixing in very young, pre-banded chicks with those produced by captive parents. Sources told Shorrock that 30 percent of peregrines declared captive-bred were actually robbed from nests. It was easy money, and less risky than trying to sell wild birds or wild eggs directly into the black market.

In October 1992, prosecutors employed crude genetic profiling to prove that Joseph Seiga, an unemployed birdkeeper in Liverpool, had passed off four baby goshawk siblings stolen from the wild as the offspring of a captive-bred female. The babies shared multiple genetic markers but had none in common with the purported mother. Seiga was convicted and fined. Three years later DNA evidence helped send Derek Canning, a peregrine breeder in Northumbria who kept maps of aeries across Scotland and Wales, to prison for eighteen months for laundering dozens of wild-trapped falcons.

Some of McWilliam's former colleagues belittled that kind of work, but McWilliam loved the challenge of the investigations—and, like so many of the men he was tracking, he enjoyed the thrill of the chase. He also believed that each sketchy breeder that he put out of business served as a warning to others—and as an incremental victory for the cause of environmental protection. In 2009, he zeroed in on John Keith Simcox, a breeder in eastern England, who claimed that the ring on his twenty-three-year-old female goshawk, which he had obtained in the 1980s from a breeder in Hungary, had fallen off the bird's leg. An animal health inspector refitted the goshawk with the ring, but an informant told McWilliam that the inspector had unwittingly ringed a wild impostor; the elderly bird had died and Simcox had pulled a switch.

McWilliam swooped in with a search warrant and took a blood sample from the goshawk. Then, using a family tree attached to the bird's Article 10 certificate, he tracked down the Hungarian goshawk's offspring, obtained additional blood samples, and sent them all to a DNA lab. The results were indisputable: the newly ringed female could not be the birds' mother. Simcox pleaded guilty to possession of a wild bird—McWilliam suspected he had stolen it from an aerie in north Wales—and to making a false declaration to obtain a registration. He received a three-month prison sentence. Simcox had allegedly engaged in such fraud for years, but this conviction "finished him off," said McWilliam, forbidding him from ever again breeding Schedule 4 birds, including goshawks.

=

The rare-bird underground was far more extensive than a handful of launderers in England sneaking into aeries in Scotland and Wales. Criminals roamed from Southeast Asia to the former Yugoslavia to the Amazon jungle, plundering birds of prey, flouting export and import regulations, smuggling chicks and mature birds abroad in often horrific conditions, and feeding a voracious market for exotic fauna. In Bangkok in 2000, Raymond Leslie Humphrey, the owner of a British birds of prey center called Clouds Falconry, squeezed twenty-three live raptors—including Thai crested serpent eagles and Blyth's hawk eagles, both previously unknown in Europe—into plastic tubes. Humphrey hid the tubes inside two large suitcases, and then checked the baggage into the unpressurized and unheated hold of an airplane to London.

Customs officers at Heathrow got a tip, pulled Humphrey aside, and seized his luggage. Inside the bags they made a terrible discovery: six of the twenty-three birds were dead (another died shortly afterward), and the other seventeen had sustained massive pressure injuries, asphyxia, and hypothermia. A search of Humphrey's residence turned up dozens more endangered birds, as well as a golden-cheeked gibbon, one of the rarest apes in the world. Humphrey was sentenced to six and a half years in prison for illegally importing protected species—an act of "extreme and sickening cruelty," in the words of the appeals court judge who upheld Humphrey's conviction in 2003. The judge reduced the sentence by one year, but it was still the longest jail term ever given out in the United Kingdom for a wildlife crime.

Another rare-bird trader, Harry Sissen, used plastic tubes to smuggle birds from black market dealers in Eastern Europe overland to France and then by ferry across the English Channel to Dover. At Sissen's breeding center in North Yorkshire, Alan Roberts seized one hundred forty protected birds, including three Lear's macaws from the Brazilian Amazon (only one hundred fifty of the all-blue parrots remain in the wild) and three blue-headed macaws from the Peruvian jungle. Sentenced to thirty months in prison for violating the regulations of the Convention on International Trade in Endangered Species, Sissen "was prepared to go to any lengths to obtain endangered species from which to breed," the presiding judge declared. The black market value of a pair of Lear's macaws, according to *PsittaScene*, a conservation journal published by the World Parrot Trust, was £50,000.

The worst of these smugglers reminded McWilliam of the "terrier men" he'd arrested in rural England, who used dogs to drive badgers from their burrows and tear them apart. Some people seemed to get pleasure out of subjecting animals to pain, he thought, or were so consumed by greed that they didn't stop to consider the suffering they were inflicting on other creatures. McWilliam struggled to maintain his equanimity in the face of such brutality. "One of the things with being a police wildlife officer," he would tell Timothy Wheeler for the 2015 documentary *Poached*, "is you've got to leave your emotions out of it, even if you are an animal lover [or] a bird lover . . . You've got to be quite clinical . . . and know if you get emotionally involved in these things, you never sleep at night."

McWilliam knew that the greatest demand for illicit rare birds was coming from the Arab world. He had read intelligence about the Siberian raptor smuggling route to the Middle East, and his colleague Alan Roberts had helped Belgian authorities bust a zookeeper who ran a bird-laundering operation across the European Union: stealing peregrine eggs from their nests in southern Spain, forging Article 10s at Belgium's Merlin Zoo in Sint-Jan-in-Eremo, and then allegedly selling the birds for nearly one million euros to rich Arab clients, as well as wealthy Chinese. "We began to pick up intelligence about wild birds going to Dubai, Qatar, and Saudi Arabia," McWilliam would say a decade later, still careful about disseminating information from an active investigation. "Dubai was the one we got most about, because of the racing" that had been growing in popularity since its introduction to the Persian Gulf in the early 2000s. "We noticed people coming in who had no history of falcon breeding, or falconry, because of the new money."

In the mid-2000s Guy Shorrock heard about two wildlife criminals who had recently been convicted in northern Canada for stealing gyrfalcon eggs, possibly for sale to clients in the Middle East. One of these men, Jeffrey Lendrum, was already in the Royal Society database for a conviction in Zimbabwe in 1984. The other, Paul

Mullin, had no previous record. Shorrock wrote to the Canadian authorities, seeking more information, but citing privacy laws, the Canadians refused to share details with the charity. Then Shorrock attended a Convention on International Trade in Endangered Species lecture in London that happened to be hosted by Canadian wildlife officials. As they narrated the story of the notorious 2002 gyrfalcon heist, Paul Mullin's name flashed on the screen, along with a home address in Southampton. *Is Mullin still stealing eggs from the wilderness?* Shorrock wondered.

Shorrock never shared the information with McWilliam. Despite their fruitful collaboration busting egg collectors in the early 2000s, jealousies and resentments had been building between the National Wildlife Crime Unit and the Royal Society for the Protection of Birds, and the two men in particular. "It's all to do with the fact that a non-government agency [gets] frustrated . . . the police can't share information [or] intelligence with them," McWilliam would tell Timothy Wheeler in his interview for *Poached*. A series of email exchanges, made public via Britain's Freedom of Information Act, would expose the wildlife unit's growing resistance to working with, and even disdain for, the charity. "I do think on occasions they have something to offer," McWilliam wrote to his colleagues in 2013, "but their expertise would have to be required and . . . the Police must keep control." He seemed to waver. "Or then again we could just say 'F*** them.'" It was an attitude the Royal Society for the Protection of Birds apparently reciprocated.

As it turned out, the National Wildlife Crime Unit had the story of Mullin and Lendrum's Canadian heist, conviction, and subsequent movements in its files as well—though nobody had checked through the piles of records at the unit's Stirling headquarters. The documents dated back to the founding of the original National Wildlife Crime Intelligence Unit in 2002, the same year that Mullin and Lendrum were arrested in Quebec, and had been transferred to Scotland after the unit shut down in 2005, where they had been all but forgotten. A perusal of the records might have revealed not only that Mullin had changed his name and was back in England, but another tantalizing development: after years of globe-trotting, Lendrum had settled with his now-wife in a suburban town in the West Midlands, within striking distance of the peregrine falcons of Scotland and Wales.

FOURTEEN

THE RHONDDA VALLEY

In the years that followed his guilty plea for stealing gyrfalcon eggs in Canada's Nunavik territory, Jeffrey Lendrum tried to settle into a normal life. In the summer of 2002, just weeks after his arrest, he married his girlfriend in Sospel, a medieval mountain village in the Department of Alpes-Maritimes, north of the French Riviera. Paul Mullin, now living under a new name in the hope of burying his conviction for wildlife crime, served as the best man. After the ceremony in the village registrar's office, 150 guests gathered outside to celebrate. Almost all were members of the bride's Algerian-immigrant family, although a handful of Lendrum's mates from southern Africa and England also made an appearance. Three days of Arabic-inflected singing, dancing, and fraternizing in and around the ancient alleys and plazas of Sospel followed. When the festivities ended, Lendrum returned to the house that his bride owned in Towcester, where together they continued to co-run AfricaXtreme. Lendrum made regular trips back to South Africa and Zimbabwe, both for business and to see friends and family. He was also serving as stepfather to his wife's two preadolescent daughters from her previous marriage. His egg snatching days seemed behind him.

But the business took a turn for the worse in 2003. The sale of African handicrafts in England had reached a saturation point, and income fell off dramatically. With losses growing, Mullin closed the shop in Southampton and transferred his remaining stake in the venture to Lendrum; he had invested many tens of thousands of British pounds, and lost the entire amount. Lendrum renamed the Towcester shop African Art & Curios and struggled to keep it going, at one point borrowing money from his sister, Paula's, husband so that he could refill his inventory in Zimbabwe. But he was forced to shut the business for good in 2008 and dispose of the unsold merchandise. That same year, Lendrum's marriage broke up and his friendship with Mullin ended. The trouble began after Mullin's South African girlfriend, who had followed her boyfriend to England, flew to Johannesburg with their infant daughter on holiday. During the visit she began a relationship with Lendrum, who by that point had drifted apart from his wife. Mullin's now-ex-girlfriend decided to remain in South Africa with Lendrum and the child. The move sparked a bitter custody fight, and Lendrum took her side.

After the collapse of his marriage, the loss of his business, and the fallout with his closest friend, Lendrum returned to a nomadic existence, dividing his time between his ex-wife's near-empty house in Towcester—which she'd stripped of furniture and was trying to sell—and a temporary place in Johannesburg. He was unmoored and looking for a new way to earn a living. And, as would happen whenever Lendrum found himself adrift, the evidence suggests that he resumed his exploits for his clients in the Middle East.

=

Mike Thomas first noticed disturbing things happening during the peregrine falcon breeding season of 2007. The leader of the South Wales Peregrine Monitoring Group, a volunteer organization with about a dozen members, Thomas spent weekends between March and May rappelling to aeries in the Garw (*Ga-ROO*) Valley and neighboring glens and gorges in the country's former coal-mining heartland, a region with one of the densest concentrations of peregrine falcons in Great Britain, about fifty breeding pairs. On a gray morning in early May, Thomas, a thickset man then in his fifties with thin wire spectacles and a lantern jaw, hiked from his home in Blaengarw through a Japanese larch forest to an abandoned rock quarry. He followed a steep trail to the summit of a sandstone cliff, fixed a rope, and climbed down the rock face to a nesting site on a ledge that he'd been monitoring since March. Approaching the "scrape," a shallow depression filled with gravel and flat pebbles to hold in heat and prevent the clutch from rolling off the ledge, Thomas made a dismaying discovery: the four eggs were gone.

Thomas's first thought was they had been snatched by one of the peregrine falcon's mortal enemies: a pigeon fancier, or a devotee of the ten-thousand-year-old practice of breeding or racing domestic pigeons, the falcon's most common prey. But this nest would have been impossible to access without rappelling equipment, and pigeon men, in Thomas's experience, tended to go after aeries that were not difficult to reach. In addition, they often left beer cans strewn about nesting sites and crushed eggs rather than make off with them. Besides, Thomas and his fellow volunteers knew almost every pigeon fancier in the Garw. The peregrine monitors had let them know, he says, "If you steal the eggs, we'll come after your pigeons."

Days after the Blaengarw eggs went missing, two other clutches disappeared nearby. The next breeding season, a peregrine clutch vanished from a high ledge across the mountains in the Rhondda Fawr Valley. The ledge was reachable only by a rappel so dangerous that Thomas believed the thief had to be a professional. "Whoever is climbing this is nobody we know," he told a fellow volunteer. The group recorded half a dozen disappearances the next year, 2009. And who knew how many more they hadn't found? Working at their own expense, the volunteers were forced to leave many remote aeries unattended.

Thomas was obsessed by the mystery of the missing clutches. Who had stolen them? And why? The thief was clearly a skilled climber and an experienced peregrine spotter, yet he must also have had help from a local. "You can spend days trying to locate these sites," he explained. He found it disturbing to speculate about how much damage the egg thief might have caused. "Some years twenty-six peregrine clutches were in the area," he said. If the nest raider had been systematically attacking peregrine aeries since 2007, Thomas reasoned, he could have stolen well over one hundred eggs.

＝

On the morning of April 28, 2010—a Wednesday—Jeffrey Lendrum placed his climbing equipment into the trunk of his Vauxhall Vectra sedan in Towcester and drove alone two hours to the southwest to rural Wales. He checked into the Heritage Park Hotel in Pontypridd, a town of ancient stone bridges where the River Rhondda flows into the River Taff, and set out shortly after dawn the next morning for the thinly populated upper reaches of the Rhondda Fawr Valley. Years later, he would admit that this was one of many trips to Wales he had made between 2002 and 2010—but this one, he would swear, was his first and only egg snatching mission.

Seven years later, I made arrangements to meet Andy McWilliam and Ian Guildford, the Wales-based investigator with the National Wildlife Crime Unit, to retrace Lendrum's steps that day. On an unseasonably chilly May morning, Guildford—a bespectacled, rangy Londoner, who'd lived in Wales for four decades—picked me up at Cardiff's central rail station. We drove north through verdant hills, past the old coal-mining town of Aberfan, to where McWilliam was waiting at a McDonald's in the town of Merthyr Tydfil. The burly, gray-haired investigator had driven down from Liverpool that morning. He had the GPS points of the four aeries that Lendrum had looted in April 2010, which would enable us to follow his tracks. McWilliam wasn't sure, though, that we'd be able to catch sight of any peregrines. His bird-spotting skills, he admitted, had grown rusty through lack of practice. "A couple of years ago," he told me, "I'd walk through woodlands and say, 'There's a lesser yellow legs.' Now I go out and I say, 'What the hell is that?'"

We began a switchback climb through denuded sandstone hills, blanketed in lichens and pale green grass and rising several thousand feet above the Rhondda Fawr. Gouged by slow-moving glaciers during the last Ice Age between eighteen thousand and ten thousand years ago, the Rhondda Fawr (the Great Rhondda) and a smaller valley just to the east, the Rhondda Fach (the Little Rhondda), had once been covered with dense woodlands. Then, in the mid–nineteenth century, geologists discovered a rich seam of coal running beneath the surface of the two valleys, anywhere from a few dozen feet to half a mile down.

Soon tens of thousands of men had swapped subsistence farming for the steady cash wages of a life underground, and the forests were razed to make "pit props," beams that support the roofs of coal mines. "The hills have been stripped of all their woodland beauty, and there they stand, rugged and bare, with immense rubbish heaps covering their surface," wrote Arthur Morris in the 1908 book *Glamorgan*. "The river Rhondda is a dark, turgid, and contaminated gutter, into which is poured the refuse of the host of collieries which skirt the thirteen miles of its course." Then, in the 1970s, the anthracite began to run out, and the collieries closed, the last in 2008. Today the two Rhondda Valleys have among the highest unemployment rates in the British Isles.

The road climbed higher, the pale green slopes covered in places by netting to prevent landslides, and darkened here and there by stands of pine recently planted by the British Forestry Commission to stop the erosion. Brecon Beacons National Park, a dramatic range of red sandstone peaks dotted with the burial cairns of Bronze Age tribes, rose a few miles to the north. A sign noting the distances to nearby villages—Abergwynfi, Blaengwynfi, Nantymoel—captured the linguistic oddity of this remote corner of the United Kingdom. The language derives from ancient Celtic, brought over to the British Isles from continental Europe more than 2,500 years ago. As late as 1800, the majority of Wales' population spoke Welsh as their first language, but it fell out of the school curriculum in the late nineteenth century, and English soon came to dominate the region. Today, though something of a revival of Welsh is going on, barely one in five people in Wales can speak it.

When I stepped out of the vehicle at the top of the escarpment, I was nearly blown off my feet by a gust of wind. Steadying myself, I followed the two officers across a meadow speckled with purple and yellow wildflowers and low-growing fruit shrubs called bilberry bushes. Bleating sheep, bells around their necks chiming, darted across our path through spongy tufts of grass. Bent against the gale, we arrived at the edge of the cliffs.

The ground fell away sharply, exposing dozens of steplike gray-black ledges sheltered from the wind—perfect spots for peregrines to lay their eggs. "We're at the end of the bloody world," shouted Guildford.

We walked around the edge of the cliffs to another lookout, this one providing a panoramic view of the escarpment. A smooth, curving ampitheater of black and tan sandstone, mottled with patches of grass, swept upward at a near-perpendicular angle from the Rhondda Valley floor. McWilliam and Guildford scanned the cloud-dappled sky with their binoculars, searching for peregrine falcons. They weren't able to spot one.

Lendrum had enjoyed much better luck. The egg thief waited patiently atop this escarpment, also peering through binoculars, looking for male falcons returning to their aeries with food for their incubating partners. At eight a.m. on Thursday, April 29, Lendrum laid a fixed rope at the top of the cliff and rappelled twenty feet down to a ledge, scooping up the clutch as the peregrine parents flew off in fright. He placed the four eggs in his thermal bag. He took a second clutch at four p.m., retired to the Heritage Park Hotel, and then returned the next morning at eight-thirty for two more rappels down the cliffs. That day, he seized seven more eggs—including one clutch at the abandoned quarry near Mike Thomas's village of Blaengarw in the adjacent Garw Valley. Back in Towcester, he wrapped the eggs snugly in woolen socks to keep them warm and well cushioned, and placed them in a carton in his carry-on bag. With his unsuspecting girlfriend—Paul Mullin's ex-partner, who was now sharing a life with Lendrum in South Africa—in the passenger seat beside him, he set out for Birmingham Airport.

"I've got a lucky ability," Lendrum would say years later when asked to explain his success at finding nests in the most remote and forbidding terrain. "I will always ask myself, 'If I were a peregrine, what would I do? Where would I breed?' I go to an area that looks good, I look carefully and I see them."

=

On Monday afternoon, May 3, responding to a tip from the vigilant janitor in the Emirates Lounge, Counter Terrorism agents detained Lendrum and seized the fourteen peregrine eggs that he had snatched from cliffsides in and around the Rhondda Valley. Thirty hours after Lendrum's arrest, on the early evening of Tuesday, May 4, Andy McWilliam and a colleague from the Counter Terrorism Unit (who cannot be named for reasons of security) sat in a borrowed office at the Solihull Police Headquarters, evaluating their notes from the afternoon's interrogations. The commanding officer at Solihull had extended Lendrum's detention period from twenty-four to thirty-six hours—a standard move in complicated cases. At the end of that period, the Crown Prosecution Service would assess the arrest report presented by the police and determine whether or not to file charges. If McWilliam and his partner failed to persuade prosecutors that Lendrum had committed a serious crime, the police would have no choice but to release him. Should Lendrum walk out of jail, McWilliam had no doubt that the suspect would "do a runner" and flee England as quickly as possible.

McWilliam and his partner in the Counter Terrorism force spent the evening going over their notes and typing a case summary. Then, at nine p.m., four hours before the deadline, they faxed the document to CPS Direct, a national 24/7 hotline that connects a duty prosecutor with police seeking to charge a suspect with a crime. The Counter Terrorism man got on the phone with the assigned prosecutor.

"We've got a man in custody who was attempting to smuggle fourteen peregrine falcon eggs out of the United Kingdom," he said.

The agent explained that the peregrine was an Appendix I bird, granted the highest level of protection by the Convention on International Trade in Endangered Species. Smuggling its eggs was a breach of the Customs and Excise Management Act of 1979, as well as the Control of Trade in Endangered Species Regulations of 1997. The suspect's acts were also violations of many other pieces of legislation: the European Union Wildlife Trade Regulations of 1996, the Endangered Species Act of 1976, the Wildlife and Countryside Act of 1981, the Theft Act of 1968, the Birds Directive of 1979, and the EU Habitats Directive of 1992. The suspect had been caught with incubators, a satnav, and climbing equipment. The circumstances of the arrest pointed to a "sophisticated one-man operation." What's more, he was not a British citizen, had no fixed address in the United Kingdom, and was traveling on a foreign passport.

"If we bail him," he said, "the guy is going on his toes."

The prosecutor listened mostly without comment.

"I just don't know the legislation," she said. "I think I need to do some research on this and get back to you."

McWilliam and his partner paced the halls, checking their watches for one hour, two, three . . . The minutes ticked by, and McWilliam's frustration grew. At the front desk of the custody suites, the night clerk gathered Lendrum's personal effects in preparation for his release. Finally, just before one a.m., with two minutes to go before the deadline, the duty inspector at the Solihull station, the highest-ranking officer in the building that night, stepped in to make an executive decision. (Though Crown prosecutors ordinarily have the final call on whether to charge a suspect, senior police officers can take on that role in emergencies.)

"Charge him," he said, overriding the usual procedure. He ordered Lendrum held overnight.

Early the next morning, at the Solihull Magistrates Court, a judge denied Lendrum's bail application, citing the gravity of his alleged offenses and the risk of flight. Court officers escorted Lendrum in handcuffs to pretrial detention in Hewell Prison, a twelve-hundred-bed maximum- and minimum-security facility on the grounds of a Victorian manor house in Worcestershire, southwest of Birmingham, to await a plea hearing in August—three months away.

—

As Lendrum remained locked up in a cellblock filled with prisoners who had likewise been denied bail, McWilliam began methodically to build the case against him. At this point, just two days after the egg thief's arrest, McWilliam had only circumstantial evidence that he was dealing with an experienced criminal—until he sat down to watch an unmarked DVD the Counter Terrorism police had discovered in one of Lendrum's carry-on bags. As the images rolled by—a Ray-Ban-wearing helicopter pilot smirking and announcing that he and Lendrum were "going on a tour," Lendrum dangling from a line seven hundred feet above a frozen lake, a Bell JetRanger hovering inches from a cliff, gyrfalcons circling overhead—McWilliam stared in amazement. Here was a video of Lendrum's pilot boasting about their being "fucking criminals," and it had fallen into the hands of the police. While it was still technically possible that Lendrum had, as he claimed, stumbled upon the Welsh peregrine eggs by chance, it was clear from the video that the risks, costs, and planning involved in this other operation must have been enormous.

McWilliam would soon learn that Lendrum's felonious missions had apparently extended to every corner of the globe—as free-ranging as the peregrine itself. On the suspect's laptop computer (which wasn't password protected), he pored through a Microsoft Word document that described a trip made to Sri Lanka in February 2010 to search for the aeries of the black shaheen falcon (*Falco peregrinus peregrinator*)—a powerful, nonmigratory peregrine subspecies that roosts on rock faces from Pakistan to northern Myanmar. Only forty breeding pairs are known to inhabit the island. "One [falcon] seen flying off rock . . . good site with large overhang, several places with droppings," read an account of a scouting mission to the jungled cliffs near Wellawaya. A nearby site proved to be less promising. "Military guarding elephants in area and every time [you] step [from] the car, they come out of the trees to ask what you are doing. Hard access to rock and military make this a no-go."

Lendrum—or whoever had written the report—then visited Sigiriya, a massive, six-hundred-sixty-foot column of congealed magma from an extinct volcano, with a stone palace at the summit carved by the fifth-century King Kasyapa. Neither this archaeological masterpiece nor the delicate sixteen-hundred-year-old frescoes of the women of the royal harem were of interest to the writer. "Good rock face not able to observe due to sun coming right into lens in morning," he wrote. "Mature male on rock face, very nice color with very small white bib." The author of the document also cased the security at Bandaranaike International Airport in Colombo. "On drive into airport there is security check and they open boots and doors of many vehicles to check inside," he noted. "A few meters inside doors to departure area there is a security checkpoint consisting of a row of standard baggage X-ray units, walk-through metal detector and just about everybody was patted down. The guy who patted me down was very good at it."

The notes left no doubt about where the author had flown to after leaving the jungled island. "Dubai customs were very iffy about the night vision glasses we had in our hand luggage," he warned, leaving the "we" unidentified. Lendrum would deny writing the report and, when asked if he had ever visited Sri Lanka, began to ramble. "I don't remember that, no," he would say a few years later, before adding, "We went to go and look at peregrines there. I can't remember when . . . I think it was probably just before Wales. They are beautiful birds. It's just a different subspecies of the peregrine. But I wasn't going out there to get them, no."

Days later, a key found in Lendrum's carry-on luggage, along with a receipt for the rental of a storage facility, led McWilliam to a Lok'nStore in Northamptonshire. Amid suitcases, duffel bags, and Sainsbury's shopping bags jammed inside a locker six feet high and five feet deep, he discovered more evidence of his quarry's outlaw life: an incubator purchased on eBay days before his mission to southern Wales, police records and a *Nunatsiaq News* account of his arrest in Canada back in 2002, and a copy of a letter Lendrum had written to the reporter behind the *Nunatsiaq News* article, in which he claimed to have been on a research project to determine "the effects of global warming" on gyrfalcons and insisted that he had planned to return the eggs to the nests. Lendrum's mischief went back decades, and, like some of the English egg collectors McWilliam had pursued, he had collected a trove of mementos documenting his bad behavior: there was correspondence from the early 1980s laying out a scheme apparently concocted by Jeffrey and Adrian Lendrum to smuggle African black eagle eggs and chicks to a breeder in Birmingham—just as Kit Hustler, the Zimbabwean ornithologist and prosecution witness at the Lendrums' 1984 trial, had long suspected. The breeder they'd been in contact with, Philip Dugmore, had been convicted and fined two years later for illegally keeping six black eagles. The raptors "in all probability, came from the supply of eggs from this defendant to him," Lendrum's new prosecutor would soon declare in court.

=

Then McWilliam secured another compelling piece of evidence. Paul Mullin, now living in southern England, learned from news reports that summer that his former friend had been arrested with falcon eggs at Birmingham Airport. Still bearing a grudge against Lendrum— "Karma's a bitch," he would say—he phoned the airport police. "If you want to know anything about Jeffrey Lendrum, I can help," he told the officer who answered the call. The policeman relayed the message to McWilliam, who called Mullin back within minutes. They met at a police station in Newbury, a market town south of Oxford, but the initial encounter didn't go well. "I was with Lendrum when he was caught in Canada," Mullin told McWilliam, as two Newbury officers hovered in the background. The constables interrupted the interview, and cautioned Mullin that anything he said could be used against him. "What I'm about to tell you is outside of your jurisdiction," Mullin snapped. "If you're not happy, I'm walking." Mullin called an early end to the encounter.

McWilliam arranged a second, private meeting at a highway rest stop in Oxfordshire. Wearing a baseball cap and sunglasses this time, and claiming to be worried that he was being followed, Mullin sat at a table across from the investigator and didn't stop talking for an hour. He brought photographs, plane tickets, receipts, field notes, maps, the business cards of the arresting officers in Kuujjuaq, and other evidence of his escapades with Lendrum and the helicopter pilot. He recounted his falling-out with his former best friend after Lendrum had taken up with his girlfriend and then written a letter to a judge in support of her application for full custody of her and Mullin's young daughter. He also showed McWilliam a photograph taken at Heathrow Airport of Lendrum and Howard Waller, whom Mullin maintained had sponsored the mission to Canada. McWilliam graded Mullin an "E41" according to police-intelligence lingo, meaning an "untested source"; there was no way to be certain that he was telling the truth. But McWilliam found him personable and credible, and the documents he presented supported his account. "I couldn't see a motivation to lie," he said.

Soon after that, Pat Lorber, formerly of the Rhodesian Ornithological Society, reached out to McWilliam from King's Lynn, in East Anglia, where she had settled after leaving Zimbabwe two decades earler. She, too, had read newspaper accounts of Lendrum's arrest. Lorber filled in another critical part of Lendrum's bizarre life story: the scandal and trial in Bulawayo in 1984.

In the meantime, McWilliam had obtained persuasive evidence that Lendrum had not been acting alone in Wales. Colin Pirie, the National Wildlife Crime Unit's chief of intelligence, tracked Lendrum's vehicle through a police system that uses a countrywide network of license-plate recognition cameras. Pirie determined that

Lendrum had been to the Rhondda Valley in early April, three weeks before robbing the nests. He'd exchanged two hundred phone calls and text messages with a local breeder, to pinpoint the exact locations of the aeries. "If you've got somebody local who's keeping an eye on them, it makes the job easier," McWilliam would later say.

Police specialists traced the calls to a man named Robert Griffiths in the village of Ton Pentre at the upper end of the Rhondda Fawr, a few miles from Lendrum's primary nest-robbing zone. Law enforcement officers knew him as a career raptor snatcher. Guildford had arrested him in Scotland in the 1980s for stealing peregrines, and again in the 1990s for laundering merlins—small, powerfully built falcons—at his breeding facility. He was still selling birds of dubious provenance, and was said to be familiar with every ledge and crag in the Rhondda and its adjacent glens. "He knows more about the wild birds than those out there protecting them," Guildford said. "He knows their breeding habits, and he knows exactly where to look." When Guildford confronted Griffith in Ton Pentre with evidence that he had provided grid points to Lendrum, the breeder denied knowing the egg thief. The National Wildlife Crime Unit decided not to pursue criminal charges against him, but the discovery of the phone messages provided insight into Lendrum's modus operandi.

There were aspects of the case that McWilliam never could figure out—like why the janitor in the Emirates Lounge had found that one red-dyed egg in the diaper bin—but that Lendrum would later explain. Before arriving at the airport, he would say, he had placed the fourteen live peregrine eggs in a nine-egg carton and a six-egg carton, and he needed to fill the last slot with a similar-looking egg. He wanted it to look as if he had just bought ordinary farm-fresh eggs at the supermarket: "If [security] opened an egg box, they would just look like a whole bunch of spotted eggs. And I would say, 'Okay, take them.'"

Despite a few unanswered questions, McWilliam's summerlong investigation had exposed the patterns of a master criminal: an adventurer, athlete, and logistician who had operated confidently for decades. He had conspired to pillage the environment with unnamed "senior members of UAE society" for "significant" financial gain, acccording to a PowerPoint display that McWilliam would put together that year for the media and fellow officers. McWilliam had a pretty good idea of who some of Lendrum's clients were, but he couldn't reveal so publicly until they had been formally charged with a crime: that would be a violation of Great Britain's privacy laws.

The investigator was developing complicated feelings for the thief. "He's well traveled, he's fearless, he's resourceful, and his preparation is superb," said McWilliam. "I respected him without wanting to condone what he did." Nevin Hunter, who would command the National Wildlife Crime Unit from 2012 to 2014, shared his colleague's respect for Lendrum's gifts. Both of them had dealt with hundreds of wildlife criminals in their careers, but neither had encountered one who had covered so much ground, employed such flamboyant methods to carry out his thefts, and been so apparently successful at moving living, fragile creatures across vast distances. "I sat down with Andy, Ian Guildford, and Alan Roberts, one hundred fifty years of experience among us, and we couldn't come up with any other individual who works like Lendrum does," Hunter would say. "He identified a marketplace that hadn't been exploited by any criminal, and he was ideally suited for it."

Perhaps it was possible to appreciate Lendrum's accomplishments without too much guilt because the thief hadn't threatened any species with extinction. "Peregrines and gyrfalcons are not going to die out because one guy takes their eggs to sell to the Arab market," McWilliam's colleague Alan Roberts said, although he did sadly concede that "the principle is there. If the sheikhs decide that a more vulnerable species is going to be what they want, Lendrum made sure that all the mechanisms are in place."

In any event, begrudging respect didn't stop McWilliam from building a strong case. To round out his picture of Lendrum for the prosecution, McWilliam asked Nick Fox, the Wales-based falcon breeder to Sheikh Mohammed bin Rashid Al Maktoum, the ruler of Dubai, to estimate the value of the thirteen live peregrine eggs found on Lendrum's person. Fox projected that ten would have survived the journey to Dubai, and half would have been female. At £10,000 for a wild female, and £5,000 for a wild male, which is two-thirds the female's size and generally a slower racer, he placed a market value, in a sworn affidavit that would be presented in court, of £75,000 on the lot, then worth about $117,000. Officials of the Convention on International Trade in Endangered Species based in the United Arab Emirates corroborated the figure. Though far more conservative than other estimates of wild falcon prices over the years, the sum would hardly have been a bad income for a single month's work.

=

At the Warwick Crown Court in Royal Leamington Spa outside Birmingham, a media-heavy crowd began forming in the hour before Lendrum's mid-morning plea hearing on August 19, 2010. Alerted by McWilliam, reporters from the BBC, Sky News, the *Independent*, the *Sun*, the *Daily Mail*, and the *Times*, as well as local TV, radio, and print journalists, converged on the eighteenth-century colonnaded courthouse, one of the oldest still in use in Great Britain. The tale of the globe-trotting thief who had rappelled down cliffs to steal live falcon eggs on behalf of Arab sheikhs was irresistible to the tabloids and the evening news. McWilliam noted the satellite trucks as he walked up the courthouse steps, pleasantly surprised by the turnout. The outcome of the appearance was not in doubt: prosecutor Nigel Williams had let it be known that Lendrum, facing a compendium of powerful evidence against him, would acknowledge his guilt on one count of theft of an endangered species and one count of smuggling in violation of the regulations of the Convention on International Trade in Endangered Species. He hoped for a lighter sentence, possibly just a fine, in return.

McWilliam walked past the gallery in the small, wood-paneled courtroom—from which eighteenth-century thieves and murderers had been delivered in irons to the hangman. A few feet away, Lendrum sat in the dock. Not a single friend or family member was present. The falcon thief nodded at the investigator in recognition. McWilliam nodded back. McWilliam had faced plenty of defendants who'd hurled obscenities at him or threatened him in the courtroom. "I've been to court where I wouldn't piss on a defendant if he was on fire," McWilliam would say. He had once arrested and brought to trial a goshawk launderer named Leonard O'Connor, "a grade-one asshole," he says, who had flashed him his middle finger from the witness box every time the magistrate wasn't looking. McWilliam responded to each insult by repeating the obscene gesture. "We were like a pair of children," he would say with a laugh. Lendrum—polite and soft-spoken—was a pleasant change from such surly characters.

"You all right?" McWilliam asked.

Lendrum shrugged. "I've been keeping okay," he replied.

"You're pleading guilty," McWilliam said.

"Well," Lendrum replied, "you caught me bang to rights."

Judge Christopher Hodson entered the courtroom. He asked Lendrum to rise.

"How do you plead?"

"I'm guilty, Your Honor."

Lendrum's advocate, Nicola Purches, told the judge that her client had been "a model prisoner" in the remand block at Hewell. He was remorseful and ashamed, and the crime was completely out of character. What was more, Lendrum's father, Adrian, a lifetime heavy smoker now in his seventies, had developed emphysema, and had only a few months to live. His son hoped to fly to Zimbabwe and see him, Purches said, before he died.

Hodson asked Lendrum to rise again and to listen while he quoted from *Costing the Earth*, a document that Lord Justice Stephen Sedley, a distinguished appeals-court jurist, had prepared the previous year as a guide for sentencing wildlife criminals. "The environmental crime strikes not only at a locality and its population but at the planet and its future," Sedley had declared. "Nobody should be allowed to doubt its seriousness." Lendrum, Hodson said, had been motivated by the basest of reasons, "commercial profit . . . The amount that you would have needed to expend, on equipment, on travel, and in preparation, in my judgment proves that," he continued. "You have had two previous warnings of the consequences of dealing in protected wild birds and their eggs; convicted in 1984 in Zimbabwe; and in 2002 in Canada."

Then Hodson pronounced his judgment. "At the end of the day, a substantial sentence . . . needs to be imposed to punish you and deter others," he said. "The sentence on the indictment will be one of thirty months' imprisonment."

"Bloody hell," muttered McWilliam from a side bench. Two and a half years. The sentence was tougher than he had been expecting. He was happy enough to take the falcon thief out of circulation for a while, but he felt unexpected ambivalence about this punishment. Like a master jewel thief or other skilled practioner of the felonious arts, the man commanded appreciation of his talents, however twisted they might be. McWilliam regarded him as an accomplished adversary. He had even come to like him, in a way. He glanced at Lendrum, who looked back, stunned.

—

Over the next days, British newspapers devoted pages of coverage to Lendrum's exploits. "Caged: The £70K Egg Snatcher," the *Daily Mirror* declared. "A Bird in the Hand, a Smuggler in Jail," ran the front-page headline in the *Times* of London. "Jailed, Former Soldier Caught Smuggling £70,000 of Falcon Eggs," the *Daily Mail* proclaimed, reporting, inaccurately, that Lendrum had served in the Rhodesian SAS. The *Independent*, also embellishing a tale that needed no exaggeration, repeated the misreporting that Lendrum was "a former member of the Rhodesian SAS." Lendrum, the paper reported, "becomes the first person in 19 years to be prosecuted in the UK for attempting to smuggle peregrine falcon eggs out of the country," a reference to the two German citizens who had pleaded guilty in 1991 to smuggling twelve live eggs hidden in the dashboard of their Mercedes. The *Daily Express* ran a photo spread of "The Rare Falcon Chicks Saved from Clutches of Daring Egg Smuggler," while spinning a sensational yarn that bore little relation to the truth.

"Police feared a terrorist attack on a British airport was underway," the piece began. "The ingredients were all there—a shady character acting in a suspicious manner who was once a special forces soldier for a foreign power. Among his possessions were thousand of pounds in cash. But it wasn't explosives he was trying to sneak onto an international airliner—it was rare bird eggs."

McWilliam gave television producers permission to use the confiscated video from northern Canada, and dramatic excerpts played and played on British TV. Back in Bulawayo, members of BirdLife Zimbabwe and others who had felt betrayed by Lendrum in the 1980s expressed satisfaction that justice had been served. "At last the fellow is in prison, though a spell in a Zimbabwean jail might be a more effective deterrent," wrote Peter Mundy, the ornithology professor and friend of Val Gargett, who had once tried to arrange Lendrum's extradition to Zimbabwe, in the magazine *Honeyguide*. Mundy acknowledged that much of the case was likely to remain a mystery. "Few of the end users of illegally obtained wildlife ever seem to get convicted," he wrote. Lendrum "has proven himself to be an unrepentant reprobate and will presumably remain tight-lipped so we may never know his contacts."

Both the media and McWilliam had left another important question unanswered: What had happened to the money? Under the provisions of the Wildlife and Countryside Act, the police had confiscated everything that Lendrum had been traveling with: his Vauxhall Vectra Estate car, laptops, incubators, a spotting scope, cameras, lenses, and climbing equipment, as well as an expensive mountain bike that he was shipping back to South Africa, and a few thousand British pounds and US dollars. The total value of the forfeiture was placed at £20,000. Lendrum had a part interest with South African friends in a Cessna aircraft and owned a four-by-four in Johannesburg, both of which were outside the jurisdiction of the British authorities. But a search for other assets under the 2002 Proceeds of Crime Act would turn up little else. A close friend in Zimbabwe had once jokingly called Lendrum "the world's poorest thief." The mystery lingered, and Lendrum wasn't talking.

McWilliam had a bite with the Counter Terorrism agent who'd worked on the case with him from the beginning and then made the 130-mile drive home to Liverpool, answering a dozen more reporters' calls along the way. After brewing coffee and watching the late-evening news on the BBC, featuring images of Lendrum dangling from a helicopter, McWilliam and his wife went to bed.

One hundred ten miles away at Hewell, Jeffrey Lendrum settled into his first night in his cell as a convicted endangered-species smuggler, still insisting that he was misunderstood, and still holding secrets that McWilliam was determined to shake loose.

FIFTEEN

PRISON

After his sentencing, Jeffrey Lendrum moved into a wing for convicted felons at the high-security "B" block of Her Majesty's Prison
Hewell. During his three months awaiting trial, his cellmate had been
Jonathan Palmer, a white-haired former businessman accused (and
later convicted) of bludgeoning his wife to death in the hallway of
their home after she discovered his multiple affairs. Now he had a
new cellmate and a new prison routine that stressed rehabilitation
and vocational workshops. Cells opened at seven forty-five. Then
came showers, breakfast, job training, lunch, cell cleaning, menial
work, classes, dinner, gym, and a lockup at six-fifteen p.m. The staff
offered prisoners a choice among courses in construction, double-
glazing manufacture, industrial cleaning, waste management, and
laundry services. Lendrum, who was forty-nine years old and had
never held a nine-to-five job since managing the cannery in Bulawayo in his early twenties, wasn't interested.

Yet Lendrum discovered certain satisfactions in his life behind
bars. As he moved through the exercise yard, cafeteria, and other
communal areas of the cellblock, he was often treated like a celebrity.

Hardened felons wanted to hear about his adventures and expressed surprise, amusement, and sympathy that Lendrum was doing two and a half years for stealing eggs. "You got hit for taking birds?" they would ask. "My God, this country is nuts." Some prisoners, amazed by the reports that peregrine eggs could be sold in the Arab world for £5,000 or £10,000 apiece, begged him for tips on finding aeries. Lendrum assured them that the stories were "grossly exaggerated" and that the market price of a peregrine egg was barely one-tenth of that.

Two months into Lendrum's sentence, Andy McWilliam made an appointment to see him. Now that Lendrum had pleaded guilty to trafficking in wild peregrine eggs, the investigator hoped that he might be more forthcoming about his Middle Eastern sponsors. McWilliam had become increasingly aware of the role of wealthy Arabs in the underground falcon market. With Lendrum's admission of culpability, he saw an opportunity to implicate specific sheikhs—and pressure the Emirates or other Gulf states to take action. Lendrum was "a guy at the top of his game," recalled McWilliam, who a few days earlier had attended a ceremony in Birmingham presided over by Great Britain's Environmental Minister, honoring the sharp-eyed Emirates Lounge janitor, John Struczynski, for his contribution to Lendrum's May 2010 arrest. "We wanted him to spill the beans." And perhaps, McWilliam acknowledges, he hoped for more than that. From his encounters with repeat offenders such as Carlton D'Cruze, who had admitted he might never be able to control the impulse to raid aeries, and Gregory Peter Wheal, who had been arrested for stealing eggs ten times in a decade, McWilliam knew how difficult it was for a recidivist egg snatcher to break from lifelong criminalty. Still, he thought that maybe—just maybe—Lendrum would find a path out of the outlaw life.

McWilliam and his colleague from the West Midlands Counter Terrorism Unit drove through the gates to the old country estate one fall afternoon and followed a road past the manor house to the high-security block. They parked the vehicle, passed on foot through several more gates, and waited for Lendrum in a private interview room just off a sprawling prisoners' lounge. The falcon thief cast them a broad smile when he appeared. He shook their hands and sat opposite them at a scuffed table, chatting amiably about conditions inside the prison. After the shock of receiving a two-and-a-half-year jail sentence, he was surprisingly relaxed and seemed to be coming to terms with his loss of liberty. He was looking to the future, he told McWilliam. He had signed up for a photo-editing course, and was learning Adobe Lightroom and Photoshop.

Lendrum also seemed willing to cooperate with the police. He turned over to McWilliam the GPS points of all four aeries that he had robbed in the Rhondda and Garw Valleys. He dropped inside information about the birds-of-prey trade in Southern Africa, mentioning species that he knew were being systematically taken from Matobo and other Zimbabwe reserves and smuggled abroad. (A decade later, McWilliam still wouldn't say whether Lendrum had identified individual trappers and smugglers by name. Such material remained "restricted intelligence" under British law, and he could be criminally prosecuted for divulging it.) He spoke emotionally about his father, Adrian, who had died on September 2, two weeks after Lendrum's guilty plea, following a long struggle with emphysema. Great Britain's Prison and Probation Service had turned down his request to attend his father's funeral in South Africa.

But when pressed for intelligence about his clients in the Arab world, Lendrum claimed not to know what McWilliam was talking about. He didn't have any business in the Middle East, he insisted. McWilliam asked about his relationship with Howard Waller, mentioning a photo he had seen of Lendrum and Waller sitting together in a bar at Heathrow. Lendrum admitted that he had known Waller growing up in Rhodesia, but denied ever smuggling eggs for him. He insisted that he had stolen the live peregrine eggs in southern Wales to save them from being destroyed by pigeon fanciers. "It was spur of the moment," he said. "If you had seen me in Africa, and seen how I rescue things, then I think you would understand me. I catch snakes. I'm nuts." He was still covering for his Arab patrons, McWilliam assumed, perhaps fearful of retribution, perhaps eager to return to business with them once he was released from prison.

Despite his continuing evasiveness, the Hewell administration considered Lendrum a model prisoner who stood a good chance of successful reintegration into society. In late autumn, shortly after the visit from McWilliam, the governess rewarded him for his good behavior by moving him across the grounds to Hewell's Grange Resettlement Unit, a manor house that had once belonged to the Earls of Plymouth. The Grange had no formal lights-out, no lockdowns, and practically no supervision; prisoners lived together in a dormitory. The governess's only caution was a half-joking warning to Lendrum that "your pilot friend" refrain from "attempting a rescue" in his helicopter. Prisoners had relaxed phone privileges as well, and one of the first people Lendrum reached out to was McWilliam. He chatted about his progress in his photo course and mounted his usual defense of his actions in the Rhondda Valley, without any prompting from McWilliam this time, rambling on about pigeon fanciers and the shootings and poisonings of peregrines. "If I hadn't saved those birds nobody would have," he told the officer. Surprised by the call,

McWilliam wondered whether any of his friends or family had been by to visit.

=

Soon Lendrum received more good news. On February 1, England's Court of Appeals ruled that his punishment was "manifestly excessive and out of step with the sentences imposed in earlier cases" of bird smuggling, including that of Harry Sissen, the North Yorkshire rare-parrot trafficker whose two-and-a-half-year sentence had been reduced to eighteen months on appeal. Citing Lendrum's willingness to plead guilty and his "family circumstances in South Africa," the court reduced his sentence to eighteen months, including time served. Providing that he could present a proper residential address and find employment, the prisoner was free to leave Hewell immediately on parole. He would, however, have to remain in the United Kingdom for another nine months, until the end of his reduced sentence, and report weekly to a court officer.

Lendrum, as it turned out, did still have friends—one of whom put him in touch with an acquaintance named Charles Graham, an entrepreneur who owned four go-kart tracks in southern England. Graham agreed to take on the parolee as a rehabilitation project, and got him a job greeting customers, giving safety demonstrations, helping with catering, and serving as a "race marshal" on the nine-hundred-meter track at his Daytona Sandown Park. Soon Lendrum, his girlfriend, and her toddler daughter, Paul Mullin's child, moved into a wing of Graham's house on the North Downs, a ridge of chalk hills running west from the White Cliffs of Dover. The three settled into a comfortable life in limbo—making ample use of Graham's swimming pool and hot tub all summer long. "He had no bills to pay, he had food on the table every night," says Graham. Lendrum entertained employees at the track with stories about his nine months in prison and even bragged about his jailhouse nickname, the Birdman. "Jeff had this South African bonhomie," remembers Graham. "He was a swashbuckling adventurer." Over beers in the hot tub with Graham, Lendrum dropped his guard and admitted that he had stolen the falcon eggs for the money, estimating that the last operation in Wales could have brought a sum "in the high five figures" if he hadn't been caught at Birmingham Airport. Yet he assured other friends that he had put that phase of his life behind him. "He told me he was finished with it," says Craig Hunt, the boyhood mate who owned the Southern Comfort Lodge in Bulawayo. "He would never do it again."

=

At the end of 2011, his parole over, Lendrum returned to South Africa and moved in with his younger sister, Paula, and her husband in Johannesburg. Lendrum's brother, Richard—who'd had little contact with his brother during his months in prison—decided to join in helping his wayward sibling get back on his feet. As the publisher and editor in chief of *African Hunting Gazette*, a glossy quarterly with a print run of sixteen thousand, Richard hired his brother to replace a departing staff member who worked on Visited & Verified, an online customer guide to lodges, camps, and safari outfitters in Southern Africa. Jeffrey Lendrum "is excited to travel and meet prospective clients and friends in the hunting fraternity," the magazine's website declared in early 2012, introducing the new employee to readers of *African Hunting Gazette*, which mostly combined reviews of the latest weaponry and ammo with personal accounts of big game shooting safaris. "He's a wildlife enthusiast with an immense love for

Africa's flora and fauna and has spent many of his fifty years in the bush. His interest and knowledge is diverse, from the Big Five" game animals—lions, leopards, rhinos, elephants, and Cape buffalo—"to birds and insects."

For the second time since leaving prison, Lendrum had been offered a fresh start—and he seemed grateful for the opportunity to turn his life around. He traveled the hunting circuit, meeting safari lodge owners, touring their properties, authenticating their claims about the big game and terrain they offered hunters, and then passing on the information to the editorial staff. He was earning a decent salary, staying out of trouble, and spending his time in the environments where he had always been most content: the mopane woodlands, riverine bush, and thornveld savanna of Southern Africa.

One day McWilliam got a call from Johannesburg. "Hey, Andy, it's Jeffrey," the caller said. It took McWilliam a moment to register that the falcon thief was on the line. McWilliam hadn't expected to hear from him again, but Lendrum laid on an odd request: he needed help resolving a dispute about a parking ticket that he'd received before leaving England. "I wasn't even driving the bloody car," he told McWilliam.

"I thought to myself, *This is strange. If he's in Johannesburg, what the hell does it matter?*" McWilliam recalled. "Whether it was just an excuse to ring me up, I don't know." McWilliam told him there was nothing he could do.

Soon Lendrum was calling him every two or three weeks. He talked enthusiastically about the wildlife he'd seen and how grateful he was for this second chance. He shared his views on wildlife conservation, criticizing a program being introduced in Zimbabwe, Namibia, and South Africa to remove the horns from live rhinos to discourage poaching. "People will still follow the trail and shoot the animal. How are they going to know?" he said, dismissing the idea as ridiculous. He blamed the Convention on International Trade in Endangered Species in part for the rhino poaching epidemic, arguing that it had forced the rhino-horn trade underground, driven up prices, and created a black market. "If there was total transparency, rhino, as well as any endangered species, could be farmed like cattle," he said. McWilliam found Lendrum knowledgable and thoughtful, and he had to admit that much of what he said sounded reasonable. Eventually Lendrum came around to discussing raptors; the laws made no sense, he maintained. Lendrum tried to get McWilliam to agree that CITES should recategorize the peregrine falcon as a less endangered species and allow a certain amount of harvesting and exporting of wild birds of prey. "Whatever," McWilliam replied. His job was to enforce the law; he was happy to let the scientists and politicians make policy.

On another call, Lendrum surprised McWilliam with an invitation to come to South Africa for a safari. "You can stay with me," he even said. He'd moved out of his sister's and was renting his own place. McWilliam declined, knowing that fraternizing with a convicted wildlife criminal, even a reformed one, was hardly appropriate for a wildlife crime investigator. But he was touched—if a little puzzled—that Lendrum was intent on maintaining a relationship with him. Lendrum would extend the offer to McWilliam several more times.

=

While Lendrum was roving the bush for *African Hunting Gazette*, McWilliam was becoming enmeshed in office politics. In early 2010, a new boss had taken command of the National Wildife Crime Unit. A former homicide detective with no wildlife experience, the man came across to some of his employees as a remote and clueless self-promoter. He disappeared from headquarters for days at a time, attending conferences in far-flung locations like China and India, burning through the unit's limited budget, and rarely explaining his absences. The staff took to calling him "the Walking Eagle" behind his back, because, McWilliam explained, "He's filled with so much shit that he can't get off the ground."

In February 2012, the *Scottish Sun* ran a puff piece about the crime unit boss called "Cop's Work on the Wild Side." The article compared him to the hero of a popular Hollywood comedy. "Unlike Jim Carrey's wacky character in *Ace Ventura: Pet Detective*, he is deadly serious about his role," the profile began. He bragged about the achievements of the unit since he had taken over, including "his greatest collar . . . an infamous smuggler who stole rare bird eggs to order." McWilliam couldn't believe that the man was taking credit for bagging Jeffrey Lendrum. McWilliam hadn't even informed him until after the arrest had gone down.

But the most insulting part of the profile was the chief's characterization of the NWCU. "Before I took over, the unit was seen as 'fluffy bunny,'" he told the reporter, "but things have changed since then." McWilliam was infuriated by the insinuation that he and the other seasoned investigators were sentimental animal huggers. He fired off several angry emails, accusing him of denigrating and demoralizing the staff. The chief claimed that the *Scottish Sun* reporter had made up the quote; McWilliam contacted the journalist, who stood by his reporting. When the chief found out, he berated McWilliam for speaking to the press without permission, and threatened to discipline him. "Bring it on," McWilliam dared. For weeks, it was unclear whether McWilliam would be fired from the unit. The dispute eventually subsided, but McWilliam and his superior never spoke to each other again.

===

In the spring of 2013, Jeffrey Lendrum passed his first anniversary working for his brother's magazine. He had, his brother, Richard, believed, finally put his days as an egg thief behind him. Then, that April, Jerome Philippe, a hunting concessionaire in Namibia and the founder of a popular website called AfricanHunting.com, posted an alert on the members' forum. "Jeffrey Lendrum of African Hunting Gazette: convicted wildlife smuggler," it declared, going on to inform the forum's twenty-thousand participants of his three convictions over twenty-six years.

Angry comments appeared on the AfricaHunting.com forum within hours. "Is *African Hunting Gazette* letting [safari camp owners] know that a convicted criminal is being sent to stay at their house with their family for the purpose of 'verifying' their outfits?" wrote one longtime subscriber. "If I was an outfitter knowing what I know now, I would not let this guy anywhere near my property!" Some readers canceled their subscriptions. Advertisers began to pull out.

Richard Lendrum had feared this day would come. Since putting out his first issue of *African Hunting Gazette* (originally called *African Sporting Gazette*) in 2000, Lendrum had successfully positioned the quarterly as a pro-conservation magazine, arguing that trophy hunting benefits wildlife by providing revenue for game management, anti-poaching patrols, and national park operations. Many big game hunters who subscribed to the *Gazette* liked to see themselves as wildlife conservationists at heart, and the revelation that a convicted thief and smuggler held a prominent position on the magazine's staff was, Lendrum understood, unlikely to go down well. "I knew I was running a risk having [Jeffrey's] association with my business," Richard would later admit, "but . . . he had served his time . . . His range of services for a division of the magazine was very restricted and limited, and to be honest, very useful. And he was my brother."

Jeffrey Lendrum begged for forgiveness. "What I did was stupid and believe me I paid for it," he posted on AfricaHunting.com, "or do I have to keep paying?" He profusely apologized, writing later in his post, "I am sincerely sorry . . . I did my time and am commited to my job." As the irate comments continued to pour in, he posted his cell number, his Skype address, and his email address, urging those who condemned him to make contact. "Please call me and after we have spoken and I have explained myself, we will be friends," he wrote. These awkward pleas for understanding failed to win over many hunters.

In early 2014, with Jeffrey Lendrum's presence at the magazine still eliciting threats of boycotts from advertisers and subscribers, Richard Lendrum informed his brother that he would have to let him go. It was a "horrific" moment for both of them, he would later acknowledge. Jeffrey felt abandoned, Richard mortified and angry that he had been given no choice but to cut his brother loose. But the survival of his business had to come first. Months later, still trying to put the controversy to rest, Richard Lendrum posted on AfricaHunting .com to reassure his readers that his generosity toward his sibling by no means implied sympathy for his crimes: Jeffrey Lendrum was a "wildlife trafficker," he acknowledged, and a "smuggler of falcon eggs." He insisted that he had nothing to do with his behavior and did not "support it in any way."

Losing his job at *African Hunting Gazette* was devastating for Jeffrey Lendrum. He sought steady employment, but his younger brother says that few opportunities were available in post-apartheid South Africa for a middle-aged white man, especially one with a felony conviction. For a while he tried a variation of his old hustle from before the days of AfricaXtreme. Reaching out to dealers in the United States and Europe, he procured spare parts for four-seat Cessna 172 Skyhawks and other single-engine planes and distributed them to aircraft-maintenance companies in South Africa. But the work was irregular, and provided him only a meager living. On an affidavit that he would later file with the police, he reported a monthly income of between $1,000 and $2,000, $500 of which went toward rent.

Bleak as things were, he found ways of keeping his connection to the natural world. He managed, somehow, to obtain an Honorary Ranger Certificate from South Africa's department of national parks, allowing him to participate in a volunteer program to place identification rings on owls, hawks, and other wild birds to study their life cycles, habits, and movements.

Richard Lendrum says that he lost track of his brother soon after his forced departure from *African Hunting Gazette*. Jeffrey Lendrum's calls to Andy McWilliam stopped, too. And so Richard Lendrum, Andy McWilliam, and everyone else in Jeffrey Lendrum's orbit were surprised some months later by the news reports from the other side of the world. Lendrum, it seemed, was in trouble again.

SIXTEEN

PATAGONIA

Early one morning in October 2015, at the start of spring in the southern hemisphere, a rented four-by-four departed the Chilean outpost of Punta Arenas and headed north across the bleak, wind-swept prairie known as the Patagonian Steppe. The vehicle followed La Ruta del Fin del Mundo, the Highway at the End of the World, a two-lane asphalt strip bordered to the west by fenced cattle and sheep ranches, and to the east by the icy blue waters of the Strait of Magellan. It passed the ghostly remains of an estancia abandoned a century ago, and a rusting freighter that had run aground in the 1930s. Lesser rheas—gray, flightless birds resembling ostriches—scurried away amid clouds of dust. Guanacos—alpaca-like wild grazers with brown fur and pale bellies—placidly munched the hardy yellow grass known as *coirón*. After two hours the asphalt ran out, and a gravel track wound through bush-covered hills. Then, just south of Chile's border with Argentina, Jeffrey Lendrum arrived at his destination: Pali Aike National Park, marked by a solitary green ranger hut with a sign welcoming visitors.

The indigenous Tehuelche tribe, hunter-gatherers who migrated to southern Patagonia after the glaciers receded ten thousand years ago, called Pali Aike both "the desolate place of bad spirits" and "the devil's country." The terrain is studded with volcanoes formed during the Jurassic era 100 million years ago by the collision of the Chile Rise and the Peru-Chile oceanic trench. A series of eruptions—the first taking place 3.8 million years ago, the most recent 15,000 years ago—covered the steppe with spills of black lava and parapets of basalt, which glow yellow, red, and greenish gray in the harsh desert sunlight. Half a dozen collapsed craters loom over the yellow plain like broken teeth.

Despite the otherworldly bleakness, the thirty-one-square-mile reserve teems with wildlife: hares, armadillos, gray foxes, pumas, guanacos, skunks, mole-like rodents known as tuco-tucos, and birds unique to Patagonia. Chilean flamingos, splashes of pink and orange in a charred landscape, gather in the park's salt lagoons. Colonies of buff-necked ibises, large rodent eaters with cream-and-russet throats and long, curving gray bills, build nests high in trees or inside the extinct volcanoes—sharing the ledges with peregrine falcons, in a relationship of mutual coexistence rare among birds of prey.

The raptors were what Lendrum had come for. After the loss of his job at the *African Hunting Gazette* eighteen months before, Lendrum had tried his hand at selling airplane parts. It had not worked out as he'd hoped, and now he had returned to the enterprise that he knew best. He had arrived in Chile at the height of the southern hemisphere's breeding season in pursuit of the eggs of one of the world's rarest birds of prey: the pallid peregrine, a snowy-white-breasted raptor found only in the wilds of the Patagonian mainland, the Falkland Islands, and Tierra del Fuego, an archipelago of hundreds of islands, many covered with volcanoes, mountains, and glaciers, at the southernmost tip of South America. Scientists had not even set eyes on the bird until 1925, when a *pallido* captured by Patagonian otter hunters near the Strait of Magellan ended up in a zoo in Münster, Germany. Otto Kleinschmidt, Germany's best-known ornithologist, triumphantly proclaimed that he had identified a hitherto unknown species, and gave it the scientific name *Falco kreyenborgi*, after Hermann Kreyenborg, the falconer who had first brought it to his attention. But field researchers in Patagonia later found the white-breasted raptors sharing nests with southern peregrine falcons, most of which have black-barred, light gray breast feathers. In 1981, scientists confirmed that the pallid falcon was a genetic fluke—a rare pale morph of the southern peregrine, the *Falco peregrinus cassini*.

=

As Lendrum slipped back into a life of crime, he had no idea that someone was watching him. Two weeks before Lendrum's arrival at the southern tip of Patagonia, the night watchman at the Hotel Plaza in Punta Arenas, Chile's southernmost city and a gateway to the Antarctic, had approached Nicolas Fernández, a young mountaineer and wilderness guide who was working part-time at the reception desk. A large black backpack had been gathering dust for a year in the storage room of the hotel, a 1920s French-neoclassical mansion built by a cattle ranching baron and overlooking the leafy Plaza de Armas. Nobody had claimed the luggage, and the guard wondered whether they could see if anything inside was worth taking. Fernández agreed that the pack had been abandoned, and said he thought that it would be fine to open it.

On their hands and knees in the storage room, the two hotel employees searched through the contents with growing curiosity: a pair of cargo pants, a pair of jeans, a six-hundred-foot-long coiled climbing rope, a two-pronged steel hook for grasping tree branches, and a black-and-yellow, shoe-box-sized device with a transparent door and an electrical cord, manufactured by Brinsea in the United Kingdom. After bringing the rope home with him to use on his next glacier expedition, Fernández searched the Internet and discovered that the piece of equipment from Brinsea was an incubator. The owner, Fernández surmised, must have come to Patagonia the previous year to steal the eggs of wild birds. But who was he? The backpack had no identification tag, and nobody in the Hotel Plaza could remember the owner's name.

Two days later, a man called from South Africa to make a reservation.

He needed a room for eight nights, he told Fernández, who was again working behind the reception desk. Then the man informed the clerk that he had left a black backpack behind during the week that he had stayed at the hotel in October 2014, with the expectation of retrieving it on his next visit.

"Is it still there?"

"Yes, we're holding it for you," Fernández replied, astonished by the timing of the call. After the caller hung up, Fernández typed his name, "Jeffrey Lendrum," into Google.

Fernández's first hit was a YouTube video of Lendrum toying with an Egyptian cobra in the bush. Next came Lendrum dangling from a helicopter in Quebec. *What kind of guy is this?* he wondered. Fernández typed in "Jeffrey Lendrum egg smuggler" and came up with five thousand hits. His concern mounting, the clerk read about the arrest at Birmingham Airport, the conviction and jail sentence, the gyrfalcon-egg-stealing escapade in Canada, and the 1984 trial for theft in Zimbabwe. The Internet had destroyed whatever anonymity Lendrum had once enjoyed on his egg-plundering capers. There on the first page of hits was Andy McWilliam of Britain's National Wildlife Crime Unit calling his quarry an international wildlife smuggler who worked "at the highest global level of wildlife crime." Guy Shorrock of the Royal Society for the Protection of Birds had told the BBC that Lendrum was "the highest level of wildlife criminal." Half a dozen newspapers, Fernández noted with alarm, had described the Irish national and South African resident as a "former member of the Rhodesian SAS."

Lendrum's reservation at the hotel began on October 13, one week away. Unsure what to do, Fernández returned the climbing rope to Lendrum's black backpack and consulted a longtime friend and former policeman, who urged him to reach out to Chile's Agriculture and Livestock Service (SAG), the government agency responsible for protecting the country's wildlife. The hotel clerk explained what he had uncovered to SAG representatives in Punta Arenas and Santiago. He mentioned that Lendrum appeared to have an elite military background. "I'm uneasy about this and hope that you could be discreet in your actions," he wrote in an email, concerned for his own safety. His contacts at the Agriculture and Livestock Service and, later, the police, advised him to watch Lendrum, remain calm, and avoid revealing to the egg thief what he knew. Maybe they could catch him in the act.

=

At the entrance to Pali Aike National Park, Lendrum paid the gatekeeper three thousand Chilean pesos (about $4.50), drove on for a couple of miles, and parked at the trailhead leading to an extinct volcano called Morada del Diablo, "the Devil's Dwelling." Carrying a backpack filled with rope, spikes, a harness, and carabiners, he set out on foot on a dirt trail that cut through a fifteen-thousand-year-old field of congealed black lava. The collapsed crater, otherwise known as a caldera, loomed directly ahead of him. Small black lizards covered with white speckles skittered over the rocks; when I retraced Lendrum's steps three years later, the skeletal remains of guanacos killed by pumas baked beneath the morning sun. He passed nobody—hardly surprising, considering that the park attracts an average of only eight visitors a day.

After a mile's hike he began a steep climb over loose gray stones, and emerged at the top of the caldera. Perched behind a guardrail at the edge of the drop-off, with pillars of basaltic lava behind him, Lendrum looked across the maw of the dead volcano. A curving wall of basaltic rock—tinted green, splattered with whitewash, and riven with fissures—formed the remnant of the volcano's lip. Steep slopes of gray scree and soil laden with red-tinted hematite fell away into the abyss, and the cries of buff-necked ibises echoed off the wall. Moments after I made the same climb, a peregrine rose, plummeted into the crater, circled back up, and disappeared inside a crevice.

Lendrum spotted an aerie, fastened a rope, and rappelled down the wall. He worked his way toward the nest, his excitement rising. But as he landed on the ledge, Lendrum identified the raptor as an ordinary cassini, not the rare pallid morph that he was seeking. He left the Morada del Diablo, one of most spectacular places he had ever climbed, exhilarated but empty-handed.

Even so, there were many more places for aeries in the rugged Patagonian landscape. He followed a dirt road through the pampas to a line of sixty-foot cliffs overlooking Posession Bay, an inlet between the mainland and the Isla Grande, the largest island of the Tierra del Fuego archipelago. The gray-sand beach below was deserted, except for a few plywood shanties inhabited by fishermen. (When I visited the area in 2018, one informed me that he had often seen a pair of the legendary *peregrino pallido* nesting on the rock face.) Lendrum hiked along a beach strewn with mussel shells, scanning the sky and the cliffs—some of them bare, some blanketed in scrub and dwarf pine. "Basically you've got to know what you're looking for, or you won't see them, because there are so many sea birds there," Lendrum would later say. "Someone who's never seen a peregrine could find a couple of nests in a day or two in the Rhondda Valley. Here it was a lot harder." A 2002 study by the Raptor Research Foundation noted that the pallid peregrines are especially difficult to spot, "being less conspicuous and gull-like when seen beneath gray, overcast skies."

Waves lapped gently over the shoal just offshore, and the sky abounded with southern giant petrels, oystercatchers, southern lapwings, cinnamon-bellied ground tyrants, austral negritos, and upland geese. It seemed like a proverbial needle-in-a-haystack search, but Lendrum soon spotted a pair of *pallidos* and they led him to what he was looking for: their clutch of four mottled brown eggs, nestled on a ledge halfway up the rock face. He carefully wrapped the prizes and carried them back to the Hotel Plaza in Punta Arenas, a two-hour drive south.

=

From behind the desk in the wood-paneled hotel lobby, up a steep flight of stairs from the street, Nicolas Fernández quietly observed Lendrum's comings and goings. He watched Lendrum leave with his large black backpack in the early mornings and return in the evenings, his clothing soiled and sweaty. He'd helped him move into a spacious room on the top floor of the hotel, hauling a second piece of luggage, a duffel bag, up two flights of stairs and feeling the hard, square edges of what he was certain was another incubator inside. Because Fernández spoke fluent English, Lendrum approached him regularly for advice. What restaurants would he recommend? Where in Punta Arenas could he get a down jacket repaired? Where could he hire a helicopter and fly to Rio Grande on the Isla Grande, in the far south of Argentina? "He was a nice, friendly guy, always wandering around the hotel," Fernández would later say. Yet despite his easygoing demeanor, the staff was on edge, having been informed of Lendrum's history by Fernández. "Every employee knew that he was up to no good, but we didn't want to say anything," Fernández recalled. "We were scared."

After a few days, Lendrum was relaxed enough to invite Fernández into his room, a sunlit chamber with French windows overlooking a Renaissance-style cathedral. Ropes and incubators lay strewn across the floor. Fernández pretended not to notice. Later, Lendrum emailed Fernández his travel itinerary and asked him to print out a hard copy. Fernández did so—and immediately forwarded the itinerary to SAG headquarters in Santiago, and the police.

SAG Director Rafael Asenjo saw that the convicted wildlife criminal was planning to fly on LATAM Airlines from Punta Arenas to Santiago in the early morning of October 21. In Santiago he would connect to São Paulo, Brazil, arriving at five-thirty p.m. From there he would continue on to Dubai. Detaining Lendrum in Santiago, Asenjo knew, would be problematic: SAG agents had no experience arresting smugglers of wild bird eggs. At worst, their actions could tip off Lendrum and give him time to dispose of his contraband—or the officers might inadvertently manhandle and kill the unhatched chicks. So Asenjo came up with another solution.

On the morning of Lendrum's departure, Asenjo contacted the Management Authority of the Convention on International Trade in Endangered Species in Brasília, the Brazilian capital. "We received the following communication about a probable case of wild egg trafficking on the part of a foreigner who is about to enter your country," he wrote in the email. "I'm sending you the accusation so that you can take all the necessary actions." Asenjo attached Nicolas Fernández's original message and Lendrum's itinerary. The authority passed the alert to the Brazilian Institute of the Environment and Renewable Natural Resources (IBAMA), the wildlife protection police. IBAMA dispatched two experienced officers to Guarulhos International Airport to await Lendrum's arrival.

Lendrum, completely unaware of the trap being set for him, checked out of the Hotel Plaza at dawn on October 21 and caught the flight to Santiago. He carried the four eggs in socks tied off with cords and concealed in the pockets of his fleece. In Santiago, Lendrum walked through the metal detector at the security checkpoint separating the domestic arrivals wing and international departures without setting off an alarm. He boarded the flight to São Paulo, landed at Guarulhos in the early evening, and entered the Emirates Lounge to await his flight to Dubai. Inside the shower room, Lendrum transferred the eggs, still wrapped in socks, to a battery-powered yellow Brinsea incubator that he kept in a carry-on bag. Then, around 8:30, as he prepared to board his flight, he hit a snag: security agents diverted him before the gate and ran his bags through an X-ray scanner. The four eggs were clearly visible. Two green-uniformed wildlife policemen descended on him. The IBAMA agents examined the incubator and removed the four mottled brown eggs from their socks.

"They're chicken eggs," Lendrum insisted. The wildlife officers summoned the federal police, who placed Lendrum under arrest.

Then, for the first time in his entanglements with authorities around the world, the falcon thief lost his composure. Almost as soon as he arrived in his airport holding cell, he complained of heart palpitations. Perhaps the realization of the criminal proceedings that lay ahead had had a physiological effect. Rushed to a nearby hospital, Lendrum was given an electrocardiogram, an examination by a heart specialist, and medication for chest pains. Then he was turned back over to police custody.

Experts would positively identify the eggs and transport them to a birds-of-prey center outside São Paulo. From there they would be hand-carried back to Patagonia and reintroduced to the wild, where only one would survive.

Meanwhile, a federal court judge in Guarulhos confiscated Lendrum's passport, set a trial date for late November, and released the multiple offender on eight thousand reais ($2,100) bail.

=

As he stepped into the crowded streets of Guarulhos in the tropical heat, Lendrum found himself in a predicament. Alone and unable to speak a word of Portuguese, he was stranded in Brazil's thirteenth-largest city, an unlovely sprawl of highway overpasses, shantytown favelas, factories, and traffic-choked boulevards. He was a multiple offender with the threat of a long incarceration in a foreign prison hanging over him. After all the ups and downs of Lendrum's last few years, nothing had prepared him for this.

He took a room at the Hotel Sables—a seven-story, $80-a-night hotel on the Avenida Salgado Filho, a busy thoroughfare—to wait out the month until his trial. The Guarulhos Federal Court had offered Lendrum a public defender, but the attorney spoke only Portuguese, so Lendrum had declined his services. As luck would have it, the young receptionist at the Sables mentioned that his father had a law practice a few blocks away, and spoke English. Lendrum went to see him that afternoon.

Rodrigo Tomei was a friendly, bearded attorney in his early forties with an easygoing manner and a command of idiomatic English. In 1990 Tomei's father, an airline pilot and union activist, had moved his family to Calgary, Alberta, to escape persecution by Brazil's military dictatorship. Tomei, who was then seventeen, had stayed in Canada for seven years—including a two-year stint in the army—before returning to Brazil after the end of military rule.

"They caught me with chicken eggs," Lendrum told the attorney.

"Look, man," replied Tomei, who had read the arrest report. "If I'm going to represent you I need to know the truth."

At their third meeting, Lendrum admitted that he'd been smuggling peregrine eggs, but refused to answer Tomei's questions about their intended recipients in the Middle East. When Tomei pressed him about his 2010 arrest at Birmingham Airport, Lendrum fell back on his standard explanation: "I wasn't trafficking the birds, I was rescuing them." The falcon eggs he had taken in southern Wales had been "dying because of pesticides," he said. "But the British authorities didn't believe me."

"The Brazilians are not going to believe you, either," Tomei replied. Plead guilty, he advised his client, and take a shorter sentence.

But Lendrum was certain, recalls Tomei, that "he could convince

the judge that he was innocent." Under oath in a courtroom in Guarulhos, Lendrum insisted, through an interpreter, that he was just
a bird-watcher. He claimed that he had taken the four eggs to save
them after finding the corpse of their mother lying near the nest,
and explained that the three incubators seized from his luggage by
the police belonged to an American photographer friend who had
used them to keep his cameras warm in the frosty Patagonian climate. He swore that he had visited Dubai just once in his life—a
sightseeing trip to the Burj Khalifa skyscraper, the world's tallest
building. Judge Paulo Marcos Rodrigues de Almeida called his testimony "laughable" and handed down the harshest possible sentence
for violating Brazil's Environmental Crimes Act: four years and six
months in prison. The defendant could remain free on bail pending
his appeal, but he would have to appear before the court secretary
every two months to register his address and account for his activities. He was also ordered to pay a fine of forty thousand reais, or
$10,500.

=

Tomei received the twenty-six-page judgment in December via an
alert sent to the online mailbox he maintained as a member of the
Brazilian Order of Attorneys. (Under Brazilian law, neither a defendant nor his counsel is required to be present for the verdict or the
sentencing.) The lawyer informed Lendrum on WhatsApp that he
had "some news" about his case. "Let's have coffee and talk about
it," he suggested.

When Tomei translated the court decision, Lendrum blinked a
few times and seemed about to cry.

"Look, we knew you would get convicted. It was a question of how much jail time you would get," Tomei said. The next step, he told Lendrum, trying to give him some hope, was filing an appeal. "We're not going to reverse the verdict, but we can try to reduce the sentence."

Where would he serve his time? Lendrum asked.

The Penitenciária Cabo PM Marcelo Pires da Silva, Tomei replied, in the remote town of Itaí, about 190 miles west of São Paulo. Nicknamed the "Tower of Babel," Marcelo Pires da Silva had opened in 2000 exclusively for foreigners, after disgruntled Brazilian prisoners in other jails had threatened to kill international inmates in an effort to embarrass the government. A total of 1,443 detainees of eighty-nine nationalities were incarcerated there by 2011, according to the Brazilian magazine *Veja*. "During [downtime] in Itaí, it is possible to see kipa-wearing Jews conversing in Hebrew," *Veja* reported, "Lithuanian and Dutch doing sit-ups, Peruvians playing dominoes surrounded by other Latinos and a Muslim kneeling toward Mecca to do one of his five daily prayers." Eighty percent of the inmates were reportedly doing time for drug trafficking. Marcelo Pires da Silva was not the worst prison in Brazil's notoriously violent and overcrowded penal system, but it was hardly an easy place. "Sometimes not even a mattress is available to you . . . You should also be aware that the conditions of toilets and showers are extremely poor," the British Consular Network in Brazil wrote in an information pack for British prisoners. Serious illnesses often went untreated: "The system is relatively overwhelmed [so] people can wait up to 12 months for a doctor's appointment."

Lendrum told Tomei that he was considering fleeing the country.

"If you're going to do something like that, I don't want to know about it," Tomei says he told him.

=

And then, just when it seemed that things could not possibly get any worse for Jeffrey Lendrum, they did.

One morning in January, shortly after learning the verdict, Lendrum awoke in the Sables Hotel in excruciating pain. A gaping wound the size of an eight ball had appeared overnight on his thigh. Alarmed, a hotel employee rushed Lendrum to a public hospital in Guarulhos. Finding nobody who spoke English, Lendrum handed Tomei's business card to a hospital social worker, and she summoned the attorney to serve as an interpreter. Physicians determined that the wound was probably the bite of a poisonous spider that had crept into his bed and attacked him while he slept.

Doctors and nurses administered painkillers and a powerful antibiotic intravenously, and advised Lendrum to remain at the hospital under supervision for one week. "There was a danger that the toxin would infect his nervous system," said Tomei, who stayed by his bedside. "He was having heart failure. He almost died." But Lendrum ignored the doctors' advice. After three days, he hobbled back to the hotel, and started self-medicating with antibiotic tablets from a pharmacy. Still, the infection was so severe that he remained weak and in frequent pain, and his wound would not heal.

"I had nothing but shit in Brazil," Lendrum would later say.

When Michelle Conway, a longtime friend from the United Kingdom, reached out to ask where Lendrum had been for so many months, he said only that a sightseeing trip in Brazil had gone awry. A rare tropical spider had bitten him, he explained, and the airline, fearing that the infection was "contagious," had refused to allow him to board a plane home to Johannesburg. Howard Waller, who had broken off contact with Lendrum after his arrest at Birmingham Airport, received an email from him around this time, asking if he could borrow $20,000. "Then I saw an article on the Internet about this guy who had been caught with eggs in Brazil," he said, "and then I thought, 'You're asking me for *money*?'"

Soon afterward, Lendrum disappeared again.

=

Lendrum knew what he had to do. He prepared a backpack, checked out of the hotel, and traveled hundreds of miles south to the edge of the country, near Iguaçu Falls. "I knew that I was going to die in that prison," he would later explain, "so I got resourceful." Carrying a GPS and a day's supply of food and water, he slipped past border police and walked "a couple of kilometers through the jungle" into Argentina. The journey, he said, took him "most of a day." That, anyway, is Lendrum's version of how he eluded Brazilian justice. Tomei says that Lendrum was too weak to escape on foot, and theorizes that the egg thief might have taken advantage of lax immigration controls between the two economically integrated neighbors, and crossed the official border without presenting a passport. "Nobody was looking for him, so there was no need for him to sneak anywhere," Tomei said. "He could have just taken a bus."

Once safely in Argentina, Lendrum traveled 780 miles south to Buenos Aires. In the Argentine capital he appeared at the Embassy of Ireland, claiming that he had lost his passport, and was issued a new one. (He had obtained Irish citizenship some years earlier through his great-grandfather.) Then, from Ministro Pistarini Airport, Lendrum flew home to Johannesburg.

Half a year after Lendrum's disappearance, Tomei received a

WhatsApp message from his missing client. "Hey Rodrigo, I'm in South Africa seeing my doctor," Lendrum announced. "My wound is slowly getting better. How's the appeal going?" Tomei replied that he still hadn't gotten an answer.

On October 24, 2016, the Brazilian Superior Tribunal rejected the appeal and ordered Lendrum to surrender immediately. "There's nothing else we can do," Tomei messaged Lendrum. But Lendrum didn't return. Brazilian authorities soon announced that Lendrum had jumped bail, and the British media picked up the news. "Ex-SAS Rare Egg Thief Who Tried to Smuggle Birds Through Birmingham Airport on the Run," the *Birmingham Mail* declared, still buying into the fiction about Lendrum's elite Rhodesian army career. "Britain's Most Protected Bird Under Threat From SAS-Trained Wildlife Hunter," proclaimed the *Daily Mirror*.

If he tried to return to Brazil, Tomei told him, he would be arrested the moment he stepped off the plane. Lendrum decided to lie low.

SEVENTEEN

GAUTENG

In May 2017, shortly after my trip to Wales, I reached out to Paul Mullin for help tracking Jeffrey Lendrum down. Friends had told him that Lendrum was holed up at a rented home in the Johannesburg area. Rumors were circulating that Brazilian authorities had requested that Interpol, the international organization that links the police forces of 190 countries, issue a Red Notice requesting his extradition. That would place Lendrum in a select club of fugitives including Roman Polanski, Julian Assange, and Vorayuth "Boss" Yoovidhya, the thirty-two-year-old heir to the Red Bull fortune who is on the run from Thai authorities after fatally running over a Bangkok policeman with his Ferrari. But South Africa has no extradition treaty with Brazil for wildlife smuggling, and nobody appeared to be hunting for Lendrum. Mullin gave me a cell phone number, and I reached Lendrum on the first try.

I introduced myself as a journalist who had just spent a day with Andy McWilliam in the Rhondda Valley. I had hoped that dropping the investigator's name would make him more receptive to my intrusion, but whatever affection Lendrum once had for the wildlife cop had curdled into resentment. "Andy McWilliam is telling people that I was selling birds for a fortune, and that I had become a multi-millionaire," he told me. "The whole press has portrayed me as the Pablo Escobar of the falcon egg trade. Everybody writes absolute rubbish about me."

McWilliam had blown the case out of proportion, he insisted, to exaggerate the importance of the National Wildlife Crime Unit. In their meeting at Hewell Prison, Lendrum claimed, McWilliam had offered his condolences for his father's death—and then confessed that Lendrum's arrest and conviction had been like "manna from heaven" for the unit. (McWilliam would call Lendrum's accusation "complete and utter rubbish.") Lendrum brought up Michael Upson, a Suffolk constable convicted in 2012 of amassing 649 rare birds' eggs and given a fourteen-week suspended sentence and 150 hours of community service. "I got two and a half years in prison. How unfair is that?" he said. McWilliam had apparently become a scape-goat for all of the disastrous turns his life had taken since his arrest at Birmingham Airport in May 2010.

I asked Lendrum if I could visit him, and he told me that he would consider it. But when I called him back a few days later, he told me that he had just been diagnosed with prostate cancer and was about to begin radiation treatment. He didn't feel up for talking further.

Seven months later, I flew to Southern Africa, with a plan to retrace Lendrum's footsteps and make one more attempt to talk to him face-to-face. I wanted to understand the roots of his obsession with birds of prey and see whether the falcon thief would finally take responsibility for what he had done. I wanted to ask him about the appeal of the outlaw life, and why he kept raiding nests around the world despite his growing profile and the increasing likelihood that he would be caught. And, yes, I hoped to persuade him to talk about the Arab connection.

My first stop on the journey was Bulawayo, Lendrum's hometown. Most of the white community had fled the lush, now-down-at-the-heels city, driven out by Robert Mugabe's destructive policies—the forceful seizures of white-owned farms by war veterans and ruling party cronies in the early 2000s, the collapse of agriculture and then the whole economy, the rampant corruption, the uncontrolled printing of money that in 2008 sent inflation soaring to 80 billion percent in a single month, wiping out the value of pensions . . . But Peggy Lendrum was still there, living in a retirement village not far from the house in Hillside where Jeffrey had grown up. She was mortified, I was told, by her son's crimes and global notoriety. "She is very stressed, brought on by Jeffrey's lack of transparency, not to mention his lifestyle," Julia Dupree, a family friend, emailed me before my arrival, informing me that Peggy had cautiously agreed to, then turned down, my request to meet with her. "How she remains sane I have no idea."

Lendrum had been through months earlier, Dupree told me, weakened by his treatments for prostate cancer and professing remorse. He'd announced his intention to build a memorial to Val Gargett for all the trouble he'd caused her. Yet during the same visit he had tried, without success, to obtain a list of nest locations from the curator of the bird egg collections at Bulawayo's Natural History Museum, and had asked to join a raptor survey in Matobo National Park—a request the ornithological society had rejected. "What f****** audacity!" Pat Lorber emailed me when I told her about Lendrum's entreaty. "Doesn't he realize how discredited he is?"

The African Black Eagle Survey was still going, nearly sixty years after the study's start, though its participants had dwindled to a handful of elderly volunteers. John Brebner, the current head of the project, agreed to take me on a search for nests inside Matobo. Beforehand, he had me sign an agreement pledging not to give away the locations of the black eagle aeries. "You're sworn to secrecy," said Brebner, a genial onetime cattle rancher turned pesticide salesman. The precaution was the most obvious legacy of the Lendrums' betrayals.

Early one morning in December, the height of the warm, dry season, we set off with Brebner's wife, Jen, in his four-by-four and headed down a potholed tarmac highway through the bush. The Zimbabwe Defence Forces had driven Mugabe from office two weeks earlier following months of escalating tensions between the ninety-three-year-old president's power-hungry wife, Grace, and the vice president, Emmerson Mnangagwa. Now Mugabe was sidelined with his wife at his villa in Harare, and some of the indignities of life under an increasingly incompetent dictator were already being addressed. For the last two years of Mugabe's rule, police checkpoints had lined this road—manned by hungry cops owed back wages who cited drivers for fake violations and extorted small fees. The day after Mugabe's forced resignation, the new president, Mnangagwa, had ordered all such roadblocks in the country removed.

John and Jen Brebner and I entered Matobo through the main gate, and bounced over a rough dirt track. Scanning a fissure-ridden cliff one hundred feet high, my guide pointed to a huge spherical bundle of twigs and branches inside a horizontal crevice seventy feet up. "That's a fairly new black eagle nest, only six or seven years old," Brebner told me. "There's one in the park that's been here for thirty-eight years." I tried to imagine young Jeffrey Lendrum rappelling down to a rock fissure like this one, disappearing into the giant stick nest, and fishing out the precious eagle eggs, excited by the adventure, the strangeness, the illicitness, and the secrecy of it all. Brebner pointed to a regal creature nearby, perched at eye level on the branch of a thorn tree. Its sharply hooked black beak, orange body, barred plumage, ruffled reddish crown, massive black-feathered legs, and fearsome talons identified it as a crowned eagle, one of the rarest raptors in the park. "They hunt in the canopy and they will take anything—black vervet monkeys, dassies, even a baby klippie [antelope]," he said. I wondered how many crowned-eagle eggs snatched by Lendrum here had ended up in the hands of birds-of-prey enthusiasts in Europe and the Middle East—and how many more eagles might have populated the park had it not been for him.

=

Through friends of Lendrum's family, I learned that the falcon thief's life had continued to disintegrate. He had broken up with his longtime girlfriend (Mullin's ex-partner) several years earlier, had no job, and was living in a rented bungalow near Pretoria, an hour north of Johannesburg. His treatments for his cancer had weakened him, and in mid-2017 someone had broadsided his vehicle at an intersection after dark, leaving him badly injured. Whatever money he had made from his falcon smuggling—and Mullin and others insist that it wasn't much—had apparently been spent long ago. Lendrum had gone from being a swaggering outlaw to suffering as the victim of a self-destructive obsession. "He's got a very tough life," Richard Lendrum told me when I met him at a coffee shop in an affluent neighborhood in northern Johannesburg. "Nothing great at all."

I asked the younger Lendrum, a trim man in his early fifties with chiseled features and fine lines around his eyes, to speculate about what had driven his brother into a life of crime. "We both love wildlife, it's just that he's gone down a slightly different path," he said with a pained smile. "It's a high adventure, high adrenaline way of eking out a living. It's just gone a little wrong." Richard had learned much over the years about his brother's egg-thieving business, but he was parsimonious with the details. "Obviously, there are breeders that . . . get intermediaries to do their dirty work for them. That's the reality. They will do anything to get birds around the world," he told me. When I prodded him, he named Howard Waller and Arab royals as his brother's clients, and warned me about approaching them: "What would you think if your world was going to be exposed and it may affect you, your family, your livelihood, and your potential future earnings?"

Richard said that he was trying to provide some direction to his brother's life and wean him off his criminal behavior. Jeffrey Lendrum was part owner of an old Cessna single-engine airplane, and had been attempting, so far unsuccessfully, to raise enough money to repair the plane and hire it out for charter flights. "I try to help him out, offering guidance and a brotherly perspective," Richard said. "But the main thing is that he's trying to come back from his cancer, and that's the focus, getting healthy." Lendrum doubted his brother would talk to me. He had ambitions to write a memoir and he didn't want to give away trade secrets. And, Richard said, his brother knew that if he revealed anything about his Middle Eastern royal partners, he could be endangering himself. "He's not going to go and squeal," he told me. "He's aware of how powerful these people are."

"And you think that Jeff is afraid of them?" I asked.

"I know that he is," he said.

=

Two hours after meeting Richard Lendrum, I reached Jeffrey Lendrum on the phone. I was flying out of South Africa that evening, I told him. This would be my last opportunity to hear his side of the story. Could he meet me for an hour?

Lendrum hesitated, and then, to my surprise, he said yes. He directed me to meet him at the Featherbrooke Shopping Centre in Roodepoort, a city a bit north of Johannesburg in Gauteng, formerly known as Transvaal, the smallest, richest, and most densely populated province in South Africa. I should look for an Ocean Basket seafood restaurant, next to an indoor ice-skating rink. (Lendrum had a particular fondness for the seafood chain: it was in another Ocean Basket in the late 1990s that he had proposed to Mullin that they go into business together selling African handicrafts.) He would be waiting for me at the entrance.

An Uber driver picked me up at my guesthouse in Johannesburg and took me across the parched plains and low rolling hills of the Highveld, past farms, tin-roofed shacks, and bus stops. It was a hazy summer day, and the temperature had climbed into the high eighties. He dropped me off outside a sprawling commercial complex, and I found an Ocean Basket. But I saw no sign of a skating rink—or of Lendrum.

Lendrum was apologetic when I called him minutes later. He had sent me to the wrong shopping mall. "My short-term memory is failing," he said. He blamed the mistake on the side effects of his cancer treatment—and, indirectly, on South Africa's growing middle class. "They're putting up so many of these malls all over Gauteng, with 'feathers' and 'brooks' and 'meadows' in the names. I can't keep them all straight," he told me. He had meant to send me to the Forest Hill City Mall in Centurion, a town formerly known as Verwoerdburg, after Hendrik Verwoerd, the architect of apartheid. I called for another Uber. The driver headed north for forty more minutes and let me out at the entrance to a massive structure near a highway interchange. Just inside I caught sight of the skating rink—and beside it, an Ocean Basket.

Lendrum walked up to me and stuck out his hand. "You probably recognized me from my photos," he said. His receding hairline, black-framed glasses, and orange-white-and-blue striped button-down shirt hanging loosely over a pair of khaki shorts made him look more like a clerk in a sporting-goods store than a daredevil adventurer. But after months of fighting prostate cancer, he was tanner and healthier-looking than I'd expected. "I haven't been doing anything, just trying to get better," he told me, sliding into a coffee-shop booth. "I haven't been well at all."

Lendrum took me through his exploits in Zimbabwe, Canada, Great Britain, Chile, and Brazil. When I pressed him to explain his crimes, he presented each egg heist as a well-meaning if overzealous rescue mission or a scientific expedition gone wrong. He told me his story persuasively, looking me in the eye. If I weren't already familiar with his pattern of falsehoods—if I hadn't seen Mullin's video from Canada and watched Lendrum tell lie after lie before a judge in his videotaped testimony in Brazil—I might have believed parts of it. Lendrum had ready explanations for all of his misfortunes, a long story of bad luck, miscarriages of justice, and victimhood. But so much still didn't add up. And one thing was clear: Lendrum had gotten sloppier. His last mission in South America had been almost comically inept: deliberately leaving a backpack filled with incriminating evidence for a year at his hotel, allowing the receptionist to see the ropes and incubators in his room, sharing his flight itinerary, and doing nothing to mask his identity. "He seems to be successful at stealing the birds' eggs, but not very successful in smuggling them out," Bob Elliot, head of investigations for the Royal Society for the Protection of Birds, had told the BBC following Lendrum's flight from Brazil. Lendrum himself admitted his planning had sometimes been less than meticulous. "The devil is in the details," he said with a shrug, when I asked him about the twenty minutes that he had stayed in the Emirates Lounge shower room in Birmingham without bothering to turn on the water, and the red-dyed egg he had discarded in the diaper bin.

But then again, there could be dozens of egg trafficking trips he'd made over the years that have gone undetected. Lendrum had traveled to Patagonia six times "as a tourist," he told me, in the decade before his South American misadventure, drawn, he said, by the region's majestic landscapes and the most bountiful and varied bird life on the planet. How many eggs might he have smuggled out with him?

"Weren't you taking a big risk by stealing eggs again?" I asked.

"I never thought that the hotel clerk in Chile would rummage through my stuff or that he'd Google me." It was, I thought, a remarkable display of cluelessness.

"And the prospect of jail didn't make you hesitate?"

"I honestly didn't think that there would be a problem if I were caught," he said, "maybe just a fine." That seemed disingenuous, or delusional, considering his recent imprisonment.

The discussion shifted to the memoir he wanted to write. I asked whether he planned to expose the wild falcon trade in the Middle East. "I can write about it," he said—acknowledging, for the first time, that the black market exists—"but I'd end up in a tunnel somewhere—killed."

I asked if he really believed his former clients were that dangerous.

"Things happen," he said darkly. "I don't know the ramifications, I could say this and they could take out my sister." He also didn't trust that Britain's National Wildlife Crime Unit or Middle Eastern governments would do anything with the information. "What do I gain out of it by besmirching a royal figure?" he asked. "All I will do is get my fifteen minutes of fame, and it will be forgotten about." Nothing significant, he was certain, would come from his naming names.

I wondered whether Lendrum was deliberately exaggerating the threat he faced in order to pump up the drama of his life, but Andy McWilliam wouldn't dismiss the danger out of hand. Lendrum had never shared such fears with McWilliam, the investigator told me, "but there could be something in what he says."

I felt sorry for Lendrum in some ways. Charming, energetic, resourceful, intelligent, and passionate about birds of prey, he could, as the Zimbabwean professor Peter Mundy had observed in the ornithological magazine *Honeyguide*, have probably made a noteworthy career in academics, field research, or wildlife conservation. But he was conflicted between his love for animals and his need to possess them. Driven by the thrill of the chase, by a juvenile need to break the rules, and by his ambition to be seen as a globe-trotting daredevil—and by financial incentives as well—he had followed a twisted path into this South African cul-de-sac. Now, despised by conservationists, fearful of his handlers, broke, and sick, he had lost almost everything.

=

"Do you imagine that there will be a time when you will get back to egg collecting?" I asked. We had been talking at the Forest Hill City Mall for nearly two hours, and Lendrum was growing restless. He had an appointment to speak to a friend about the charter airline company he was trying to get off the ground. I knew it was time to end the meeting.

He said he doubted that he would return to the field. He was on the run from Brazil, had been banned from Dubai, wasn't welcome in Canada, couldn't travel to the United States (for reasons he never explained), and was under scrutiny in the United Kingdom. Besides, he wasn't the formidable outdoorsman that he'd once been. "I'm getting too old for it," he said. "Look at me." Prostate cancer had depleted his energy, and the car wreck had damaged the nerves in his neck and limbs.

We said our goodbyes. Lendrum shook my hand and moved slowly off. Then, before disappearing around the corner, he turned and hit me with a proposition. "Do you want to steal some eggs sometime?" he asked, grinning. "We'll go into the Rhondda Valley and see how many peregrines we can get—right under Andy McWilliam's nose. You do the climbing. We'll make millions."

It was, I thought, all bluster and self-mockery. Lendrum's egg snatching days were finally behind him. But I turned out to be wrong.

EPILOGUE

On June 21, 2018, I was sitting in a stifling auditorium, watching my oldest son's graduation ceremony at the John F. Kennedy International School in Berlin, when my iPhone went off in my pocket. The caller's ID had been blocked, and, over the valedictorian's amplified speech I heard a muffled voice with a South African accent speaking my name. I didn't register who it was. "I'm at my son's graduation," I told the caller. "I'll have to call you back."

Only after hanging up did I realize that it must have been Lendrum, calling to chat, as he had done periodically in recent months, about peregrine falcons and pigeon fanciers, a proposed trip with me to Matobo National Park, my impending visit to South America, or some questions I had about his childhood. Minutes later I found a message in my in-box:

"Call if you want. Cheers jeff."

"Sorry Jeff!" I typed back. "I just couldn't make out who it was. Will call when I get home." In spite of Lendrum's long history of environmental pillaging, and his many attempts to bamboozle me, I, like McWilliam, had found it hard not to like him. He was cheerful, garrulous, and full of energy. His lying was so transparent that it made it easier to shrug off. His haplessness in recent years also made him seem less toxic: he was the thief who couldn't steal straight. Talking to Lendrum at length had made me realize something else, too: he was always dancing on the edge of a confession, as if prevaricating so consistently for so long had worn him out.

Distractions came up, and it wasn't until four days later that I finally got around to ringing Lendrum's cell.

The phone was off.

I tried the next day, and couldn't get through. That was unusual: Lendrum hadn't let his phone go unanswered for so long before. Three more attempts over the next several days went directly to voice mail.

It didn't take me long to discover where Lendrum was.

On June 29, the British Home Office issued a press release: "Rare Bird Eggs Importation Prevented by Border Force at Heathrow." Three days earlier a passenger from South Africa identified as a "56-year-old Irish national" had aroused the suspicion of Border Force agents. They had stopped him, searched him, and discovered seventeen eggs from endangered birds of prey—African fish eagles, black sparrow hawks, Cape vultures, and African hawk eagles, similar to crowned eagles but more common—as well as two fish eagle chicks that had hatched in transit, in a customized belt hidden beneath his clothing. The Convention on International Trade in Endangered Species lists the fish eagle as an Appendix I bird, threatened with extinction; the other three species are Appendix II. The suspect had no documentation for any of them. British law doesn't allow a suspect to be identified until he is charged in court, but I had little doubt about who it was.

Sure enough, in late July, British newspapers reported that Jeffrey Lendrum had been charged with four counts of fraudulently evading prohibition—i.e., importing protected wildlife—and that he had been packed off to the Dickensian-sounding Wormwood Scrubs Prison in London to await a plea hearing in August. The National Crime Agency, founded in 2013 to combat "serious and organized crime," has a close relationship with Heathrow's Border Force and had immediately taken control of the investigation, relegating McWilliam, who probably knew more about Lendrum than any other law enforcement officer in England, to the sidelines. The details from the court appearance were skimpy—Lendrum's lawyer had argued that his client was on his way to declare the eggs and chicks before he was intercepted—and I had a wealth of questions that, for the moment, couldn't be answered. How had he procured the eggs? Who was he delivering them to? Why had the Border Force stopped him? And, most of all, what the hell had he been thinking?

I flew to London for Lendrum's pretrial hearing on August 23. His solicitor, Keith Astbury, had told me that his client intended to plead not guilty. But risking a jury trial could result in a tougher jail sentence than a plea bargain would—up to the maximum penalty of seven years. Had Lendrum rejected his solicitor's advice, as he had in Brazil? Astbury wouldn't comment.

At Isleworth Crown Court, in a drab London suburb directly beneath the flight path of jets landing at Heathrow Airport, I sat in the empty public gallery of a tiny second-floor courtroom, waiting for Lendrum to appear. I knew from Astbury that Lendrum had no interest in talking to me, but I hoped to make eye contact, at least. It wasn't to be. Court officers escorted Lendrum from a holding cell to a bulletproof booth at the rear of the courtroom, out of sight of the gallery. I heard his disembodied voice—faint, downcast—say, "I'm not guilty." When I stood in an attempt to get a look at him, a court officer motioned furiously for me to sit back down. Tony Bell, Lendrum's in-court lawyer, or barrister, promised to provide the judge with records about his client's ongoing cancer treatment to expedite a request for bail—a request that would be denied. Then his trial was set for January 7, 2019.

=

Four and a half months later, on a cold, drizzly morning, I traveled by tube to Snaresbrook Crown Court, a mid-nineteenth-century Gothic-revival manor house on eighteen acres of manicured grounds at the eastern edge of London. Barristers wearing white wigs and black robes walked along paths past stone turrets and arched entryways, looking like extras on a Georgian-era movie set. The third and climactic day of *The Queen v. Jeffrey Lendrum* was scheduled to unfold in Courtroom 15, a modern chamber with coral-colored upholstered chairs, blond-wood desks, gray carpeting, and soft track lighting on a white-paneled ceiling. I sat in the gallery a few feet from the glass-partitioned section reserved for defendants, and had a close-hand view of Lendrum as the bailiff escorted him into the courtroom. Dressed in sneakers, jeans, and a shapeless gray sweatshirt over a white cotton polo, he sat down, expressionless.

Craig Hunt, Lendrum's childhood friend who owned the Southern Comfort Lodge, would later speculate that Lendrum, floundering in the outside world, had deliberately engineered his own arrest at Heathrow, trading away his liberty for "free medical care, three meals a day, and a television set." If so, Lendrum had badly miscalculated the conditions of his incarceration. Wormwood Scrubs had become notorious for filth, narcotics, and gang warfare. After half a year awaiting trial, working as an orderly, or trusted assistant to the staff, in the segregation unit, which was reserved for disruptive prisoners or for those who faced a threat from other inmates, Lendrum looked paler, thinner, and more disheveled than the last time I had seen him. Still, when he had caught my eye the first morning of the trial, he flashed a smile. I smiled back.

At ten o'clock the usher rapped three times on the door separating the courtroom from the judge's chambers and called the session to order for the trial's third and penultimate day. All the attendees—Lendrum; his barrister, Tony Bell; the prosecutor, Sean Sullivan; four journalists; and Michelle Conway, a friend from his Rhodesian childhood who lived in England and had visited him frequently at Wormwood Scrubs ("Jeff is gentle as a lamb," she would tell me)—rose for the judge's entrance.

"God save the Queen," the usher intoned.

Judge Neil Saunders, a silver-haired jurist in his sixties, swept in with a bow. The previous afternoon, during a discussion of procedural issues, Saunders had derailed Lendrum's barrister's plans to try the case before a jury, which was still waiting in another room to be empanelled. Lendrum was not acting criminally, Bell had planned to argue to the jury, because his intention all along had been to hand the eggs over to British authorities upon arrival. The judge had ruled that what mattered in establishing culpability was not the defendant's alleged "intention," but the simple act of bringing prohibited goods into the country and not immediately declaring them. (To my surprise, this issue hadn't been dealt with before the proceedings began.) With his defense thrown out of court, Lendrum had been forced to plead guilty on the spot, uttering the plea to the judge from behind the glass barrier. The jury pool was dismissed without even setting foot in the courtroom. Now, on day three, the trial would head straight to the sentencing phase; prosecutor and barrister would each call witnesses and present their arguments for and against a lengthy incarceration directly to the judge.

Birds-of-prey expert Jemima Parry-Jones, the first prosecution witness to be called, told the court that the birds Lendrum had stolen came from a wide range of South African habitats—cliffs, mountain peaks, old-growth forests, and riparian woodlands (forests near rivers or lakes)—indicating that his latest project had covered significant territory and had probably lasted days or even weeks, quite an achievement for a man who claimed to suffer from nerve damage in his arms and neck. Parry-Jones placed a street value on the eggs at between £80,000 and £100,000, or between $104,000 and $130,000.

Lendrum had raised the suspicions of Heathrow's Border Force the moment he stepped up to the immigration counter, a customs offical testified in an affidavit read aloud in court. He had worn a heavy winter coat during a brutal summer heat wave (better to conceal his belt filled with eggs), held a return ticket to Johannesburg for six o'clock that same evening, and offered a flimsy story about coming to purchase airplane parts in Luton, a London suburb. He may also have been on a watch list, though border officials would neither confirm nor deny this. Lendrum certainly thought so—although, troublingly, Lendrum claimed that this hadn't stopped customs officials from letting him through in the past. "A couple of times coming into the UK, I joked with the guys, and they let me go," Lendrum told the court when summoned to the stand in the afternoon. "'I know what you're here for,' they said."

Lendrum again cast himself as a misunderstood animal savior.

He had rescued the eggs from forests because "South Africa was cutting down all the trees," he testified, "destroying their habitat." He had told customs officers at Heathrow that his intention all along had been to turn the eggs over to them and to request that they deliver them to Parry-Jones's birds-of-prey center in Gloucestershire, where they would be hatched under close supervision and protected. There were rumors, however, that the intended recipient was an unscrupulous Welsh breeder and longtime friend of Lendrum's, who'd been waiting just outside Heathrow that morning, and who had fled when he realized that Lendrum had been arrested. Lendrum's unpersuasive performance on the stand reminded me of the classic definition of insanity: doing the same thing over and over and expecting different results.

"You are a convicted smuggler of rare birds around the globe for profit, are you not?" Sullivan, a young, sandy-haired Oxford graduate, challenged Lendrum as the cross-examination phase got under way. "In Brazil you are convicted of those offenses, and you run. You flee jurisdiction, is that right?"

"On—on the advice of my lawyer, yes," Lendrum stammered.

"You are an absconded smuggler of birds eggs, and that's what you were when you arrived at Heathrow, weren't you? You were on the run, as a convicted smuggler."

"I spoke to my lawyer and I thought I had won the appeal."

"It's not the case, is it?"

"Now I know."

When it came time to pronounce his sentence, at ten o'clock the following morning, Saunders, echoing several judges before him, called Lendrum's testimony "completely implausible." The judge asked him to rise. He had weighed the gravity of Lendrum's offense, he said, against his age, precarious health, last-minute change of plea to guilty, and the character references submitted by Michelle Conway and Craig Hunt. Conway had compared Lendrum admiringly to "Crocodile Dundee," while Hunt had described his gentle, fun-loving, but "impulsive" nature, ever since his school days.

"The sentence I pass," Saunders said, "is one of thirty-seven months' imprisonment on each count, to run concurrently." Lendrum would serve his sentence at Pentonville Prison in North London, a hulking, high-walled fortress erected during the early Victorian era, where the Irish poet and playwright Oscar Wilde had spent two months of his two-year sentence at hard labor for homosexuality. A 2018 report by the Independent Monitoring Board declared the penitentiary crumbling and "rife" with vermin and complained that inmates went weeks without getting exercise in fresh air.

Lendrum rose without expression and left the courtroom, holding the best-selling nonfiction book that Conway had given him during her most recent jailhouse visit: *Factfulness: Ten Reasons We're Wrong About the World—and Why Things Are Better Than You Think*. Lendrum's own prospects offered little reason for optimism. With his five convictions on four continents, two terms in prison, a flight from a felony conviction in Brazil, and an Interpol Red Notice, it was hard to imagine that any prospective employer would be willing to give the hapless thief another chance once he got out. He faced the threat of extradition to Brazil, though the authorities had yet to file a request at the Westminster Magistrates Court in London, the clearinghouse for all such petitions. He was on immigration watch lists around the world, and his criminal record was all over the Internet. "There's more hits on my name than the Yorkshire Ripper," he had complained, near tears, once again the self-proclaimed victim, at one point in his testimony. Lendrum had made an attempt to cover his tracks, yet it demonstrated the same degree of ineptitude and half-heartedness as his latest egg smuggling escapade. In 2017, it had emerged in court that morning, the falcon thief had officially changed his name to "John Smith." Lendrum was a man trapped in an endless loop of criminality, unable to outrun his past.

====

Andy McWilliam had followed the Lendrum proceedings from Liverpool, sidelined from the investigation by the National Crime Agency. For a brief time in the run-up to the trial, McWilliam had thought that the prosecutor might summon him to court to provide evidence of Lendrum's "bad character." But by autumn his hopes of playing a useful role had faded. The day after Lendrum's sentencing, I caught a train from London Euston to Liverpool Lime Street to get his take on the trial.

McWilliam was waiting for me at the end of the platform. I almost didn't recognize him: He was thirty pounds lighter than the last time I had seen him, having embarked on an extreme bicycling regimen after a health scare. He was not surprised by Lendrum's relatively modest punishment, which all but guaranteed that he would walk out of prison, on parole, in thirteen months. "The prisons are so damned bloody crowded," he told me, as we ambled through the Victorian heart of Liverpool, a time capsule of the port's glory days. "As long as you're not considered a 'threat to society' the judge will grant you some leeway." Unlike Craig Hunt, who believed that Lendrum had intended to get caught at Heathrow Airport that June morning, the investigator was convinced that Lendrum had made the smuggling journey from Johannesburg to London several times—until his luck

had run out that June. This time, McWilliam didn't offer any optimism that Lendrum would stay out of trouble after his release on
parole in the winter of 2020. (In the late spring of 2019 Lendrum
would be transferred from the grim purgatory of Pentonville to the
category "D," or minimum security, Ayelesbury Prison, in Bucking-
hamshire, north of London.)

We walked past St. George's Hall, a colonnaded concert venue
built of sandstone. McWilliam had stood on its steps on December
9, 1980, keeping watch over the thousands of Liverpudlians griev-
ing for John Lennon, who'd been murdered in New York City the
night before. As McWilliam spoke, I wondered, not for the first time,
whether intertwining his story so closely with Lendrum's diminished
his accomplishments. He'd been around long before Lendrum—
and would keep investigating crimes now that his quarry was locked
away.

The National Wildlife Crime Unit was entering its thirteenth
year, having survived a series of bruising funding battles. In the winter of 2014, only a last-minute plea by Head of Unit Nevin Hunter
to the Home Ministry and the Department for Environment, Food
& Rural Affairs (DEFRA) had saved the unit from dissolution and
McWilliam and his colleagues from unemployment. Nearly the same
scenario had occurred when funding lapsed two years later. This
time the government had, in the final hours, committed to keeping
the unit active until 2020.

McWilliam seemed confident that the existential struggles were
over. The unit had achieved headline-making successes in recent
years. An international investigation had resulted in the convictions
and jailing of members of the Rathkeale Rovers, an Irish organized
crime gang that had carried out a series of brazen rhino-horn robber-

ies in museums across England, selling the artifacts to China. Some of the thieves got eight years. McWilliam had also become ever more skilled at scrutinizing the Internet for evidence of wildlife crime; two weeks earlier, photos that he'd spotted on Facebook had led to a raid and an arrest in Merseyside for that peculiar British scourge, badger baiting. He and his colleagues had expanded their investigation into the illegal falcon trade, too. McWilliam hinted that he'd gotten intelligence on some of the biggest financiers in Dubai and other Emirates; once again, though, he wasn't allowed to name names. Efforts to persuade Arab governments to act on the intelligence collected by the National Wildlife Crime Unit had so far led nowhere. "It's out of our control," McWilliam said with resignation.

McWilliam's appearance in *Poached* had made him something of a law-enforcement celebrity—much like the heroes of his favorite police drama from his childhood, *Dixon of Dock Green*. The documentary focused in part on the relationship between the wildlife officer and John Kinsley, a prolific Merseyside egg collector turned bird photographer. In 2002, McWilliam had blocked Kinsley's application for a license to photograph birds' nests, skeptical about his claim that he had reformed; four years later, police in South Wales arrested Kinsley for disturbing goshawks while climbing a tree to take pictures without a permit. "I got twelve months' probation and was banned from every national park and reserve . . . because of Andy McWilliam," Kinsley told the director bitterly early in the film.

After that setback, Kinsley had self-published a book, *Scourge of the Birdman*, a long attack on McWilliam that contained a doctored photograph of his nemesis with a Hitler mustache. The book, according to the jacket copy, "reveals the issues of corruption and dishonesty [of] some of those with positions of authority." But in recent years, McWilliam and Kinsley had set aside their animosity, and the officer had evolved into something of a confidant for the egg thief. At the film's conclusion, Kinsley, a haunted-looking figure who struggled for years with depression and unemployment, seeks to take advantage of an offer of amnesty and break from his criminal past. He summons McWilliam to his home and voluntarily turns over to him on camera his entire collection of thousands of eggs.

=

Several egg collections that McWilliam confiscated from Merseyside criminals in the 1990s and 2000s are held under lock and key in a storage room at the Liverpool World Museum, a bounty of archaeological and natural history wonders opened in 1860, at the height of the British Empire. I asked McWilliam if he could give me a tour, and, after a scramble on the phone to obtain permission, we rendezvoused with a curator in the museum's cavernous central gallery.

The curator led McWilliam and me down a corridor, past administrators' offices and storage rooms, to a door marked NO ENTRY. We followed him into a refrigerated chamber where the museum stores nearly ten thousand clutches. Almost all the specimens are kept in Tupperware-type plastic containers or glass-topped wooden trays on shelves in long rows of steel cabinets, which are compressed together and slide open with a turn of a handle, like a bank vault.

McWilliam opened drawers filled with trays of eggs belonging to Dennis Hughes, a daring peregrine egg collector who had been killed in a fall in a rock quarry in 1991. The collection had remained hidden for a decade after his death. In 2000, an informant told McWilliam that Hughes's mother had kept her son's bedroom locked since the day he died. "I went round and gently persuaded his mum, 'Let's have a look,'" McWilliam recalled. Inside a false bottom in Hughes's bed, McWilliam found hundreds of eggs. A magistrate ordered their forfeiture, and McWilliam turned them over to the museum.

Here, too, were the collections of Anthony Higham and Carlton D'Cruze, the two Merseyside miscreants who'd been among the first significant collars of McWilliam's wildlife-crime-fighting career. But the most impressive cache had belonged to Dennis Green, the destitute bird portraitist and onetime member of the Royal Society for the Protection of Birds who'd amassed four thousand eggs, one of the largest collections ever seized in Great Britain.

We cast our eyes over Green's artfully arranged clutches of oystercatchers, stone curlews, peregrine falcons, and other endangered species: gem-like orbs resting on beds of cotton, fragile spheres of white, cream, and violet spotted and speckled with dark pigment. For a year I had been speaking to McWilliam about the compulsiveness and self-destructiveness of the collectors, had interviewed Lendrum about his relentless pursuit of live raptor eggs, at the risk of his freedom and sometimes his life, and viewed the famous oological collection at the British Natural History Museum in Tring, packed with the trophies gathered by eighteenth- and nineteenth-century obsessives. There, in Hertfordshire, I'd seen the peregrine eggs that Derek Ratcliffe had used to document the lethal effects of DDT, one example of egg collecting serving, however inadvertently, the cause of science. I had also inspected perhaps the collection's greatest treasures: six freckled, pale yellow, pyriform or pear-shaped eggs of the great auk, a flightless seabird that had lived across the upper latitudes and been driven into extinction by excessive hunting in the mid-nineteenth century. These eggs included an eighteenth-century specimen once owned by the famed Italian biologist Lazzaro Spallanzani, which

Walter Rothschild, the museum's founder, had purchased for a substantial sum in 1901.

I had dived deep into the esoteric world of the oologist, and begun to understand the eggs' remarkable power: the beauty of their many shapes, textures, colors, and patterns, each the product of natural selection, the better to perpetuate the species . . . The complex metabolic system wrapped in a delicate casing, from the protein-rich albumen that cushions and nourishes the developing embryo to the microscopic pores on the surface of the shell that draw in oxygen and expel carbon dioxide . . . The egg, a symbol of new life and fertility, a self-contained miracle of genesis and development, requiring only heat and air to thrive, was "incorporated as a sacred sign in the cosmogony of every people on the earth," wrote Helena Blavatsky, a nineteenth-century Russian occultist and philosopher, "and was revered on account of its form and inner mystery." McWilliam sometimes ridiculed the collectors for their bizarre attachment to "a piece of calcium," but I was coming to see that he, too, grasped their mysterious allure. "I think that if required on pain of death to name instantly the most perfect thing in the universe, I should risk my fate on a bird's egg," declared the clergyman and political activist Thomas Wentworth Higginson in 1862.

Next to the rows of cabinets, McWilliam recognized an antique wooden display case with forty thin drawers that he had seized from Green's bedroom on a spring day in 1999, almost exactly twenty years earlier. "It's like meeting an old friend," McWilliam said. He opened the drawers to reveal the speckled buff-colored eggs of black-legged kittiwakes; the marble-like, lily-white eggs of Dartford warblers; and the black-and-purple-splattered eggs of red-backed shrikes, whose disappearance from Britain in the 1970s had turned public opinion decisively against the oologists. Each clutch had a story behind it—of human obsession and nature's fragility, of man's perpetual insistence on imposing his will upon the wildness of our world, and of the tiny handful of investigators, most unrecognized, working to safeguard the environment's bounty and wonder.

The curator closed the cabinets and sealed the vault, and McWilliam led me back to the museum's main gallery and out into the world.

ACKNOWLEDGMENTS

When I set out to enter the world of the fugitive Jeffrey Lendrum in the spring of 2017, I had no idea whether I would be successful. Fortunately, dozens of people around the globe whose paths had crossed the egg thief's opened doors for me and brought his story to life. Over four interviews in Liverpool, bird-watching expeditions, and many phone conversations, Andy McWilliam vividly recounted his journey through the wildlife-crime underworld, his pursuit of Lendrum, and the complex relationship that developed between him and his quarry.

Overcoming his initial hesitation, Paul Mullin hosted me three times in southern England, and spoke to me for a total of ten hours on the phone. He described in detail everything from the nuts and bolts of the African handicrafts business to the felonious journeys that he and Lendrum took to the subarctic in 2001 and 2002.

Plenty of others provided guidance, inspiration, and stories as I followed Lendrum's trail across four continents. In the United Kingdom, Pat Lorber drew a portrait of the ornithological community in Rhodesia and post-independence Zimbabwe, and her encounters during that period with young Lendrum and his father. Ian Guildford of the NWCU guided me on two trips through the Rhondda Valley—once with Andy McWilliam, and the second time with Mike Thomas, the peregrine watcher who first suspected that an egg thief was plundering local nests. Jemima Parry-Jones, founder of the International Centre for Birds of Prey, taught me the essentials of falcon breeding and other raptor-related arcana, with assistance from Holly Cale. Guy Shorrock of the Royal Society for the Protection of Birds answered every question I had about ornithological crime. I'm also grateful to Nick Fox; Howard Waller; Douglas Russell, the curator of the egg collection at the Natural History Museum at Tring; Martin Sims, Alan Roberts, and Nevin Hunter, all of the National Wildlife Crime Unit; Steve Harris; Bob Elliot of the RSPB; Darren Turner at the Warwick Crown Court; the staff of the British Library; Charles Graham; Michelle Conway, Phil and John Struczynski; and Jake Hulyer, a talented young British journalist who traded observations with me at Lendrum's trial in London.

I had half a dozen lengthy conversations over Skype with Kit Hustler, the former ornithologist at Hwange National Park in Zimbabwe, now living in New Zealand, who had near-perfect recall of Adrian and Jeffrey Lendrum's trial in 1984 and the events leading up to it. In Zimbabwe, John and Jan Brebner spent a memorable day with me in Matobo National Park, pointing out eagles and nests, and sharing with me their love of African landscapes and birds of prey. Peter Mundy, Julia Dupree, Carolyn Dennison, and Vernon Tarr helped bring the African part of Lendrum's story to life. Fredi and Rita Ruf of the Hornung Park Lodge in Bulawayo and the staff at the York Lodge in Harare were wonderful hosts during my stay in Zimbabwe.

In Brazil, Rodrigo Tomei shared documents and videos with me and related the tale of Lendrum's arrest and his months in Guarulhos.

Rafael Asenjo and Nicolas Soto Volkart of Chile's Agriculture and Livestock Service provided key information about the trap they'd laid for Lendrum, while Nicolas's son, Alvaro Soto, served as my guide in the wilds of Chilean Patagonia—imparting his knowledge about the resident birdlife and giving my Spanish a three-day work-out. Nicolas Fernández at the Hotel Plaza recounted Lendrum's sojourn there and gave me a personal tour of Punta Arenas. Dorothea Cist, a resident of Santiago, was instrumental in making the Chile trip happen. In Dubai, the estimable Pranay Gupte provided introductions to key contacts. Linda El Sayed Ahmed and Suad Ibrahim Darwish of the Hamdan bin Mohammed Heritage Center arranged visits to falcon breeders and trainers working for the Al Maktoum family; in Abu Dhabi, Bryn Close and his daughter Natalie allowed me to shadow them for three days at the President Cup, and Angelique Engels, an official at the Abu Dhabi Falconer's Club, answered all my questions about the sport.

I'm grateful to Timothy Wheeler, the director of *Poached*, who shared the raw transcript of his long interview with Andy McWilliam; and to Paula Lendrum Maughan and Richard Lendrum, who filled in details about their brother's early years. Jeffrey Lendrum met with me near Pretoria for three hours and continued conversing with me by phone for six months, making me understand his genuine passion for birds of prey and even turning over the GPS coordinates of the nests he plundered in the Rhondda Valley and Patagonia.

Kevin Cote was involved in this project from its early days, serving as an enthusiastic listener, problem solver, and sounding board over dozens of hours of bike riding along the Havelchaussee and through the Grunewald in Berlin. Philip and Terrie Stoltzfus hosted me at their home during my frequent visits to London, serving me fantastic dinners, putting me up in a guest room, and listening to my tales of egg collectors, bird smugglers, and falcon racers. Their daughter, Ellie Chamberlain Stolztfus, and her husband, Dan Chamberlain, often joined us and also lent an ear to my ramblings. Kathleen Burke, Janet Reitman, Lee Smith, Yudhijit Bhattacharjee, Diane Edelman, David Dobrin, and Melissa Eddy helped to assuage anxieties and self-doubt. Alex Perry provided keen advice and, with his family, hosted me at his lovely home in Hampshire. David Van Biema, a fellow bird enthusiast, kept me excited about the project; Terry McCarthy was a pal and soul mate during his too-brief sojourn in Berlin. Geoffrey Gagnon in New York and Claudio Edinger in São Paulo also offered friendship and support.

Jon Sawyer and Tom Hundley at the Pulitzer Center, Ian Buruma, formerly of the *New York Review of Books*, and Suzanne MacNeille of the *New York Times* underwrote my trip to Southern Africa in December 2017; Suzanne also assigned me pieces from Chile and Dubai, further helping me defray the costs of my global odyssey. The gang at *Outside*—Chris Keyes, Alex Heard, Reid Singer, Luke Whelan, and my longtime editor Elizabeth Hightower Allen—commissioned, edited, and published my article "The Egg Thief," which became the basis for *The Falcon Thief*.

I'm deeply indebted to my editor, Priscilla Painton at Simon & Schuster, who believed in this project from its inception and pushed me onward. Megan Hogan edited the manuscript line by line, vastly ramping up the quality of the narrative, shepherded it along from start to finish, and took care of countless production-related details. Emily Simonson also contributed valuable comments and questions, as did production editors Samantha Hoback and Yvette Grant. Flip Brophy, my longtime agent, was an eager listener over breakfasts at

Barney Greengrass and other eateries in New York City. Nell Pierce, Flip's assistant, cheerfully and efficiently dealt with contract issues and other details.

Finally, great thanks to my mother, Nina Hammer, my father, Richard Hammer, my stepmother, Arlene Hammer, and my sister, Emily Hammer, for being there for me on the other side of the pond. In Berlin, my sons, Max, Nico, and Tom abided my frequent absences, and understood—even shared a bit—my growing fascination for birds. Above all, Cordula Kraemer believed in me, stood by me, kept me focused when I was seized by structural problems and anxieties, and gave endlessly to me. Without her love, generosity, and patience, this story would never have taken flight.

NOTES

Prologue

xi *"Thief Who Preys on Falcon Eggs"*: John Simpson, the *Times*, January 5, 2017.

xii *"A glimpse of dense brush"*: Jonathan Franzen, "My Bird Problem," *The New Yorker*, August 8, 2005.

Chapter One: The Airport

2 *"gave me a background"*: John Struczynski, interview by author, April 14, 2018.

4 *"Are you carrying"*: Mark Owen, Midlands-Birmingham Police, interview by author, October 4, 2017; Andy McWilliam, interview by author, Liverpool, August 22, 2017.

6 *"What kind of eggs"*: Owen, interview, October 4; McWilliam, interview, August 22.

Chapter Two: The Investigator

9 *"We're not quite sure"*: Andy McWilliam, interview by author, Liverpool, January 21, 2017.

11 *"a spectacular crash"*: Derek Ratcliffe, *The Peregrine Falcon* (London: A&C Black, 1993), 66.

11 *"all peregrine eyries"*: David R. Zemmerman, "Death Comes to the Peregrine Falcon," the *New York Times*, August 9, 1970, p. 161.

11 *"as crude a weapon"*: Rachel Carson, *Silent Spring* (New York: Houghton Mifflin, 1962), 297.

12 *"This sudden silencing"*: Carson, *Silent Spring*, 103.

13 *"As an apex predator"*: Guy Shorrock, interview by author, Sandy, England, August 26, 2017.

15 *"I always say"*: Mark Jeter, quoted in "The Egg Thief" by Joshua Hammer, *Outside*, January 7, 2019.

16 *"All living things"*: Alfred Russel Wallace, *The Malay Archipelago: the Land of the Orang-utan and the Bird of Paradise: A Narrative of Travel with Studies of Man and Nature* (London: Macmillan, 1890).

16 *"To the bird watcher"*: Carson, *Silent Spring*, 86.

17 *"Don't let the man go"*: Andy McWilliam, interview by author, August 23, 2017.

20 *"That's alive"*: Lee Featherstone, phone interview by author, March 3, 2018.

21 *"He knew what he was doing"*: Featherstone, interview, March 3.

21 *"They're fertile, they're alive"*: Featherstone, interview, March 3.

Chapter Three: The Interview

24 *"She was in a terrible state"*: Jeffrey Lendrum, phone interview by author, March 16, 2018.

24 *"Okay, you were arrested"*: Andy McWilliam, interview by author, Liverpool, January 21, 2018.

24 *"This is ridiculous"*: McWilliam, interview, January 21.

24 *"They're duck eggs"*: McWilliam, interview, January 21.

27 *"Let's go find that car"*: McWilliam, interview, January 21.

27 *"Smash open the window"*: McWilliam, interview, January 21.

28 *"If you're just an egg collector"*: McWilliam, interview, January 21.

Chapter Four: The Art of Falconry

31 *"a falconer bearing a hawk"*: Austen Henry Layard, *Discoveries Among the Ruins of Ninevah and Babylon* (London: Harper, 1853), 112.

32 *"For the Bedouin"*: Mark Allen, *Falconry in Arabia*, with a foreword by Wilfred Thesiger (London: Orbis, 1980), 15.

32 *"a swift dog and a splendid hawk"*: Robin S. Oggins, *The Kings and Their Hawks: Falconry in Medieval England* (New Haven, CT: Yale University Press, 2004), 38.

32 *"falcon gentle"*: Oggins, 38.

33 *"is to have his horse"*: Oggins, 38.

33 *"was surrounded by hawks"*: Layard, *Discoveries*, 409.

34 *"is generally made"*: Layard, 412.

34 *"Although the smallest"*: Layard, 410.

35 *"The peregrine swoops"*: J. A. Baker, *The Peregrine* (London: HarperCollins, 1967), 40.

35 *"The hawk breaks"*: Baker, 40.

36 *"so events in time"*: Helen Macdonald, *Falcon* (London: Reaktion Books, 2006), 31.

36 *"between black-and-white"*: Macdonald, 32.

40 *"on a downward spiral"*: Sarah Townsend, "Sheik Hamdan's Bid to Revive the Glorious Arab Sport of Falconry," *Arabian Business*, June 13, 2015.

40 *"drawing gasps from breeders"*: Townsend.

40 *"Any strong falcon"*: Anonymous falconry expert, interview by author, Abu Dhabi, United Arab Emirates, January 9, 2018.

41 *"back-to-nature quest"*: Fernanda Eberstadt, "Falconry's Popularity Soars in England and Scotland," *Condé Nast Traveler*, January 15, 2013.

Chapter Five: Rhodesia

44 *"hyperactive and aware"*: Pat Lorber, interview by author, King's Lynn, England, August 23, 2017.

44 *"I'm Pat Lorber. Who are you?"*: Lorber, interview, August 23.

45 *"My father was passionate"*: Jeffrey Lendrum, interview by author, Centurion, South Africa, December 18, 2017.

46 *"I've climbed to more nests"*: Jeffrey Lendrum, phone interview by author, March 16, 2018.

47 *"tons of sticks, and build a rudimentary nest"*: Vernon Tarr, interview by author, Bulawayo, Zimbabwe, December 10, 2017.

47 *"I'd climb a tree"*: Howard Waller, interview by author, Inverness, Scotland, January 22, 2018.

49 *"He saw the way things were going"*: Richard Lendrum, interview by author, Rosebank, South Africa, December 18, 2017.

51 *"were likable, smooth, gregarious, and chatty"*: Lorber, interview, August 23.

52 *"They can fly in a gale"*: Rob Davies, "The Verreaux's Eagle—An Interview with Dr. Rob Davies," *African Raptors: The Online Home of African Raptor Interests*, August 12, 2010, http://www.africanraptors.org/the-verreauxs-eagle-an-interview-with-dr-rob-davies/.

52 *"like watching jet fighters"*: Davies.

53 *"Val could go put her hand gently"*: Lorber, interview, August 23.

53 *"The eagle didn't flinch"*: Tarr, interview, December 10.

53 *"Do not stay"*: Valerie Gargett, *The Black Eagle: A Study* (Randburg: Acorn Books, 1990), 22.

53 *"We are visitors"*: Gargett, 22.

53 *"It paid to be physically fit"*: Gargett, 22.

54 *"Jeff was cocky"*: Lorber, interview, August 23.

54 *"The Lendrums are so active"*: Lorber, interview, August 23.

55 *"kow-kow"* . . . *"bombing-diving-and-stooping"*: A. Lendrum and J. Lendrum, *Augur Buzzard Study*, Ornithological Association of Zimbabwe, ninth annual report, 1982.

55 *"They would throw up a claw"*: Lorber, interview, August 23.

57 *"My dad used to go up on call-ups"*: Richard Lendrum, interview, Rosebank, South Africa, December 18.

57 *"Being a nonconformist"*: Paula Lendrum Maughan, Facebook Messenger interview with author, April 17, 2019.

57 *"hot extractions"*: Jeffrey Lendrum, testimony, *The Queen v. Jeffrey Lendrum*, Snaresbrook Crown Court London, January 9, 2019.

57 *"He saw some terrible things"*: Michelle Conway, interview by author, London, January 9, 2019.

58 *"Some of these impostors"*: "Wall of Shame," The C Squadron 22 Special Air Service web page, http://www.csqnsas.com/dishonour.html.

58 *"One thing you get to know"*: Paul Mullin, phone interview by author, May 9, 2018.

59 *"incomplete breeding cycles"*: Lorber, interview, August 23.

59 *"This had never happened before"*: Lorber, interview, August 23.

61 *"Have you just been to the crowned eagle nest?"*: Christopher "Kit" Hustler, phone interview by author, September 12, 2017.

Chapter Six: Liverpool

64 *"I thought, I can do this"*: Andy McWilliam, interview by author, Liverpool, August 22, 2017.

65 *"What is the Ku Klux Klan?"*: McWilliam, interview, August 22.

65 *"the active side"*: Andy McWilliam, phone interview by author, May 17, 2018.

65 *"They must have been"*: McWilliam, interview, August 22.

66 *"You, boots!"*: Andy McWilliam, interview by author, Liverpool, January 11, 2019.

66 *"policing by consent"*: British Home Office, "Definition of Policing by Consent," December 10, 2012, https://www.gov.uk/government/publications/policing-by-consent/definition-of-policing-by-consent.

66 *"to talk down"*: McWilliam, interview, January 11.

67 *"That's it, mate"*: McWilliam, interview, August 22.

67 *"Don't you like the police?"*: McWilliam, interview, August 22.

68 *"the New York of Europe"*: *The Bankers' Magazine*, vol. 11 (London: Groombridge & Sons, 1851).

69 *"faced stretches of waste ground"*: Andy Beckett, *Promised You a Miracle: Why 1980–82 Made Modern Britain* (London: Penguin, 2016).

71 *"It was us against them"*: McWilliam, phone interview, May 17.

71   *"You're going to the Linby Colliery"*: McWilliam, interview, August 22.

71   *"There are fathers"*: Andy McWilliam, interview by author, Liverpool, October 2, 2017.

73   *"an old shat of a car"*: McWilliam, interview, August 22.

73   *"You become detached"*: McWilliam, interview, August 22.

74   *"Listen here, you bastard"*: McWilliam, interview, October 2.

74   *"Do you remember me?"*: McWilliam, interview, October 2.

74   *"Christ! This is murder"*: McWilliam, interview, October 2.

75   *"the opposition"*: McWilliam, interview, August 22.

Chapter Seven: The Trial

79   *"a pair of live bird eggs"*: Christopher "Kit" Hustler, phone interview by author, May 7, 2018.

79   *"Leave as fast as you can"*: Hustler, phone interview, May 7.

80   *"Are you Adrian Lendrum?"*: Hustler, phone interview, May 7.

80   *"We had no warning"*: Jeffrey Lendrum, interview by author, Centurion, South Africa, December 18, 2017.

81   *"Thank God you're here"*: Hustler, phone interview, May 7.

82   *"Have you got the standard?"*: Hustler, phone interview, May 7.

82   *"We just got them today"*: Hustler, phone interview, May 7.

83   *"What do you think this is?"*: Pat Lorber, interview by author, King's Lynn, England, August 23, 2017.

83   *"one single red blotch"*: Lorber, interview, August 23.

84   *"chicks growing well"*: Lorber, interview, August 23.

84   *"Val is being over-the-top"*: Hustler, phone interview, May 7.

85   *"misunderstanding"*: Anonymous former colleague of Peggy Lendrum at Girls' College, Bulawayo, email to Pat Lorber, April 10, 2019, sent to author.

85   *"Adrian had thought"*: Lorber, interview, August 23.

87   *"irregular"*: Prosecutor, *State v. Adrian Lloyd Lendrum and Jeffrey Paul Lendrum*, case number 7904-5/6, transcript, October 1, 1984.

87   *"There was a trust placed in you"*: Giles Romilly, *State v. Adrian Lloyd Lendrum and Jeffrey Paul Lendrum*, case number 7904-5/6, transcript, October 1, 1984.

88   *"face just fell"*: Lorber, interview, August 23.

88   *"People didn't want"*: Lorber, interview, August 23.

88   *"He would be gone"*: Hustler, phone interview, May 7.

89   *"British police asserted"*: "A Matter of Trust," *Honeyguide: Journal of Zimbabwean and Regional Ornithology* 31, no. 2 (September 1985).

89   *"is organized internationally"*: "A Matter of Trust."

90   *"a very personable"*: P. C. Mundy, "The Lendrum Case: Retrospective 2," *Honeyguide: Journal of Zimbabwean and Regional Ornithology* 56, no. 2 (September 2010).

90 *"sense of entitlement"*: Christopher "Kit" Hustler, phone interview by author, April 10, 2019.

90 *"They couldn't climb, so they came to me"*: Jeffrey Lendrum, phone interview by author, May 18, 2018.

91 *"he slipped away in the gloom"*: Mundy, "The Lendrum Case: Retrospective 2."

91 *"The guy has been reading"*: Jeffrey Lendrum, interview, December 18.

Chapter Eight: The Collectors

94 *"Their pointless pursuit"*: Guy Shorrock, "Operation Easter: The Beginnings," *Royal Society for the Protection of Birds Blog*, May 9, 2018, https://community .rspb.org.uk/ourwork/b/investigations/posts/operation-easter-the -beginnings.

96 *"a misunderstanding"*: Andy McWilliam, interview by author, Liverpool, January 21, 2018.

96 *"as a gift"*: Guy Shorrock, phone interview by author, May 23, 2018.

96 *"Nazi storm troopers"*: McWilliam, interview, January 21.

97 *"a Cabinet of rarities"*: Tim Birkhead, *The Most Perfect Thing: Inside (and Outside) a Bird's Egg* (London: Bloomsbury, 2017), 10.

97 *"Acquisition in the name"*: Birkhead, 12.

98 *"As he rode headlong"*: Carrol L. Henderson, *Oology and Ralph's Talking Eggs: Bird Conservation Comes Out of Its Shell* (Austin: University of Texas Press, 2009), 30.

98 *"Daring Act of American Ornithologist"*: Mark Barrow, *A Passion for Birds: American Ornithology After Audubon* (Princeton, NJ: Princeton University Press, 1998), 42.

99 *"the sad ending of an active"*: Frank Haak Lattin, et al., *The Oologist* 26 (1908): 92.

99 *"a passion for beauty"*: Birkhead, *Most Perfect Thing*, 13.

99 *"I have vivid memories"*: *British Birds: An Illustrated Monthly Magazine*, vol. 51, 1958, pp. 237–38.

100 *"ogling his eggs"*: Birkhead, *Most Perfect Thing*, 15.

100 *"Perhaps their wonderful curves"*: Birkhead, 15.

100 *"distinct menace"*: Julian Rubinstein, "Operation Easter," *The New Yorker*, July 22, 2013.

100 *"Are we English people"*: Eric Parker, "Ethics of Egg Collecting," *The Field* (London), 1935.

101 *"the cloak-and-dagger"*: Patrick Barkham, "The Egg Snatchers," *The Guardian*, December 11, 2006.

101 *"pariah of the bird-watching world"*: Mary Braid, "Birds Egg Society Faces Inquiry," *The Independent*, January 15, 1995.

101 *"little Hitlers"*: Stephen Moss, ed., *The Hedgerows Heaped with May: The Telegraph Book of the Countryside* (London: Aurum Press, 2012).

102 *"It's very rare"*: Rubinstein, "Operation Easter."

102 *"Britain's foremost wildlife detective"*: *The Field* magazine, cited on back cover of Alan Stewart, *Wildlife Detective: A Life Fighting Wildlife Crime* (Edinburgh: Argyll Publishing, 2008).

102 *"I heard that when they reached wherever they were going"*: Andy McWilliam, interview by author, Liverpool, October 2, 2017.

103 *"We laid them out like a macabre jigsaw puzzle"*: Guy Shorrock, phone interview, May 23.

103 *"Abbott and Costello"*: Barkham, "The Egg Snatchers."

104 *"I pass the brochures out in the countryside"*: Steve Harris, phone interview by author, September 13, 2017.

105 *"became a bit of a hero"*: McWilliam, interview, January 21.

105 *"Don't you need a CITES"*: Andy McWilliam, interview by author, Liverpool, August 22, 2017.

106 *"The collectors couldn't bullshit"*: Harris, phone interview, September 13.

106 *"Andy was a no-nonsense"*: Guy Shorrock, interview by author, Sandy, England, August 26, 2017.

106 *"Has Mr. Higham asked"*: McWilliam, interview, January 21.

107 *"They're beautiful, aren't they"*: McWilliam, interview, January 21.

107 *"It's the sixty-four-thousand-dollar"*: *Poached*, directed by Timothy Wheeler (Ignite Channel, 2015), transcript of interview with Andy McWilliam.

108 *"the pseudo-protectionists"*: W. Pearson, *The Osprey: Nesting Sites in the British Isles*, (Brighton, England: Oriel Stringer, 1987), 11.

108 *"obsessed with the peregrine"*: Shorrock, interview, August 26.

108 *"I traveled elsewhere"*: Barkham, "Egg Snatchers."

109 *"the pinnacle of egg collecting"*: Shorrock, interview, August 26.

109 *"In memory of Jock—The Man"*: Rubinstein, "Operation Easter."

109 *"I was well and truly hooked"*: Rachel Newton, "Jailed Egg Thief 'A Threat to Wildlife,'" *Daily Post* (Liverpool), April 11, 2003.

110 *"Britain's most ruthless"*: Rubinstein, "Operation Easter."

110 *"Nest in Peace"*: Rubinstein.

110 *"top secret"*: McWilliam, interview, January 21.

110 *"The sight which met"*: Rachel Newton, "Jailed egg thief 'a threat to wildlife,'" *Liverpool Daily Press*, April 11, 2003, p. 11.

111 *"My body felt cold"*: "Jail For Prolific Collector of Eggs," extract from field notes, *Legal Eagle: The RSPB's Investigations Newsletter*, January 2003, no. 35.

111 *"The [mother] bird's"*: Holly Cale, interview by author, Newent, Gloucestershire, England, August 22, 2017.

112 *"loners and social misfits"*: McWilliam, interview, October 2.

112 *"from butter to packets of instant custard"*: Rubinstein, "Operation Easter."

112 *"I can't believe"*: McWilliam, interview, October 2.

112 *"They are somehow"*: Emma Bryce, "Inside the Bizarre, Secretive World of Obsessive Egg Thieves," *Audubon*, January 6, 2016.

112 *"rare and difficult"*: Menelaos Apostolou, "Why Men Collect Things? A Case Study of Fossilized Dinosaur Eggs," *Journal of Economic Psychology* 32, no. 3 (June 2011): 410–17.

113 *"They're good, aren't they?"*: McWilliam, interview, October 2.

113 *"If I pick this bloody"*: McWilliam, interview, October 2.

114 *"just didn't seem"*: McWilliam, interview, October 2.

114 *"Is this going to be it?"*: McWilliam, interview, October 2.

114 *"egg collecting just fell"*: Shorrock, interview, August 26.

114 *"Put him before the beak"*: Harris, phone interview, September 13.

115 *"was regarded as trivial"*: Harris, phone interview, September 13.

Chapter Nine: AfricaXtreme

118 *"I had nothing to do"*: Jeffrey Lendrum, phone interview by author, February 23, 2018.

118 *"collecting black sparrowhawks"*: Lendrum, testimony, *The Queen v. Jeffrey Lendrum*, Snaresbrook Crown Court London, January 9, 2019.

119 *"Wouldn't it be"*: Paul Mullin, interview by author, Hampshire, England, August 27, 2017.

121 *"If you're a border controller"*: Mullin, interview, August 27.

122 *"There's something wrong"*: Mullin, interview, August 27.

123 *"You could blindfold"*: Mullin, interview, August 27.

123 *"Throw some meat"*: Mullin, interview, August 27.

124 *"I've always rescued animals"*: Lendrum, phone interview by author, March 16, 2018.

124 *"Do you want it?"*: Mullin, interview, August 27.

125 *"turn your garden"*: Radio commercial, recorded by Paul Mullin and Jeffrey Lendrum, played for author by Mullin.

126 *"I'm so in love"*: Mullin, interview, August 27.

126 *"proof of concept"*: Mullin, interview, August 27.

126 *"It's the most beautiful"*: Jeffrey Lendrum, interview by author, Centurion, South Africa, December 18, 2017.

128 *"What the fuck"*: Mullin, interview, August 27.

128 *"I can hear"*: Mullin, interview, August 27.

129 *"a complete flight"*: Lendrum, phone interview, February 23.

129 *"He lived a very basic"*: Mullin, interview, August 27.

Chapter Ten: Dubai

131 *"If the nest is"*: Frederick II, *The Art of Falconry* [De arte venandi cum avibus], trans. and ed. Casey A. Wood and F. Marjorie Fyfe (Palo Alto: Stanford University Press, 1943), 129.

131 *"seven days after hatching"*: Robin S. Oggins, *The Kings and Their Hawks: Falconry in Medieval England* (New Haven, CT: Yale University Press, 2004), 21.

131 *"because the longer"*: Frederick II, *Art of Falconry*, 129.

132 *"the [malleability] of youth"*: Mark Allen, *Falconry in Arabia, with a Foreword by Wilfred Thesiger* (London: Orbis, 1980), 47.

135 *"the whole thing snowballed"*: Jemima Parry-Jones, interview by author, Newent, Gloucestershire, England, August 21, 2017.

136 *"I remember being nine"*: Howard Waller, interview by author, Inverness, Scotland, January 22, 2018.

136 *"We actually hated each other at first"*: Jeffrey Lendrum, interview by author, Centurion, South Africa, December 18, 2017.

137 *"I said that I'd like"*: Waller, interview, January 22.

138 *"Suddenly an Arab"*: Wilfred Thesiger, *Arabian Sands* (New York: Penguin Digital Editions, 2007), chapter 14.

139 *"What I remember most"*: Tom Bailey and Declan O'Donovan, "Interview with His Excellency Sheikh Butti bin Maktoum bin Juma Al Maktoum," *Wildlife Middle East News* 5, no. 4 (March 2011).

140 *"would go out onto"*: Waller, interview, January 22.

141 *"They don't care"*: Anonymous falcon breeder for Crown Prince Hamdan, interview by author, Dubai, October 31, 2017.

141 *"a killing machine"*: Emma Ford, *Gyrfalcon* (London: John Murray, 1999), 13.

142 *"a predatorial mash-up"*: T. Edward Nickens, "What One Magnificent Predator Can Show Us about the Arctic's Future," *Audubon*, January-February 2016.

142 *"a large and faire"*: Thomas T. Allsen, "Falconry and the Exchange Networks of Medieval Eurasia," *Pre-Modern Russia and Its World: Essays in Honor of Thomas S. Noonan* (Wiesbaden, Germany: Otto Harrassowitz Verlag, 2006), 39.

143 *"she feels the heat"*: Husam Al-Dawlah Taymur Mirza, *The Baz-Nama-Yi Nasiri, a Persian Treatise on Falconry*, trans. D. C. Philliott (London: Bernard Quaritch, 1908), 36.

144   *"Almost like a long-married"*: Peter Gwin, "Inside a Sheikh's Plan to Protect the World's Fastest Animal," *National Geographic*, October 2018.

144   *"arguably . . . one of the most"*: Gwin.

146   *"I put my hands"*: Waller, interview, January 22.

146   *"If the female is sucking"*: Waller, interview, January 22.

146   *"You can't just put"*: Waller, interview, January 22.

147   *"I am a falconer"*: Bailey and O'Donovan, "Interview with His Excellency."

147   *"There was one mountain gazelle"*: Bailey and O'Donovan.

148   *"Howard and his wife"*: Jeffrey Lendrum, phone interview by author, February 2018.

148   *"a very nice guy"*: Lendrum, interview, December 18.

148   *"The birds would get stressed"*: Lendrum, interview, December 18.

149   *"It's ninety-nine percent"*: Lendrum, interview, December 18.

149   *"Lendrum and I may have"*: Waller, interview, January 22.

150   *"worldwide, multi-million dollar"*: George Reiger, "Operation Falcon: The Anatomy of a Sting," *Field & Stream*, January 1985, p. 23.

151   *"like having someone"*: Ford, *Gyrfalcon*, 144.

151   *"Many Arabs still believe"*: Roger Cook, "The Bird Bandits," *The Cook Report*, ITV, February 1996.

151   *"trying desperately"*: The Hawk Board, press release, "Summary of Events Leading Up to and Following the Cook Report," February 10, 1996.

152   *"Eyes can be sewn shut"*: Tanya Wyatt, "The Illegal Trade of Raptors in the Russian Federation," *Contemporary Justice Review: Issues in Criminal, Social, and Restorative Justice* 14, no. 2 (2011).

153   *"There were several Arabs"*: Tom Parfitt, "Smuggling Trade Threatens Falcons with Extinction," *The Telegraph*, March 27, 2005.

153   *"There's huge, huge money"*: Anonymous falcon breeder, interview by author, undisclosed location, August 2017.

154   *"laundering illegal birds"*: Anonymous falcon breeder, interview by author, August 2017.

154   *"anyone who believes"*: Jemima Parry-Jones, interview by author, Newent, England, May, 2017.

155   *"Inbreeding has reduced survivability"*: Nick Fox, interview by author, Carmarthen, Wales, May 2, 2018.

155   *"regular infusion of genes"*: Toby Bradshaw, "Genetic Improvement of Captive Bred Raptors," University of Washington faculty website, October 2009, http://faculty.washington.edu/toby/baywingdb/Genetics%20of%20captive-bred%20raptors.pdf.

155   *"The thing they would worry about"*: Jeffrey Lendrum, phone interview by author, March 16, 2018.

Chapter Eleven: Operation Chilly

158 *"It's going to be the adventure"*: Paul Mullin, phone interview by author, October 31, 2018.

158 *"a dream on my bucket list"*: Jeffrey Lendrum, interview by author, Centurion, South Africa, December 18, 2017.

158 *"The gyrfalcons are like bluebottle flies"*: Paul Mullin, phone interview by author, June 4, 2018.

159 *"Because we grew up together"*: Howard Waller, interview by author, Inverness, Scotland, January 22, 2018.

159 *"I told him"*: Waller, interview, January 22.

159 *"a complete liar"*: Jeffrey Lendrum, phone interview by author, February 23, 2018.

159 *"They are the biggest"*: David Anderson, interview with Luke Whelan for author's article, "The Egg Thief," *Outside*, January 2019.

160 *"one of them to go extinct"*: Robinson Meyer, "The Battle over 2,500-Year-Old Shelters Made of Poop," *The Atlantic*, July 24, 2017, https://www.theatlantic.com/science/archive/2017/07/falcon-battle-over-nests-of-bird-poop/534510/.

160 *"[I am a] utility bush pilot"*: LinkedIn profile of "bush pilot."

162 *"Look at us"*: Video of "Operation Chilly," shot by Paul Mullin, June 2001, https://www.youtube.com/watch?v=lWce39190B0.

163 *"They're beautiful"*: Lendrum, video of "Operation Chilly," shot by Mullin, June 2001.

163 *"That is a fucking noise"*: Lendrum, video of "Operation Chilly," shot by Mullin, June 2001.

164 *"dangling from a helicopter"*: Paul Mullin, phone interview by author, May 3, 2019.

165 *"The nest was . . . the most filthy"*: Ernest Blakeman Vesey, *In Search of the Gyrfalcon: An Account of a Trip to Northwest Iceland* (London: Constable, 1938), 69.

165 *"The nest of these hawks"*: John James Audubon, *Birds of America* (New York: Welcome Rain Publishers, 2001; first edition published 1828).

166 *"The ground color"*: Arthur Cleveland Bent, *Life Histories of American Birds of Prey Part II*, Smithsonian Institution Bulletin 170 (Washington, DC: Government Printing Office, 1938), 12.

166 *"You're dependent on air flow"*: Paul Mullin, interview by author, Hampshire, England, August 27, 2017.

167 *"A lake, a mountain"*: Ronald Stevens, *The Taming of Genghis* (London: Hancock House, 2010; first edition published 1956).

167 *"Are you down?"*: Video of "Operation Chilly," shot by Paul Mullin.

168 *"He was always protective"*: Mullin, phone interview, June 4.

169 *"We never bothered"*: Mullin, phone interview, June 4.

169 *"It was a total success"*: Mullin, interview, August 27.

Chapter Twelve: Busted

172 *"the* Star Wars *effect"*: Paul Mullin, interview by author, Hampshire, England, August 27, 2017.

172 *"This is getting too much"*: Pete Duncan, phone interview by author, October 29, 2017.

173 *"I'm planning to come back"*: Duncan, phone interview, October 29.

174 *"Any wildlife photographer"*: Duncan, phone interview, October 29.

174 *"There's something fishy"*: Duncan, phone interview, October 29.

174 *"These guys are stealing eggs"*: Dave Watt, phone interview by author, October 27, 2017.

175 *"it was enough"*: Mullin, interview, August 27.

176 *"This is it, Jeff"*: Mullin, interview, August 27.

176 *"Have you been stealing"*: Mullin, interview, August 27.

177 *"You can either plead"*: Watt, phone interview, October 27.

178 *"He wanted to destroy the evidence"*: Watt, phone interview, October 27.

178 *"He would risk his own life to save them"*: Paul Mullin, interview by author, Hampshire, England, May 3, 2018.

178 *"He was the weakest"*: Mullin, interview, May 3.

178 *"out of jealousy"*: Mullin, interview, May 3.

179 *"Poachers Fined for Illegal Possession"*: Jane George, *Nunatsiaq News*, May 15, 2002.

179 *"Poached Eggs Seized from Fake Film Crew"*: *National Post*, May 18, 2002.

180 *"That was it"*: Mullin, interview, May 3.

Chapter Thirteen: The Unit

182 *"Mad Mullah of the Traffic Taliban"*: "Mad Mullah of the Traffic Taliban Breaks into His OWN Police Station in Bizarre Security Stunt," *Evening Standard*, December 17, 2007.

183 *"use investigative tactics"*: Jason Bennetto, "Police Set Up Wildlife Crime Squad to Hunt Down Gangs Muscling in Lucrative Trade," *The Independent*, April 22, 2002.

183 *"Most officers would say"*: Andy McWilliam, interview by author, Liverpool, August 22, 2017.

184 *"Don't knock it"*: Andy McWilliam, email to author, October 20, 2017.

185 *"Have you thought"*: McWilliam, interview, August 22.

185 *"Suddenly I was moved"*: McWilliam, interview, August 22.

186 *"Give it a go"*: McWilliam, interview, August 22.

186 *"people who think"*: "UK Wildlife Crime Centre Launched," BBC News, October 18, 2006.

187 *"The [Home Office] didn't"*: Alan Roberts, phone interview by author, September 7, 2017.

188 *"Those killing birds"*: Guy Shorrock, *Royal Society for the Protection of Birds* blog, May 23, 2018, https://community.rspb.org.uk/ourwork/b/investigations/posts/op-easter-3-of-3-nearly-cracked.

189 *"antique ivory carvings"*: Andy McWilliam, interview by author, Liverpool, October 2, 2017.

189 *"It still smelled bad"*: Roberts, phone interview, September 7.

190 *"academic zeal"*: Simon Winchester, "The Bone Man: A Skull Collector Reveals His Extraordinary Private Collection," *The Independent*, October 12, 2012.

190 *"back from the brink"*: "Back from the Brink: Together We Can Bring Our Threatened Species Back from the Brink," website of Buglife, https://www.buglife.org.uk/back-from-the-brink.

191 *"There's not a lot"*: McWilliam, interview, October 2.

193 *"finished him off"*: McWilliam, interview, October 2.

194 *"extreme and sickening cruelty"*: Lord Justice Laws, Mr. Justice Gray, and Judge Rivlin QC, *Regina v. Raymond Leslie Humphrey*, Court of Appeal, June 23, 2003.

194 *"was prepared to go to any lengths"*: "Bird Smuggling Racket Netted £160,000," *Yorkshire Post*, August 2, 2001.

195 *"One of the things with being a police wildlife officer"*: *Poached*, directed by Timothy Wheeler (Ignite Channel, 2015), transcript of interview with Andy McWilliam.

195 *"We began to pick up"*: McWilliam, interview, October 2.

196 *"It's all to do with the fact"*: *Poached*.

196 *"I do think on occasions they have something to offer"*: Andy McWilliam, email to Alan Roberts and other NWCS personnel, February 26, 2013, obtained and originally published in the British press through the Freedom of Information Act.

Chapter Fourteen: The Rhondda Valley

201 *"If you steal the eggs"*: Mike Thomas, interview by author, Garw Valley, Wales, May 1, 2018.

202 *"Whoever is climbing this"*: Thomas, interview, May 1.

202 *"You can spend days"*: Thomas, interview, May 1.

203 *"A couple of years"*: Andy McWilliam, interview by author, Rhondda Valley, Wales, May 3, 2017.

204 *"The hills have been stripped"*: Arthur Morris, Glamorgan, cited in the *GENUKI Gazetteer, UK and Ireland Geneology*, GENUKI charitable trust, https://www.genuki.org.uk/big/wal/GLA/Rhondda/HistSnips.

205 *"We're at the end"*: Ian Guildford, interview by author, Rhondda Valley, Wales, May 3, 2017.

206 *"I've got a lucky ability"*: Jeffrey Lendrum, phone interview by author, March 16, 2018.

207 *"We've got a man in custody"*: Andy McWilliam, interview by author, Liverpool, August 22, 2017.

207 *"If we bail him"*: McWilliam, interview, August 22.

208 *"Charge him"*: McWilliam, interview, August 22.

208 *"going on a tour"*: Video of "Operation Chilly," shot by Paul Mullin, June 2001, https://www.youtube.com/watch?v=lWce39190B0.

209 *"One [falcon] seen flying"*: Jeffrey Lendrum, account of February 2010 Sri Lanka journey, found by Andy McWilliam on Lendrum's computer, shared with author.

209 *"Good rock face"*: Lendrum, account of February 2010 Sri Lanka journey.

210 *"Dubai customs were very iffy"*: Lendrum, account of February 2010 Sri Lanka journey.

210 *"I don't remember that"*: Lendrum, interview by author, Centurion, South Africa, December 18, 2017.

210 *"the effects of global warming"*: McWilliam, interview by author, Liverpool, January 21, 2018.

211 *"in all probability, came from the supply of eggs"*: Prosecutor, *Regina v. Jeffrey Paul Lendrum*, before His Honour Judge Hudson, Crown Court Warwick, August 19, 2010.

211 *"Karma's a bitch"*: Mullin, phone interview by author, May 3, 2019.

211 *"I was with Lendrum"*: Mullin, interview, May 3.

212 *"untested source"*: McWilliam, interview, January 21.

213 *"If you've got somebody local"*: McWilliam, interview, May 3.

213 *"He knows more about the wild birds"*: Ian Guildford, interview by author, Garw Valley, Wales, May 1, 2018.

213 *"If [security] opened"*: Jeffrey Lendrum, phone interview by author, February 23, 2018.

214 *"senior members of UAE society"*: McWilliam, PowerPoint display, NWCU, shared with author.

214 *"He's well traveled"*: Nevin Hunter, phone interview by author, October 25, 2017.

214 *"I sat down with Andy"*: Hunter, phone interview, October 25.

215   *"Peregrines and gyrfalcons"*: Alan Roberts, phone interview by author, September 7, 2017.

216   *"I've been to court"*: McWilliam, interview, January 21.

216   *"You all right?"*: McWilliam, interview, January 21.

217   *"The environmental crime"*: Judge Christopher Hodson, *Regina v. Jeffrey Paul Lendrum*, Crown Court Warwick, August 19, 2010.

217   *"At the end of the day"*: Hodson, *Regina v. Jeffrey Paul Lendrum.*

218   *"Bloody hell"*: Andy McWilliam, phone interview by author, May 2018.

218   *"Caged: The £70K Egg Snatcher"*: *Daily Mirror*, August 20, 2010, p. 3.

218   *"A Bird in the Hand, a Smuggler in Jail"*: the *Times*, August 20, 2010, p. 1.

218   *"Jailed, Former Soldier Caught"*: *Daily Mail*, August 20, 2010, p. 30.

218   *"a former member"*: Mark Hughes, "Ex-Soldier Jailed for Theft of Rare Falcon Eggs," *The Independent*, August 20, 2010, p. 7.

218   *"The Rare Falcon Chicks Saved"*: *Daily Express*, August 20, 2010, p. 3.

219   *"Few of the end users"*: P. C. Mundy, "The Lendrum Case: Retrospective 2," *Honeyguide* 56, no. 2 (September 2010).

220   *"the world's poorest thief"*: Michelle Conway, interview by author, London, January 9, 2019.

Chapter Fifteen: Prison

222   *"You got hit for taking birds?"*: Jeffrey Lendrum, phone interview by author, March 16, 2018.

222   *"a guy at the top of his game"*: Andy McWilliam, interview by author, Liverpool, August 22, 2017.

224   *"It was spur of the moment"*: Lendrum, phone interview, March 16.

224   *"your pilot friend"*: Lendrum, phone interview, March 16.

224   *"If I hadn't saved those birds"*: Andy McWilliam, interview by author, Liverpool, January 21, 2018.

225   *"manifestly excessive and out of step"*: Lord Justice Moore-Bick, Mrs. Justice Cox, and Sir Christopher Holland, *Regina v. Jeffrey Paul Lendrum*, Court of Appeal (Criminal Division), February 1, 2011.

225   *"He had no bills"*: Charles Graham, phone interview by author, January 14, 2019.

226   *"Jeff had this South African"*: Graham, phone interview, January 14.

226   *"He told me he was finished"*: Craig Hunt, phone interview by author, January 20, 2019.

226   *"is excited to travel"*: *African Hunting Gazette*, notice posted on AfricaHunting .com, April 8, 2013, https://www.africahunting.com/threads/jeffrey -lendrum-of-african-hunting-gazette-convicted-wildlife-smuggler.10615/.

227 *"Hey Andy, it's Jeffrey"*: McWilliam, interview, August 22.

227 *"I thought to myself"*: McWilliam, interview, August 22.

228 *"People will still follow"*: McWilliam, interview, August 22.

228 *"You can stay with me"*: Lendrum, phone interview, March 16.

229 *"He's filled with so much shit"*: Andy McWilliam, interview by author, Martin Mere Wetlands Reserve, England, October 2, 2017.

229 *"Cop's Work on the Wild Side"*: Douglas Walker, "Cop's Work on the Wild Side," *The Sun*, February 11, 2012.

229 *"Before I took over"*: Walker, "Cop's Work."

230 *"Bring it on"*: McWilliam, interview, October 2.

230 *"Jeffrey Lendrum of African Hunting Gazette"*: Jerome Philippe, post on message board, AfricaHunting.com, April 8, 2013, https://www.africahunting.com/threads/jeffrey-lendrum-of-african-hunting-gazette-convicted-wildlife-smuggler.10615/.

230 *"Is African Hunting Gazette letting"*: "africauntamed," post on AfricaHunting.com, April 8, 2013.

231 *"I knew I was running"*: Richard Lendrum, post on AfricaHunting.com, July 5, 2017, https://www.africahunting.com/threads/jeffrey-lendrum-of-african-hunting-gazette-convicted-wildlife-smuggler.10615/.

231 *"What I did was stupid"*: Jeffrey Lendrum, as "Bell407," post on AfricaHunting.com, April 10, 2013.

231 *"horrific"*: Richard Lendrum, interview by author, Rosebank, Johannesburg, South Africa, December 18, 2017.

231 *"wildlife trafficker"*: Richard Lendrum, post on AfricaHunting.com, July 5.

Chapter Sixteen: Patagonia

234 *"the desolate place of bad spirits"*: *The Rough Guide to Chile* (London: Rough Guides UK, September 2015), https://www.roughguides.com/destinations/south-america/chile/southern-patagonia/parque-nacional-pali-aike/.

236 *"Is it still there?"*: Nicolas Fernández, interview by author, Punta Arenas, Chile, October 19, 2018.

237 *"at the highest global"*: Andy McWilliam, quoted in "Award for Birmingham Cleaner Who Caught Egg Smuggler," BBC News, October 6, 2010.

237 *"the highest level"*: Guy Shorrock, quoted by Claire Marshall, "Egg Smuggler Was Wildlife Criminal," BBC News, August 19, 2010.

237 *"I'm uneasy about this"*: Nicolas Fernández, email provided to author, October 19, 2018.

239 *"Basically you've got to know"*: Jeffrey Lendrum, phone interview by author, February 23, 2018.

239 *"being less conspicuous"*: David Ellis, Beth Ann Sabo, James F. Fackler, and Brian A. Millsap, "Prey of the Peregrine Falcon (*Falco Peregrinus Cassini*) in Southern Argentina and Brazil," *Journal of the Raptor Research Foundation*, 2002, Vol. 36, no. 4: 318.

240 *"He was a nice, friendly"*: Fernández, interview, October 19.

241 *"We received the following"*: Rafael Asenjo, email provided to author by Rodrigo Tomei (Lendrum's attorney), October 14, 2018.

242 *"They're chicken eggs"*: Rodrigo Tomei, interview by author, Guarulhos, Brazil, October 14, 2018.

243 *"They caught me"*: Tomei, interview, October 14.

243 *"he could convince"*: Tomei, interview, October 14.

244 *"laughable"*: Judge Paulo Marcos Rodrigues de Almeida, Federal Justice Court, judgment and sentence, Guarulhos, Brazil, December 14, 2015.

244 *"Let's have coffee"*: Tomei, interview, October 14.

245 *"During [downtime] in Itaí"*: João Batista, Jr., "Os presos que vêm de fora: Torre de Babel carcerária guarda 1,443 detentos de 89 nacionalidades. Populacão nunca foi tão grande e não para de aumentar," *Veja* (Brazil), August 6, 2011.

245 *"Sometimes not even"*: "Information Pack for British Prisoners in Brazil," British Embassy Brazil, July 21, 2015.

246 *"There was a danger"*: Tomei, interview, October 14.

246 *"I had nothing but shit in Brazil"*: Jeffrey Lendrum, phone interview by author, March 16, 2018.

246 *"contagious"*: Michelle Conway, interview by author, London, January 9, 2019.

247 *"Then I saw an article"*: Howard Waller, interview by author, Inverness, Scotland, January 23, 2018.

247 *"I knew that I was going to die"*: Lendrum, phone interview, March 16.

247 *"Nobody was looking"*: Tomei, interview, October 14.

248 *"Hey Rodrigo, I'm in"*: Tomei, interview, October 14.

248 *"Ex-SAS Rare Egg"*: Ben Hurst, "Ex-SAS Rare Egg Thief Who Tried to Smuggle Birds Through Birmingham Airport on the Run," *Birmingham News*, January 6, 2017.

248 *"Britain's Most Protected"*: Abigail O'Leary, "Britain's Most Protected Bird Under Threat From SAS-Trained Wildlife Hunter," *Daily Mirror*, January 5, 2017.

Chapter Seventeen: Gauteng

250 *"Andy McWilliam is telling"*: Jeffrey Lendrum, phone interview by author, May 10, 2017.

250   *"manna from heaven"*: Jeffery Lendrum, phone interview, May 10.

250   *"complete and utter rubbish"*: Andy McWilliam, email to author, April 3, 2018.

251   *"She is very stressed"*: Julia Dupree, email to author, December 3, 2017.

251   *"What f****** audacity!"*: Pat Lorber, email to author, November 16, 2017.

252   *"You're sworn to secrecy"*: John Brebner, Black Eagle Project, interview by author, Bulawayo, Zimbabwe, December 11, 2017.

252   *"That's a fairly new"*: Brebner, interview, December 11.

253   *"He's got a very tough life"*: Richard Lendrum, interview by author, Rosebank, South Africa, December 18, 2017.

254   *"We both love wildlife"*: Richard Lendrum, interview, December 18.

254   *"Obviously, there are breeders"*: Richard Lendrum, interview, December 18.

255   *"My short-term memory is failing"*: Jeffrey Lendrum, phone interview by author, December 18, 2017.

256   *"You probably recognized"*: Jeffrey Lendrum, interview by author, December 18, 2017.

257   *"He seems to be successful"*: Bob Elliot, RSPB, interview, "Notorious Bird Egg Thief on the Run in Brazil," BBC Today radio program, January 6, 2017.

257   *"The devil is in the details"*: Jeffrey Lendrum, interview, December 18.

258   *"Things happen"*: Jeffrey Lendrum, interview, December 18.

259   *"Do you want to steal"*: Jeffrey Lendrum, interview, December 18.

Epilogue

261   *"I'm at my son's graduation"*: Author's notebook, June 24, 2018.

261   *"Call if you want"*: Jeffrey Lendrum, email to author, June 24, 2018.

262   *"Rare Bird Eggs Importation"*: "Rare Bird Eggs Importation Prevented by Border Force at Heathrow," National Wildlife Crime Unit press release, June 28, 2018.

264   *"free medical care"*: Craig Hunt, phone interview by author, January 20, 2019.

265   *"Jeff is gentle as a lamb"*: Michelle Conway, interview by author, London, January 9, 2019.

266   *"A couple of times"*: Jeffrey Lendrum, testimony, *The Queen v. Jeffrey Lendrum*, Snaresbrook Crown Court, January 10, 2019.

267   *"South Africa was cutting"*: Jeffrey Lendrum, testimony, *The Queen v. Jeffrey Lendrum*, January 10.

267   *"You are a convicted smuggler"*: Sean Sullivan, prosecutor, cross-examination of Jeffrey Lendrum, *The Queen v. Jeffrey Lendrum*, January 9, 2019.

267   *"completely implausible"*: Judge Neil Saunders, judgment, *The Queen v. Jeffrey Lendrum*, January 10, 2019.

268   *"rife"*: "Pentonville Is 'Crumbling and Rife with Vermin,'" BBC News, August 22, 2018.

268 *"There's more hits"*: Jeffrey Lendrum, testimony, *The Queen v. Jeffrey Lendrum*, January 9, 2019.

269 *"bad character"*: Andy McWilliam, interview by author, Liverpool, January 11, 2019.

269 *"As long as you're"*: McWilliam, interview, January 11.

271 *"It's out of our control"*: McWilliam, interview, January 11.

271 *"I got twelve months' probation"*: *Poached*, directed by Timothy Wheeler (Ignite Channel, 2015), on-camera interview with John Kinsley.

271 *"reveals the issues"*: *Poached*, on-camera interview with Kinsley.

272 *"I went round"*: McWilliam, interview, January 11.

274 *"incorporated as a sacred sign"*: H. P. Blavatsky, *The Secret Doctrine* (New York: Penguin, 2016; original edition published 1888), 265.

274 *"I think that if required"*: Tim Birkhead, *The Most Perfect Thing: Inside (and Outside) a Bird's Egg* (London: Bloomsbury, 2017), 15.

274 *"It's like meeting"*: McWilliam, interview, January 11.

INDEX

ABOUT THE AUTHOR

Joshua Hammer is the *New York Times* bestselling author of *The Bad-Ass Librarians of Timbuktu*. He has written for the *New York Times Magazine*, *GQ*, *The New Yorker*, *National Geographic*, *The Atlantic*, *Smithsonian*, and *Outside*.